READING ISAIAH

READING ISAIAH

Poetry and Vision

Peter D. Quinn-Miscall

Westminster John Knox Press
LOUISVILLE
LONDON • LEIDEN

Book design by Sharon Adams
Cover design by Lisa Buckley

First edition
Published by Westminster John Knox Press
Louisville, Kentucky

This book is printed on acid-free paper that meets the American National Standards Institute Z39.48 standard. ∞

PRINTED IN THE UNITED STATES OF AMERICA

Library of Congress Cataloging-in-Publication Data

Quinn-Miscall, Peter D., 1943–
    Reading Isaiah : poetry and vision / by Peter D. Quinn-Miscall.
        p. cm.
    Includes bibliographical references and index.
    ISBN 0-664-22369-9 (alk. paper)
    1. Bible. O.T. Isaiah—Criticism, interpretation, etc. 2. Hebrew poetry, Biblical—History and criticism.   I. Title.

BS1515.52 .Q56 2001
224'.1066—dc21   2001026092

Contents

Acknowledgments

The beginnings of this poetic voyage into Isaiah's imagery and vision lie in my classes of twenty and more years ago. Its development occupies the following years in both my teaching and writing. Innumerable people, both colleagues and students, have aided me through encouragement and with many insights and criticisms. From colleagues I single out Danna Nolan Fewell, David Gunn, and David J. A. Clines to express my appreciation for their consistent support of my attempts to make a new thing from Isaiah. From my students I acknowledge Art Ondrejka and Wayne Viguerie, who helped initiate the study with probing, and at times disturbing, questions and with excellent papers. Their traces are evident in my book. Last, and certainly not least, is my wife Michele, who initially urged me to write this book; she was the first reader and editor of the manuscript in its earliest and latest forms.

Introduction

One Isaiah, One Vision

"The vision of Isaiah son of Amoz that he envisioned concerning Judah and Jerusalem." The opening to the book of Isaiah announces that the <u>book is a vision </u>and not a narrative work or a collection of proverbs. We see and imagine it just as much as we hear and understand it. The vision that is the book of Isaiah is a grand poem that encompasses God, the entire universe, humanity, and the sweep of history from creation on. Within this panorama the poet focuses on the fortunes of one people, Israel, in two trying periods of their history: the Assyrian invasions of the late eighth century B.C.E. and the Babylonian invasions of the sixth century B.C.E.[1] plus the following Persian period of reconstruction. The Babylonian invasions ended in the destruction of Jerusalem, the end of the Davidic monarchy, and the forced exile of many of the ruling elite to a site near Babylon. The Persians, under Cyrus, let Judea rebuild itself as a Persian province; returning exiles, such as Ezra and Nehemiah, played a significant role in the new era. These events and peoples are patterns and characters in the vision that has a strong dramatic aspect to it. The poet composed the poem and the vision known as the book of Isaiah sometime after these events. He employs the events to present the vision of God and humanity, of God's ways with the world, especially the choice of one people, and of what life lived in God's presence, on God's holy mountain, is like.

The type of reading I employ represents a decided change from the way that many commentators have treated the book of Isaiah for the past century or more. Since the development of historical criticism in the eighteenth century C.E., scholars have assumed that the distinct parts of the book are to be regarded as referring directly to these different periods in Israel's history and therefore as having been

1

composed at roughly the same time as those periods. Thus speeches that refer to events or characters of the eighth century B.C.E. were composed at that time or soon thereafter; the same applies to speeches that point to events or characters of the sixth century B.C.E. Because of this assumption, a significant amount of the study of Isaiah has been devoted to debating what the separate sections of the book are, what specific times they refer to, and when they were composed.

At the end of the eighteenth century C.E., historical critics divided the book into two parts, chapters 1–39 (mainly eighth century B.C.E.) and 40–66 (mainly sixth–fifth century B.C.E.). The two parts were studied as two separate works that had been combined, perhaps only by chance, into one scroll or book. At the close of the nineteenth century C.E., Bernhard Duhm refined this view and proposed a hypothesis that, in varying forms and ways, has since been the dominant model for studying Isaiah. This is the theory of three Isaiahs: First Isaiah (1–39), Second or Deutero-Isaiah (40–55), and Third or Trito-Isaiah (56–66). The theory is based on the movement from the Assyrian crisis of the late eighth century B.C.E. to the Babylonian invasion and destruction of Judah of the early sixth century B.C.E. Reconstruction of the community, with many leaders returning from Babylon, occurred in the last half of the sixth into the fifth century B.C.E. In this theory, most of First Isaiah is dated to the late eighth century, although some of it (e.g., chaps. 24–27) is regarded as the latest material in the whole book. Second Isaiah is dated to the rise of Persia and the end of Babylonian dominance, 550–530, and Third Isaiah to the first fifty or so years of rebuilding Judah as a Persian province, 520–450.

In this approach critics read passages in Isaiah in terms of their reference to a specific historical period and even to specific events and people if the material allows this. To put it simply, Isaiah is read as a poetic and impressionistic representation of Israel's history, and the goal of a commentator is to speak first of that history and then of the representation itself, that is, the vision of the book of Isaiah.

Since 1980 an increasing number of studies look at Isaiah as a whole and not just as the combination of independent works. These studies break into two categories. First, some combine this interest with the theory of three Isaiahs and focus on how the total book was edited and reedited to establish some unity and continuing relevance for it. Second, others regard Isaiah as one book that is to be studied and read for its own sake, for what it says and presents, and not as a variety of ways of addressing different periods in Israel's history. The present work fits solidly in the latter camp.

This shift from historically focused modes of reading to others that are more literary, whether concerned with narrative or poetry, is a shift occurring throughout biblical studies, but it is not a total or simple shift. Historical modes of reading are by no means dead and gone. Biblical studies are marked by a variety of approaches, interests, and goals and by an incredible range of debate and controversy between different groups and within the same group. Literary critics of the Bible disagree and argue among themselves just as much as historical critics do.

One major result of the variety and debate is the increasing practice of authors introducing their work with a brief discussion of what they are doing and why and not just assuming that every reader shares their approach and goals. This is what I am doing in this introduction: describing briefly what I am not doing, and at more length what I am doing.

I am reading the book of Isaiah as a sweeping vision written in poetry. We will pay attention to literary and poetic issues such as parallelism, figurative language, imagery, and characterization. There is one book, one Isaiah, and not three; therefore, I do not refer to First, Second, and Third Isaiah. This assumption of one book does not, however, deny or overlook the major differences in both style and content that occur throughout the book. Chapters 40–66 are not the same as 1–39, but I deal with the variations in other ways than by positing a work written later by another poet. The outline of Isaiah in the next chapter presents many of the diverse parts, and the rest of the book offers ways of assessing the diversity.

I often refer to history in the readings; this is history in the sense of our knowledge of the geography, nations, people, and events of the eighth century B.C.E. on. I do not read Isaiah as though its different parts were contemporary with and directly addressed to different periods in Israel's history. The first part of the next chapter reviews that history; the role history plays in my approach will be clear as we progress. A final issue is the date of the composition of Isaiah. This is a major issue in historical-critical studies. I assume a fifth or even fourth century B.C.E. date and therefore read the entire book as a retrospective on Israel's history from the mid-eighth century to the end of the sixth century. I do not pursue the issue since I do not think that we know enough about Judah in the Persian period to argue for more than this.

A Way of Reading

We read Isaiah as a vision *written*, for the most part, in poetic form. Whatever the relation may be between this written work that we have and earlier materials, oral or written, my focus is on the present work, not on these supposed earlier sources. I note many of the abrupt shifts in style and content in Isaiah that may occur from one verse to the next without transition or comment, but I do not explain them as due to some chance combination of previously separate speeches or poems.

The focus of my book is more on explaining and exemplifying this way of reading than it is on presenting a developed interpretation of Isaiah based on this way. My book is not a commentary or other type of full interpretation of Isaiah whether historical, literary, or theological. I still present a particular way of reading, imagining, and understanding Isaiah that has its own assumptions, methods, and implications. This way is more obvious in some sections (e.g., the final chapter). I do not argue for the approach to the same extent and in the same detail as in a commentary or full interpretation, but I am not claiming that this is a neutral or value-free approach.

I guide readers into a new way of reading Isaiah and then leave them free to pursue it further and in more detail on their own. Although I do cite and comment on a large number of both short and long passages from Isaiah, they are only part of Isaiah and not a majority part. I also quote a small number of passages several times to demonstrate their richness through the presence in them of a variety of poetic devices, themes, and imagery.

I want to reveal, through this approach and its categories, the richness, intricacy, and complexity of Isaiah. This will frequently result in disclosing problematic passages, ambiguities, and even contradictions; but, true to my purposes of revealing the complexity, I will generally leave the problems and ambiguities unresolved. I may state my preference for a particular translation or interpretation, but I will note other ways and not reject or argue against them. This may be troublesome for readers who prefer to have such problems, especially contradictions, resolved or explained in some fashion and not left as an essential part of Isaiah's vision.

Although we are reading religious poetry with many implications for spirituality and theology, I am not going to develop those implications. At a few points, I will note traditional Jewish and Christian interpretations, especially of the Messiah and the Servant, but I do not pursue them to argue for or against them. This passing mention of traditional interpretations is not a claim that they are invalid interpretations; they are part of other ways of reading Isaiah that I am not dealing with in this book. Again, I want to guide my readers in a way of reading this grand poem and vision and leave it to them to develop their own theological and spiritual conclusions and applications. This includes making their own judgments about how to understand and appropriate or not these traditional interpretations. This openness will be troublesome for the readers who want these implications clarified and resolved. I particularly have in mind the contradictory portraits of the Lord as a God of both mercy and justice, a God of all and a God of one people, and a God of love and compassion and a God of violence and destruction.

Finally, in the majority of my readings I do not adhere tightly to the sequential order of Isaiah. I draw parallel and contrasting texts from throughout the book of Isaiah to exemplify an image, theme, and so on. The procedure is solidly rooted in my understanding of the book of Isaiah as a vision that is a simultaneous panorama of movement across time; of themes and images of sin, punishment, and restoration; and of a large cast of characters. Isaiah develops all his different aspects by repeating them and expanding them, not usually by developing them in a progressive fashion. Isaiah's vision of God and humanity (whether all nations or only Israel) and the many relationships that can exist between them is the same in his closing and opening chapters. The vision does not present a simple story of past sin, present punishment, present-future repentance, and finally future restoration.

Translating Isaiah

Isaiah is written in Hebrew, and the text used in English translations is the Masoretic Text (MT) represented in the major manuscripts from the tenth and eleventh centuries C.E. From the third century B.C.E. on, when Greek became the common language of the ancient Near East, Jews produced a series of Greek translations of the Hebrew Bible; the modern practice of revising translations has ancient roots. The earliest translation is the Septuagint (abbreviation: LXX or Gk) produced in the third to second centuries B.C.E.; it does not always agree in detail with the MT and sometimes makes better sense.

A modern English translation at points can agree with the Septuagint rather than with the Hebrew of the Masoretic text and may note the change. For example, the New Revised Standard Version renders 5:17b "fatling and kids," notes that the Hebrew has "aliens" for "kids," and in a note refers to the *Gk* to support "kids." Not all translations make this change (e.g., the Tanakh), and some translations that do make the change, do not note it (e.g., the New Jerusalem Bible).

The Dead Sea Scrolls include two manuscripts of Isaiah: 1QIsa[a] and 1QIsa[b].[2] The latter agrees closely with the MT, while the former often differs in details and, as with the Septuagint, many times makes better sense. A translator can choose to represent 1QIsa[a] in the translation and may note the change. For example, the New Revised Standard Version renders the last phrase in 3:24 "instead of beauty, shame," and notes that the Masoretic text lacks "shame" but that it is found in the *Q Ms*, which is their siglum for 1QIsa[a]; the Tanakh makes a similar note. Such variations between the Hebrew Masoretic text and the Septuagint and the Hebrew Qumran scrolls account for a small number of the differences among contemporary translations of Isaiah.

I discuss some of the major contemporary translations of Isaiah. I include the KJV from a sense of tradition, but I do not include earlier versions of present-day translations mainly for reasons of space. I briefly note how and why translations differ and how these differences, both major and minor, affect our reading of Isaiah whether we are aware of it or not. "Translation" means not just the language used but how it is printed on the page, including poetic or prose form, punctuation, breaks between sections, and headings. Following are the Bibles referred to in the rest of the book. I give the abbreviation and the full title here and use the abbreviation in the rest of the book. Each of these Bibles has a brief introduction in which the style and goals of the translation are detailed.*

GNB	Good News Bible—Today's English Version
KJV	King James Version
NAB	New American Bible
NIV	New International Version
NJB	New Jerusalem Bible
NRSV	New Revised Standard Version
REB	Revised English Bible
TNK	Tanakh: The Holy Scriptures—The Jewish Bible[3]

*For a full discussion of contemporary translations, consult Sheeley and Nash's *The Bible in English Translation: An Essential Guide* (Nashville: Abingdon Press, 1997).

Modern Bibles divide the books into chapters and numbered verses; the system developed in the thirteenth century. It was first used in the Latin Bible and then transferred to Hebrew manuscripts. The division into chapters does not always reflect agreed-upon divisions in the content of Isaiah; Bibles vary in how they mark chapter breaks beyond using the actual number. Reading in translation is characteristic of Bible study partly because of the large number and availability of different translations. There are different translations of the Bible for a variety of reasons, including national and denominational concerns. I focus on general issues of language and translation. Why do translations of a biblical book, or even of a chapter of a book, differ?

No two languages express human thought and speech in the same way. A translator rendering Biblical Hebrew into English will always have a choice of ways to translate a word, a sentence, and a whole book. The choice depends on a number of factors, not only accuracy. A literal translation attempts to mirror the original language as closely as possible in word order, number of words, and exact rendering of each word even if it is not always in flowing, modern English. An idiomatic or free translation attempts to capture the basic meaning of the Bible in flowing, modern English even if it does not mirror the Hebrew. Individual translations can be at one extreme or the other, but most are somewhere in between. Translation is an art of choice and compromise, not an exact science. The variety and the level of the vocabulary and grammar used is another choice. What audience and how wide an audience does the translator want to appeal to?

For example, in the opening verse of Isaiah, NRSV renders the Hebrew word-for-word:

> The vision of Isaiah son of Amoz, which he saw concerning Judah and Jerusalem in the days of Uzziah, Jotham, Ahaz, and Hezekiah, kings of Judah.

GNB is at the opposite end of the spectrum:

> This book contains the messages about Judah and Jerusalem which God revealed to Isaiah son of Amoz during the time when Uzziah, Jotham, Ahaz, and Hezekiah were kings of Judah.

TNK is in between:

> The prophecies of Isaiah son of Amoz, who prophesied con-
> cerning Judah and Jerusalem in the reigns of Uzziah, Jotham,
> Ahaz, and Hezekiah, kings of Judah.

Translators understand their task differently and target different audiences. Each translation has its strengths and weaknesses; one is not better than another in an absolute sense. Different translations can be equally accurate translations. My translations are literal and designed to fit the context in this book.

There are, in addition, factors involved with understanding the Hebrew text itself. As with any written work, the Hebrew Bible (HB)[4] is at points easy to read, at others difficult to understand, and at most times somewhere in between these two poles. Translators will usually be closer to each other in how they render a clear passage and farther apart with a difficult passage. In a related way, a passage can be clear in the sense that it says only one thing and does not suggest anything else; such a text is univocal and unambiguous. At the other pole is a passage that says and suggests a variety of things; such a text is rich and ambiguous.

Since Isaiah is mainly a work of poetry, much of it is rich and ambiguous. Even when a passage in Isaiah is clear, it may have several levels of meaning. A translator of Isaiah is faced with questions such as: Can the richness be rendered in English? How much of it should I try to translate?

The vision of the peaceable kingdom in 11:1–9 NRSV opens with an allusion to the line of David through the mention of his father Jesse.

> A shoot shall come out from the stump of Jesse, and a branch
> shall grow out of his roots.

GNB makes the allusion a direct reference.

> The royal line of David is like a tree that has been cut down; but
> just as new branches sprout from a stump, so a new king will arise
> from among David's descendants.

The different translations of Isaiah are anchored in the Hebrew text and reflect varied ideas of both what the translation should be and how the Hebrew text should be understood. In the rest of the book I will expand this introduction at points by showing how other topics discussed relate to translation.

Most of Isaiah is poetry. Probably mainly for reasons of space, ancient manuscripts of the Hebrew Bible, whether in Hebrew or in a translation such as Greek, print very little of the poetic material, such as Psalms and Isaiah, in the versified form that we are used to in modern Bibles. (KJV does not use poetic form because it renders each verse as a separate paragraph. GNB prints select portions of Isaiah in poetic form, e.g., 2:2–4; 11:2–9; all of chaps. 40–55 and 60–62; no comment is made by the translators.) Most translations print the narratives in Isaiah 6–8 (Ahaz and Isaiah), 22:15–25 (Shebna and Eliakim), chapters 36–39 (Hezekiah and Ahaz), and 44:9–20 (the idol maker) in prose. TNK does print the last one wholly in poetic form, while NRSV prints it in prose.

> The makers of idols
> All work to no purpose;
> And the things they treasure
> Can do no good,
> As they themselves can testify.
> They neither look nor think,
> And so they shall be shamed.
> (44:9 TNK)

All who make idols are nothing, and the things they delight in do not profit; their witnesses neither see nor know. And so they will be put to shame. (44:9 NRSV)

The length of a poetic line, the connection between consecutive lines, and the division into subsections are other issues. This includes punctuation and printing with spaces. In 9:11–13[5] TNK uses a separate line for each phrase, while NRSV combines two or more into a single line:

> So the LORD raised adversaries[6] against them,
> and stirred up their enemies,
> the Arameans on the east and the Philistines on the west,
> and they devoured Israel with open mouth.
> For all this his anger has not turned away;
> his hand is stretched out still.
> The people did not turn to him who struck them,
> or seek the LORD of hosts.
> (NRSV)

> So the LORD let the enemies of Rezin
> Triumph over it

>   And stirred up its foes—
>   Aram from the east
>   And Philistia from the west—
>   Who devoured Israel
>   With greedy mouths.
>   Yet His anger has not turned back,
>   And His arm is outstretched still.
>   For the people has not turned back
>   To Him who struck it
>   And has not sought
>   The LORD of Hosts.
>
>   (TNK)

The differences between these two translations include: synonyms (adversaries, enemies and foes; hand and arm); people as a collective (they; the Philistines) or as an individual (it; Philistia); the use of "it" rather than "he" to depersonalize the people; and the use of lowercase (his; hosts) or capital letters (His; Hosts) to refer to God. A translation, including the precise way it is printed on the page, affects our understanding of Isaiah. The differences in translations derive from the complex process of interpreting the Hebrew text, of translating that interpretation into English, and then printing that translation in a particular form in a book.

Parallelism/Repetition

Poetry is an intense and complex use of language. It draws attention to itself so that how a poem looks, its form, is an integral part of what it means, its content. With poetry we pay close attention to what words and how many words are used, how they are arranged, and what is said clearly and what is not. Poetry is marked by recurring patterns whether the repeated aspects are meanings, the actual words used and their arrangement, or the sound of the words. Features such as versification, unusual syntax, and strange uses of words highlight the words on the page to a degree that prose does not. Prose is the ordinary form of written expression. The distinction between poetry and prose in the Hebrew Bible is not rigid. Although there is much in the Hebrew Bible that is obviously prose or poetry, there is much that lies in between the two and can be called poetic prose or prosaic poetry.

In Hebrew poetry one of the main features that draws attention to the poetic language is the use of parallelism or repetition. The occurrence of parallelism in the Hebrew Bible fits on a spectrum; it is obvious and consistent in poetry but not absent in prose. I follow the general trend in contemporary biblical studies to move away from attempts to define set patterns for parallelism and rather to describe the general types of repetition that occur in Hebrew poetry and to show how specific passages of poetry both fit with and depart from the general types. Petersen and Richards, in their *Interpreting Hebrew Poetry*, employ the balance or tension between regularity and variety as a central feature of their presentation. I will illustrate the feature at points in my discussions.[†]

In line with the same trend I do not speak of meter in Hebrew poetry. This is a major aspect of classical and other poetry whose presence no scholar, despite earnest attempts, has been able to demonstrate in Hebrew poetry to the satisfaction of other scholars. Nor do I refer to rhythm, more general patterns of large-scale repetition and flow, since it is outside the scope of my presentation.

A translator has to decide how to represent parallelism in general and each specific repetition in translation. The decision depends in part on how the translator views the role of parallelism in the Hebrew text. How important is it to the poem? How many features of parallelism in the Hebrew need to be and can be rendered in the English? How should the English be printed to highlight the chosen features? The differences between NRSV and TNK in the passages just cited are instructive. With 11:1 NRSV captures the parallelism; GNB bypasses it to make the allusion to David explicit.

Finally, many specific features of parallelism cannot be rendered in English without the use of some sort of notations because of the differences between the languages. These include gender, number, and various types of wordplay. At relevant points in my reading I comment on gender and number, particularly as they appear in the use of the second person pronoun "you"; Hebrew distinguishes gender and number in the pronoun and English does not (see p. 165). For example, in 57:1–5 the prophet denounces "you offspring of a sorceress" and "you children of rebellion"; the pronouns are masculine plural. In verses 6–13 the prophet shifts and addresses a woman: "Among the idols in the valley is your portion; they, they are your lot." All of the second person pronouns in the denunciation are feminine singular.

[†] David L. Petersen and Kent Harold Richards, *Interpreting Hebrew Poetry* (Guides to Biblical Scholarship; Minneapolis: Fortress Press, 1992).

The change in addressees is not observable in the English pronouns and is not noted in the translations we are considering.

With regard to wordplay, I note a pun in 61:3 between *pe'er*, "crown," and *'eper*, "ashes" (see pp. 207 and 213). In 1:23 the equation "your princes are rebels" is literal in Hebrew: *sarayik sorerim*. In Hebrew much of the terminology of chapter 1 comprises various combinations of *s* and *r* sounds. Verses 25–26 offer one final example that plays on the related meanings of to "turn against" and to "return"; in the passage they are the same word in Hebrew: "I turn [*'ashivah*] my hand against you. . . . And I (re)turn [*'ashivah*] your judges as at the beginning."

Figurative Language

Figures of speech are expressions that depart from the ordinary sense and use of words and phrases; they use words in striking ways. Figurative language is a distinctive trait of biblical poetry because of its frequency and intensity. It is not present in prose with the same frequency and intensity. The following figures of speech are the main ones that play a role in my discussions of Isaiah; note the parallelism in the examples.

Simile makes an explicit comparison using *like* or *as*.

> [Your land] is desolate, *as* overthrown by aliens.
> And daughter Zion is left
> *like* a booth in a vineyard,
> *like* a lodge in a cucumber field,
> *like* a besieged city.
>
> (1:7–8)

His heart and the heart of his people shook *as* the trees of the forest shake before the wind. (7:2)[7]

The poet can develop a comparison by building a simile on a simile.

> Therefore this sin will be for you
> *Like a spreading break* in a high wall whose crash comes suddenly,
>   in an instant.
> Its crash is *like the crash of a potter's vase*, ruthlessly smashed,
> And among the smashed pieces there is not found a fragment
> To scoop fire from an oven or to dip water from a cistern.
>
> (30:13–14)[8]

In a *metaphor*, the poet refers to one thing, person, or idea using a word or phrase that normally refers to something else. The reference suggests that the two share a common quality or essence. In a limited sense, a metaphor is a simile without "like" or "as." This is that not because of a chance resemblance, but because this *is* that through a shared attribute or nature.

For example, in Isaiah 1:9 the people assert, in a simile, that they could have been "like Sodom" and become "like Gomorrah," that is, totally destroyed. In 1:10 the prophet employs the comparison and turns it into a metaphor, an assertion of the people's nature, that is, totally wicked: "You rulers of Sodom! You people of Gomorrah!" He does not say that they are *like* rulers of Sodom.

Apostrophe is direct address to an absent or dead person, an element of nature, an entire nation, or something that would not otherwise be addressed. It is generally introduced by "O!" "Hear, O heavens, and give ear, O earth!" (1:2),[9] "O house of Jacob!" (2:5). It is accompanied by *personification*. God, natural objects, abstract ideas, and the dead are endowed with human qualities, attributes, and actions; they are talked of as individuals. Nations such as Israel, Assyria, and Babylon are personified; they can hear, speak, and act as a human in a variety of ways.

"Alas, O proud crown of the drunkards of Ephraim!" (28:1). Ephraim is the main tribal area in Israel, the northern kingdom, and the name refers to the whole kingdom. (This use of a part to refer to the whole is a *synecdoche*.) The proud crown is Samaria, the capital, that by synecdoche can stand for its inhabitants, in this case, the nobility. Even abstract ideas such as God's word and teaching are personified to the extent that they move and act. For example, "teaching goes forth from Zion and the word of the Lord from Jerusalem" (2:3); and "as the rain and snow come down . . . so will be my word that goes forth from my mouth" (55:10–11).

Personification is connected with naming, especially naming to mark a changed status. "Afterward you will be called The City of Righteousness, The Capital Faithful" (1:26).[10] "Whoever is left in Zion and remains in Jerusalem will be called Holy" (4:3). "There Is Not There a Kingdom they name her, and all her princes are Nothing" (34:12). The most elaborate names are in the latter part of Isaiah.

> You [Jacob] will be called "Breach-Mender,"
> "Restorer of streets to be lived in."
> If you refrain from breaking the Sabbath,

> From taking your own pleasure on my holy day,
> If you call the Sabbath "Delightful,"
> And the day sacred to Yahweh "Honourable."
>   (58:12–13 NJB)‡

> They shall call you City of the Lord,
> Zion of the Holy One of Israel.
>   (60:14 NAB)

> You [Zion] will be called by a new name,
> A name given by the LORD himself.
> You will be like a beautiful crown for the LORD.
> No longer will you be called "Forsaken,"
> Or your land be called "The Deserted Wife,"
> Your new name will be "God Is Pleased with Her."
> Your land will be called "Happily Married."
>   (62:2–4 GNB)[11]

Narrative and Speeches

A narrative is a story told by a narrator, a storyteller. A story is comprised of plot, characters, and setting. Genesis is a prime example with stories of creation and the patriarchs, Abraham, Jacob, and Joseph. In the Bible, extended narratives are in prose; the Hebrews reserved poetry for prayers, songs, proverbs, and prophetic literature.

Speeches in narrative are *reported speech*; the narrator reports who is speaking and cites the speech.

> In the beginning God created the heavens and the earth. . . . And God said, "Let there be light," and there was light. (Gen. 1:1–3)

The narrator tells when this happened and what God did; he tells us that God spoke, what was said and, finally, the result of the speech. We have a story in a nutshell: setting, plot, and character. The Lord's statement is marked in translation with quotation marks.

At the other pole, there is *dramatic or lyrical speech* that has little or no indication of who is speaking and to whom. Information about the

---

‡ See p. 13 for a discussion of the two different names for God in the HB: God ('elohim) and the LORD (YHWH). The NJB uses "Yahweh" instead of "the LORD."

speaker, the addressee, and the situation addressed must be inferred from the speech itself. Although some of the speeches in Isaiah fit at the extreme end of this pole, most include some hints about the speaker and the settings. But they are hints; seldom are we given full introductions to a speech. The opening verses of Isaiah are a good illustration. With the exception of verse 1, they also exemplify parallelism.

1. The vision of Isaiah son of Amoz, which he envisioned concerning Judah and Jerusalem in the days of Uzziah, Jotham, Ahaz, and Hezekiah, kings of Judah.
2. Hear, O heavens! and give ear, O earth!
    for the Lord speaks:
    "Children I rear and bring up, but they rebel against me.
3. The ox knows its owner, and the donkey the crib of its master;
    Israel does not know, my people do not understand."

4. Woe! Sinful nation; iniquitous people;
    Offspring of evildoers; children who act corruptly!
    They have forsaken the Lord; they have despised the Holy One
    of Israel; they have turned back.

Because of the superscription to the book in verse 1 we assume that Isaiah, the poet-prophet, speaks in verse 2, but we do not have a narrative introduction like that of Genesis: "And Isaiah said. . . ." We do have an introduction when the Lord is cited. The quotation marks that I use are not in the Hebrew text and there are no clear indications of them, especially for closing the quotation after verse 3.[12] TNK, NIV, GNB, and NJB employ such marks; they are not used in NRSV, REB, or NAB. The use of quotation marks is a matter for the translator's discretion. The added space between verses 3 and 4 occurs in TNK, NIV, GNB, and NRSV. It gives the reader the impression that there is a change of speaker, of subject matter, or of addressee—or perhaps of all these. The break does not occur in the other translations even if they, like NJB, use quotation marks in verses 2–3. The lack of the space gives the reader the impression of continuing speech.

The discussion highlights, once again, the decisions that a translator makes from interpreting the Hebrew text to printing the English on a page. Use of quotation marks, added spaces, and so on are all legitimate aspects of translation; this is not a claim that one of the above translations is more accurate in the way it prints the passage. The difficulties and the possibilities are part of the original Hebrew.

We as readers are affected by what is said, how it is said, and how it is printed on the page. I point the last out at times because we are not always aware of its effects on our reading and understanding. As an example of the effect of printed arrangement, let us reread the same translation with a different presentation.

> The vision of Isaiah son of Amoz, which he envisioned concerning Judah and Jerusalem in the days of Uzziah, Jotham, Ahaz, and Hezekiah, kings of Judah.
>
> Hear, O heavens! and give ear, O earth! for the Lord speaks: Children I rear and bring up, but they rebel against me. The ox knows its owner, and the donkey the crib of its master; Israel does not know, my people do not understand.
>
> Woe, sinful nation; iniquitous people; offspring of evildoers; children who act corruptly! They have forsaken the Lord; they have despised the Holy One of Israel; they have turned back.

Verb Tense

This is a complicated and highly debated area in Hebrew studies, and I deal with it only as it affects English translations of Isaiah. The two conjugations in the Hebrew verb system indicate the type of action just as much as the time of the action, that is, the verb tense, past, present, or future. Examples of types of action are a simple action seen as a whole or an action seen as a process or a series of smaller acts. One of the conjugations also expresses the mode of the action; this is translated into English using helping verbs such as "can," "might," and "ought to."

For example, after the initial call to heavens and earth, NRSV renders the rest of verses 2–3:

> For the Lord *has spoken*:
> I *reared* children and *brought* them *up*, but they *have rebelled* against me.
> The ox *knows* its owner. . . .
> But Israel *does not know*, my people *do not understand*.

In Hebrew all of the verbs belong to the conjugation that indicates a simple action. The Lord's speaking and rearing and the ox's knowing are presented as accomplished fact.

NRSV translates the one Hebrew conjugation with three English forms. First is the English perfect tense, *has spoken* and *have rebelled.* Second is the past tense, *reared* and *brought up.* Third is the present tense, *knows, does not know,* and *does not understand.* Other translations, such as NAB, NJB, and REB, render the first phrase, "for the LORD speaks," which highlights the Lord's speaking as a continuing fact, not just a past event. All understand the opening quotation as a story of past actions (raising and rebelling) with present consequences (not knowing).

I translate the last part of verse 2, "Children I rear and bring up, but they rebel against me," to stress the immediacy and temporal inclusiveness of the passage. Isaiah's vision spans past, present, and future. It is not a simple tale of past grace and sin, past and present punishment, and future restoration. This simple tale is a pattern in Isaiah that is present in chapter 1. The Lord raises them (grace) but the people rebel (sin); they are beaten (punishment: vv. 4–9) and then promised restoration (vv. 26–27). This pattern or plot can begin at any point in time, not just in the past. Whenever the Lord raises children, they rebel, they are punished, and at times they are ultimately restored. My translations, with their frequent use of the present tense, are a logical result of this understanding of the book of Isaiah.

The other Hebrew conjugation, which indicates action as process, is generally translated with the future tense that casts Isaiah's vision into a future that is yet to be. The conjugation is used in 2:2–4. NRSV renders it with the future tense:

In days to come
    the mountain . . . *shall be established* as the highest of the mountains,
    and *shall be raised* above the hills;
    all the nations *shall stream* to it. . . .
He *shall judge* between the nations,
    and *shall arbitrate* for many peoples;
they *shall beat* their swords into plowshares; . . .
nation *shall not lift* up sword against nation.

In the vow of the peoples in verse 3, NRSV uses modal forms:

    Let us go up to the mountain of the LORD . . .
    that he *may teach* us his ways
    and that we *may walk* in his paths.

By contrast, if translated with present and modal tenses, the passage presents a vision that we see now even though it is a vision of a world that does not exist but that is filled with potential and possibility. The future is captured in the opening phrase, and we are transported to those times to see this marvelous event.

> This will be in the latter times:
> The mountain of the house of the Lord is established
> as tallest of the mountains, as the highest of the hills,
> And all the nations flow to it, many peoples come and say,
> "Come, let us go up to the mountain of the Lord,
>   to the house of the God of Jacob,
> That he may teach us his ways and that we may walk in his paths;
> For teaching comes forth from Zion and the word
>   of the Lord from Jerusalem."[13]
> He judges among the nations and decides for many peoples;
> They beat their swords into plowshares and their spears
>   into pruning hooks;
> Nation does not lift a sword against nation,
>   and they no longer learn war.[14]

My translations of this passage and of others accentuate the immediacy of Isaiah's vision by preferring the present tense. We see the scene now even though it is not or is yet to be. These are possible renderings, possible ways of reading Isaiah, but they are not the only ones. As with other translation issues, this is part of the translator's philosophy of translation and of the understanding of Isaiah as a whole and of the particular passage's place in that whole.

"Isaiah"

I use the name "Isaiah" in two ways. First, "Isaiah" refers to the whole book and its implied author. "Implied" means that I am not arguing for a particular historical author of the book. In this use, "Isaiah says . . ." and "Isaiah employs imagery . . ." are shorthand ways of saying that the whole book presents a certain message or imagery. To avoid constant use of "Isaiah," I often refer to the poet or the prophet as the unnamed writer of a section.

This generic sense of "Isaiah" differs from the specific use of the name Isaiah to refer to the eighth-century prophet named in 1:1, 2:1, and 13:1 and who appears in chapters 6–8, 20, and 36–39. This is the individual prophet associated with the events of 735–700 B.C.E. As we will see, he and this period provide many of the major patterns, themes, and imagery for the entire book; and he, in particular, lends his name to the entire book. Isaiah (the whole book) speaks of Isaiah (the eighth-century prophet).

The Vision of Isaiah

The drama of Isaiah is the poet-prophet's vision. A vision presents things seen and imagined just as much as thought and conceptualized. Sin and punishment are concepts; Isaiah presents them in vivid and dramatic fashion, employing parallelism and figurative expressions.

> The way of peace they do not know,
> And there is no justice in their paths.
> Their roads they have made crooked;
> Whoever walks in them does not know peace.
> Therefore justice is far from us,
> And righteousness does not reach us;
> We wait for light, and lo! darkness;
> And for brightness, but in gloom we walk.
> We grope like the blind along a wall,
> Like those who have no eyes we grope;
> We stumble at noon as in the twilight,
> Among the vigorous as though we were dead.
> (59:8–10)

Isaiah is a vision that reaches in time from God's original creation to the creation of a new heavens and new earth. Isaiah, the poet and prophet, seeks ways to bring together and to understand all the places, both in the heavens and on the earth, and all the people and things involved in the world. The people include God and all humanity, and the vision traces the various relationships that they can have with each other. Isaiah focuses on particular periods in time and on a particular cast of characters, especially Israel and their neighbors near and far. The focus still has a significance that reaches beyond those periods and those characters.

The vision encompasses past, present, and future. This is one of the reasons why different translations can vary the verbal tenses between past, present, and future and still be reliable translations. Isaiah is not trying to describe an actual world, present or past, but an ideal world, a dream world, that never existed "but that is filled with the possibility of what might be."[15] In the rest of this book, we will, at the same time, enter this world of Isaiah, see the vision, and read the book.

We start with reading the book. The next chapters examine three different, but overlapping, ways of reading and understanding Isaiah. These are themes, imagery, and characters. *Themes* are the abstract ideas or concepts that we encounter and talk about when we read Isaiah, for example, righteousness, justice, sin, and servanthood. *Imagery* refers to concrete and perceptible aspects, objects, scenes, and actions of the book. The sun, the moon, fire, and gleaming jewels are all part of the imagery of light. *Characters* are those whom we meet on the pages of Isaiah mainly through what they say and what others say about them. The term *character* is used in a broad sense since those we meet in the pages of Isaiah can be personified nations, peoples, and cities. At other times the character can be the historical entity or site without any hint of personification.

Social injustice is an abstract theme; "crushing my people, grinding the face of the poor" (3:15) is an image that embodies the theme. In the brief scene of 3:13–15 the Lord, a major character, "rises and stands in court" to bring these charges of exploitation against "the elders and princes of his people." The latter are occasional characters in the book. This passage is a good example of how these three— themes, imagery, and characters—go together. (The above passage from 59:8–10 is another fine example.) I will focus on the three elements one at a time, but I will not be able to exclude the others from the discussion.

Endnotes to Introduction

1. I follow a common convention in biblical studies and use B.C.E. (Before the Common Era) and C.E. (the Common Era) in place of the traditional Christian designations B.C. (Before Christ) and A.D. (Anno Domini, "the year of the Lord").
2. Eleven major caves were found at Qumran, numbered 1–11. The siglum 1QIsa[a] refers to the first manuscript of Isaiah found in cave 1 at Qumran. 1QIsa[b] is the second manuscript of Isaiah also found in cave 1. Isaiah was a popular book at Qumran; there were at least twenty separate scrolls of the book.
3. This is published by the Jewish Publication Society and is frequently referred to with the abbreviation JPS.
4. Following another common practice in biblical studies, I refer to the "Hebrew Bible" rather than the "Old Testament."
5. This is the versification in NRSV; in TNK it is 9:10–12. In Isaiah, chaps. 9 and 64 differ by one verse in the numeration in the MT from that in the LXX, which under-

lies most English translations. In both chapters the traditional English translations, following the Septuagint, count what is the last verse in both chaps. 8 and 63 in the MT as the first verse of chaps. 9 and 64. Several English translations, e.g., NAB, NJB, and TNK, follow the Hebrew versification.

6. Both NRSV and TNK note that the Hebrew text needs to be changed for this phrase. TNK refers to this as an *emendation*; NRSV, as a *correction* (Cn); both terms mean a change in the Hebrew text that does not have support in any other Hebrew manuscript or ancient translation. NRSV prints "adversaries" and notes "adversaries of Rezin"; TNK prints "enemies of Rezin" and notes "its enemies."

7. 2 Kgs. 16:5 reports the event but 2 Kings is prose narrative. It does not include Isaiah's simile.

8. See J. Cheryl Exum, "Of Broken Pots, Fluttering Birds, and Visions in the Night: Extended Simile and Poetic Technique in Isaiah," *Catholic Biblical Quarterly* 43 (1981): 331–52.

9. This contrasts with the prose of Genesis that describes heavens and earth rather than addressing them: "In the beginning God created the heavens and the earth."

10. Translations differ in whether they set names off by capitalization or by quotation marks. For example, NAB renders the verse, "After that you shall be called city of justice, faithful city," but 58:12:

> "Repairer of the breach," they shall call you,
> "Restorer of ruined homesteads."

11. NJB renders the four titles: Forsaken, Desolation, My Delight is in her, and The Wedded. REB retains the KJV rendering, which transliterates the Hebrew terms underlying the last two titles: Forsaken, Desolate, Hephzibah, and Beulah.

12. GNB includes all of vv. 2–3 as a speech of the Lord: "The LORD said, 'Earth and sky listen to what I am saying. . . . They don't understand at all.'"

13. KJV and GNB include the last part of v. 3 in the people's exhortation as in my translation; the other translations close the quotation after "in his paths." Note the change in meaning if we would extend the quotation marks for another line or to the end of the passage.

14. Isa. 2:2–4 and Mic. 4:1–3 are almost literally identical. Critics debate who has borrowed from whom or whether both Isaiah and Micah are using a third source. It is not necessary to address this problem, since whether the passage is original to Isaiah or taken from another source, it does fit solidly within the vision of Isaiah in terms of words, themes, and imagery.

15. Edgar Conrad, *Reading Isaiah*, 161.

Chapter 1

What Is the Book of Isaiah?

History of Israel

The book of Isaiah alludes to many of the stories of the Hebrew Bible: Eden (51:3), Noah (54:9), and Abraham and Sarah (29:22; 51:2; 63:16). The "formless void" (Hebrew *tohu wabohu*) of Genesis 1:1 is alluded to in the "line of confusion [*tohu*]" and the "plummet of chaos [*bohu*]" in Isaiah 34:11. The references to Exodus are more numerous, and I note a few examples.

> The Lord creates over Mount Zion . . . a cloud by day,
> and smoke and a brightly flaming fire by night.
> (4:5; see Exod. 13:21–22)

> He made water flow from the rock for them;
> he split the rock and water gushed forth.
> (Isa. 48:21; see 11:15–16; 43:2)

> Where is he who put his holy spirit in their midst?
> Who made his glorious arm march at Moses' right hand?
> Who split the waters before them? . . .
> Who led them through the depths?
> (63:11–13)

The division of the land in Joshua 13–21 is alluded to in "He has cast the lot for them, and his hand has divided her for them with the line" (Isa. 34:17; see 34:11).

Little is said of the events of 1–2 Samuel and 1 Kings, although the establishment of the monarchy, the founding of Jerusalem, and the building of the temple are taken for granted as past events. The name David is mentioned a few times (e.g., 7:2, 13; 9:7; 37:35), but there is no reference to any of the events of his life or to him as a person. The main periods of Israel's history referred to in detail in Isaiah are narrated in 2 Kings 15–20 (2 Chr. 28–32) and in Ezra and Nehemiah.

The following synopsis of these periods of Israel's history is background for the treatment of Isaiah. For reasons of space and simplicity, I do not deal at length with Isaiah's geography either in a technical discussion of its accuracy or as his picture of the world, his visualized map of the universe. His human world comprises the lands stretching from Egypt in the south to Assyria and Babylon in the northeast; this world includes Israel and their immediate neighbors such as Edom, Moab, and Aram. There are references to other distant lands of both Africa and Asia. Beyond the human, Isaiah's geography includes the heavens and the mythic regions of the waters above the heavens and below the earth.

Assyria was a country in Mesopotamia whose power had waxed and waned over the centuries. In 745 B.C.E. Tiglath-pileser III began to establish an empire that would rule the Near East for over a century. From 734 on, he was campaigning in the west and was opposed by a coalition headed by Rezin of Aram, with his capital of Damascus,[1] and Pekah, king of Israel, whose capital was Samaria (Isa. 7–8). Judah, ruled by Ahaz from his capital, Jerusalem, did not join the coalition. The allies threatened to invade Judah, depose Ahaz, and replace him with a new king, the son of Tabeel (Isa. 7:6), who would join the coalition. Tiglath-pileser responded to Ahaz's pleas and payment of tribute. He destroyed Damascus, incorporated Aram into his empire, and invaded Israel. Israel was spared total conquest because Hoshea (732–722) paid tribute. At the time Judah apparently became a loyal Assyrian subject. This conflict in 734–732 is referred to as the Syro-Ephraimite War.

Within a few years Israel rebelled against Assyria, was destroyed by the Assyrian king Sargon in 722 (Isa. 20), and incorporated into the empire. Judah remained a loyal subject. Hezekiah succeeded Ahaz on the Judean throne in 715. In about 704 he joined a coalition against Assyria. Sennacherib, the Assyrian king, invaded Judah in 701, devastated the country, besieged Jerusalem, but did not capture the city (Isa. 36–37). The period of time from approximately 735 to 700 B.C.E. forms the background for much of Isaiah 1–39. Isaiah passes over the next century of Judah's history and, in its references to historical events, jumps from the Assyrian crisis of the late eighth century to the Babylonian conquest, in the early sixth century, of Judah and Jerusalem.

Babylon, both the city and its king, play a central role in Isaiah. It was part of the Assyrian Empire and was frequently an instigator of rebellion, above all with King Merodach-baladan (710–700; Isa. 39). The Chaldeans controlled Babylon in the seventh–sixth centuries; their main monarch was Nebuchadnezzar (605–562). In 605 the Babylonians destroyed the last of the Assyrian Empire. Nebuchadnezzar invaded Judah. In the succeeding years, he took a large number of Judeans into exile at a site near Babylon. He destroyed Jerusalem in 587. This begins the period referred to as the exile, which is usually dated about 600–540. The events of the conquest of the land, the destruction of city and temple, and the exile into Babylon are threatened and anticipated in parts of Isaiah 1–39 and looked back on in 40–66, where their imminent end is predicted. The book of Isaiah, however, says nothing explicit about these events. Chapter 39 closes with a forecast of the Babylonian invasion and exile, and chapter 40 opens with the declaration that the time of exile is over.

About 550 *Cyrus of Persia* appeared on the scene. He conquered Babylon in 539 and incorporated that empire into his own. One of Cyrus's policies was to allow conquered peoples to reestablish themselves in their homeland as long as they would be loyal to him. The Jews were one of these peoples; the books of Ezra and Nehemiah relate one version of their story. Cyrus's career, the return from exile, and the rebuilding of the city and the community form the background for much of Isaiah 40–66.

Historians debate the exile as a historical event. Debated issues include the status and number of exiles (few or many? only the ruling elite or others?), the condition of Judah (both the land and the community: Devastated? Prospering? Somewhere in between?) and the event of "the return" (Who? How many? What effect on Judea?). Regardless of the historical reality of "the exile" and "the return," Isaiah employs them as major patterns and images throughout his book. This is analogous to his transformation of the events of 735–700 into a central pattern. At many points I will speak of the exile and the return as Isaiah speaks of them and depicts them, but I will not thereby be taking a stand on the actual history of an exile or return.

The latter parts of Isaiah 40–66 and earlier parts of the book, such as 24–27, depart from ancient history and look off into a distant future, or into a never-never time, for the final judgment of the wicked, the vindication of the righteous, and the creation of new heavens and new earth. This look into the future is matched by the glance to the distant past of creation mainly in 40–45. Thus the book of Isaiah scans the history of the world from its creation to its end and re-creation with a particular focus on the period from about 735 to 500.

Outline of Isaiah

There is a large degree of agreement in biblical studies about larger divisions within Isaiah, although there is debate about the significance of the sections for understanding the book. In the following, I divide Isaiah into sections to present, in summary form, its contents and styles and the issues and problems encountered in reading it. As discussed in the introduction, however, I do not employ the usual division into three parts, the three Isaiahs—1–39, 40–55, and 56–66. The discussion is a way to look at this large, complex work, but the divisions are not the only way to break up the book into separate parts.

1. 1:1–12:6

Similar style and content bind these chapters. Whether speeches or narratives, the material is mostly descriptive and presents its scenes with sufficient detail so that we can easily imagine them. The content is largely denunciations of sin and evil, whether that of Israelites or of others, and announcements of the disasters that are rushing upon them. The latter are depicted mainly as military invasion and social anarchy.

> For Jerusalem stumbles and Judah falls,
> Because their speech and their deeds are against the Lord
>   to defy his glorious presence.
> The look on their faces bears witness against them;
> They proclaim their sin like Sodom, they do not hide it.
> Woe to them! They have brought evil on themselves.
>
> (3:8–9)

Woe! You who rise early in the morning in pursuit of strong drink,
    you who linger in the evening to be inflamed by wine;
Lyre and harp, tambourine and flute and wine comprise your feasts.
But the work of the Lord they do not regard, and the deed
    of his hands they do not see!
Therefore my people go into exile without knowledge;
    their nobles are dying of hunger, and their multitude is parched
    with thirst.

Therefore Sheol has enlarged her throat and opened her mouth
  beyond measure;
her [Jerusalem's and/or Sheol's] honored and her multitude go down,
  her throng and all who exult in her.

(5:11–14)

The gloomy picture of chapters 1–12 is punctuated by visions of glorious times and concluded by a hymn (12:1–6).

This will be in the latter times:
The mountain of the house of the Lord is established
As tallest of the mountains, as the highest of the hills,
And all the nations flow to it, many peoples come. . . .
They beat their swords into plowshares and their spears
    into pruning hooks;
Nation does not lift a sword against nation,
    and they no longer learn war.

(2:2–4)

A shoot goes forth from the stump of Jesse,
    and a sprout blossoms from its roots.
The spirit of the Lord rests upon it, a spirit of wisdom
    and understanding,
A spirit of counsel and strength, a spirit of knowledge
    and fear of the Lord. . . .
They do no evil and they do not act corruptly
    in all my holy mountain,
For the earth is filled with the knowledge of the Lord
    as waters cover the sea.

(11:1–2, 9)

Assyria, with minor roles given to Egypt, Moab, Edom, and others, is the major enemy, first introduced in chapter 7. "The Lord whistles . . . for the bee that is in the land of Assyria" (v. 18). His destruction is announced in chapter 10. "I will punish the arrogant mind of the king of Assyria" (v. 12). There are a group of other named characters, whether individuals, for example, God, Ahaz, Isaiah, Rezin (7:1–8), and Zechariah son of Jeberechiah (8:2); nation or city, for example, Jerusalem-Zion, Israel, and Jacob; or undefined, unnamed characters, such as the child in 9:6 and 10:19 and the shoot in 11:1–5.

There is a basic plot in the chapters that includes a threat of attack, the attack itself, and finally promised removal of the attacker and the resulting restoration of the people. The elements of the plot do not occur in strict narrative sequence, however, but are found in varying arrangements throughout the chapters. Threat, invasion, and promise, for example, occur in chapters 1 and 10. We will encounter this throughout our reading of the whole book. Isaiah does not present a narrative following a chronological or logical sequence. This is a vision, a poem, that presents, repeats, and continues to repeat themes and images. It is appropriate to refer to Isaiah as a collage or as variations on themes. Therefore, as already stated in the introduction, in my reading of Isaiah I will consistently compare and contrast passages from throughout the book (see pp. 4–5); I will repeat this notice at relevant places. This outline is the main place in my book where I strictly follow the sequential order of Isaiah.

Isaiah compresses the events of 735–700 into a major image and pattern. Because of human evil, the Lord calls for invasion and devastation, yet with a surviving remnant (1:7–9). An overwhelming force sweeps through the land (5:26–30) and, taking on the form of the Assyrian army, destroys all before it, including Damascus and Israel. It rushes into Judah like a swarm of insects (7:18–19), like a flood that reaches to the neck (8:8) and leaves the head as the image of the survivors. The pattern appears in the image of the forest being cut down and the remaining stumps producing new shoots (10:15–11:1). Once the Assyrian is removed, the overwhelming force takes the form of the Babylonian army (chaps. 13–14 and 39).

2. Chapters 13–23

There is a new superscription in 13:1, "An oracle on Babylon that Isaiah son of Amoz saw." "An oracle on . . ." is repeated in most of the chapters with different nations addressed (e.g., Moab, 15:1; and Tyre, 23:1). The style can be descriptive and graphic as in chapters 13–14 and 20, impressionistic as in 15–16 and 21, and mixed as in 22:1–14 and 23:1–18. The impressionistic poems present the reactions to the devastation and are in an abrupt style. Ar and Kir are Moabite sites.

> Alas! In a night Ar is laid waste,
> Moab is ruined;
> Alas! In a night Kir is laid waste
> Moab is ruined. . . .
> On every head is baldness,

> Every beard is shaved.
> In the streets they wear sackcloth;
> On its roofs and in its squares,
> All are wailing,
> Streaming with tears.
>
> (15:1–3)

Chapter 13 expands in striking fashion the depiction of the approach of the overwhelming force (5:26–30) because of the sin of the world (13:9–11). The force now causes worldwide devastation, depicted in terms of natural disaster and military invasion.

> Indeed, the stars of the heavens and their constellations
>   do not gleam with their light;
> The sun is dark when it rises and the moon does not shine
>   with its light.
> I punish the world for its evil, and the wicked for their iniquity. . . .
> Whoever is found is thrust through, and whoever is captured
>   falls to the sword.
>
> (13:10–15)

These dark tones reverberate in the following chapters that focus on the devastation and on the evil that led to it. Babylon moves to center stage as the enemy; Assyria is not gone and shares the scene with Babylon. Just as soon as Babylon enters the stage, however, its days of glory and destructive power are known to be already past, for the poet announces its destruction at the start (13:19–14:23). "Fallen, fallen is Babylon! All the images of its gods lie broken on the ground" (21:9). Isaiah never depicts Babylon as a present invading force.

The disaster that befalls the world is concentrated on Babylon and Assyria, and the ripple effects spread to the surrounding peoples, including Israel, Moab, Egypt, and Tyre. They have surviving remnants even if very small and weak (16:14). Because of this concern with other peoples, chapters 13–23 are called The Oracles against the Nations. The title is limiting since the section deals with all humanity and also with Israel, both negatively and positively. Destruction of others both includes Israel (17:1–6; 22:1–25) and means their survival (14:1–3; 19:23–25). The balance and tension between the fates of Israel and others is found throughout the book.

Besides the personified nations and their rulers, other named characters have already appeared in chapters 1–12 or are introduced for

the first time. Ahaz (14:28) and Isaiah (20) are among the former, and
Sargon (20), Shebna, and Eliakim (22:15–25) among the latter. The
brief tale of the last two presents another Isaianic pattern. A time of
power for one nation or person ends in their fall; another rejoices in
the fall as they enjoy their time in power. But this is not a permanent
state since the pattern repeats itself and the latter falls. Those who
think that they are in a safe place can soon be cut down. This applies
to all, whether Assyrian, Babylonian, or Israelite.

3. Chapters 24–27

Chapter 24 presents a vivid scene of desolation that is similar to
chapter 13 in its cosmic reach, except that the focus is now on the desolation and the human evil accompanying it, not on the invading army
that produces it.

> The earth dries up, it withers; the world shrivels, it withers;
>   the heavens shrivel with the earth.
> The earth lies polluted beneath its inhabitants, for they have violated
>   laws, they have broken statutes, they have destroyed
>   the eternal covenant.
> Therefore a curse consumes the earth, and its inhabitants
>   suffer for their guilt.
>
> (24:4–6)

Destruction befalls the earth and the city of chaos (24:10); the destruction is both natural disaster and social disorder. Chapters 24–27 stand
out in their context of 15–23 and 28–33 because of the limited number of specific names and places. The city of chaos has no name and
contrasts with Tyre, the arrogant city (23:7). Short chants and songs
in the first person (e.g., 24:16, 25:1–5; 26:1–6; 27:2–5) present reactions, although they are more celebration than lamentation.

> O Lord, my God, you, I exalt you and I praise your name,
> For you have performed wonders, plans of old, entirely reliable.
> Indeed, you turned the city into a heap, the fortified city
>   into a ruin. . . .
> For you were a fortress for the poor, a fortress for the needy
>   in their distress,
> A shelter from the storm, shade from the heat.
>
> (25:1–4)

Balancing the section's distinctiveness, chapters 24–27 are, at the same time, a repetition of many of the images and themes of chapters 13–23, now placed in a more inclusive and less specific setting. In a sense, chapters 13 and 24–27 are like statements of principle while 14–23 are the specific examples.

4. Chapters 28–33

These chapters comprise a variety of speeches and declarations of varying length, including a poem on the wisdom of farmers (28:23–29). It is not always easy, if at all possible, to decide who is speaking and to whom or to see what is being described or spoken about. This general and unspecific aspect ties the section to the preceding, chapters 24–27. The speeches are dominated by denunciation of corruption and violence and the announcement of the matching natural, military, and social disasters; in this the section is related to chapters 1–12 and parts of 13–23. The image of the oncoming army is alluded to at points (28:2, 17–19; 29:5–8).

Alas, O proud crown of the drunkards of Ephraim;
The fading bloom of its glorious beauty,
Which is on the head of those bloated with rich food, drunk with wine.
See! the Lord has one strong and powerful like a hailstorm,
    a destructive wind,
Like a storm of water, mighty and flooding—
He will hurl them to the earth with force.
You will be trampled underfoot, O proud crown
    of the drunkards of Ephraim;
And the fading bloom of its glorious beauty, which is on
    the head of those bloated with rich food,
Will be like the first fig before summer that, as soon as someone
    sees it, they eat it right from their hand.

(28:1–4)

Like the previous sections, these chapters include glimpses of far better times, mainly in 28:5–6, 16; 29:17–24; 32:1–8, 15–20; and 33:17–24.

In that day the Lord of Hosts will be a beautiful crown
    and a glorious wreath for the remnant of his people,

A spirit of justice for those seeking justice, and of strength
  for those turning back the battle at the gate.

(28:5–6)

Is it not just a little while before Lebanon becomes farmland,
  and farmland is thought of as a forest?
On that day the deaf will hear the words of a book,
  while from their deep gloom the blind will see;
The poor will continually rejoice in the Lord, while the needy
  of humanity will celebrate in the Holy One of Israel.

(29:17–19)

The grim fates awaiting humans include others than just Israel and Judah, mainly Egypt (30:1–7; 31:1–3) and Assyria (30:29–33; 31:8–9), but they do not play roles as important as they do in chapters 1–12 and as Babylon does in 13–23. Indeed, chapters 28–33 do not have the number of named characters, individual and national, that 1–23 do. God is the sole major named character; David is noted in a reference to the past in 29:1.

5. Chapters 34–35

This is a poem comprising two distinct parts, 34:1–15 and 35:1–10, with 34:16–17 as a transition.[2] The poem is in the center of the book of Isaiah and is indicative of the prophet's frequent combination and contrast of destruction and restoration, of judgment and salvation. To some extent, this mirrors the division of the book into two large segments. In Isaiah 1–33 the dominant picture and tone are of evil, sin, and the accompanying destruction and punishment; positive and hopeful scenes and proclamations interrupt the gloom at many points. In Isaiah 40–66 the emphasis switches. The dominant picture and tone are of forgiveness, return, and restoration; at the same time, negative scenes and proclamations of sin, desolation, and continued rebellion mar the hope at many points.

Isaiah 34:1–15 depicts a gory slaughter and the resultant eery, tranquil ruins and their strange inhabitants. The description is reminiscent of chapters 13 and 24. The Lord's rage encompasses the world. It focuses on Edom but does not lose its universal scope. The ruined land of 34:9–15 is "her" land, and she can be Edom, Zion, and the entire earth.[3]

Yes, the Lord's wrath is against all the nations,
    and his fury against all their armies.
He has doomed them, he has given them to the slaughter. . . .
Yes, a day of vengeance for the Lord, a year of retribution
    for Zion's case.
Her wadis turn to pitch, and her dust to brimstone.
And her land is burning pitch. . . .
But they possess her, the desert owl and the screech owl. . . .
Demons meet with phantoms, and a hairy beast calls to his friend.
Indeed, there Lilith [a female demon] reposes and finds rest
    for herself.
There the owl nests and delivers, for she hatches and broods
    in her shade.

(34:2, 8–9, 11, 14–15)

The picture of joy, restoration, and return to Zion in the second part of the poem forms a sharp contrast to the first part. The picture includes many of the positive images of the hopeful passages in chapters 28–33, especially the transformation of nature and the healing of the blind and deaf. The joy of the closing scene is tempered by the following stories of war and sickness in chapters 36–39.

Let wilderness and dry land rejoice; desert, shout and bloom. . . .
They see the glory of the Lord, the splendor of our God. . . .
Then are opened the eyes of the blind, and the ears
    of the deaf are opened. . . .
Indeed, waters break forth in the wilderness and streams
    in the desert. . . .
There emerges there a highway, yes, a way; it is called
    The Holy Way. . . .
The redeemed walk there, the ransomed of the Lord, they return;
They come to Zion with song, with everlasting joy on their heads.
Rejoicing and joy reach out, and grief and sighing flee.

(35:1–2, 5–6, 8–10)

6. Chapters 36–39

The narratives, involving Hezekiah and Isaiah, are almost the same as those in 2 Kings 18:13–20:19. Hezekiah's psalm of thanksgiving in Isaiah 38:10–20 is the most noticeable difference; it is not in 2 Kings. Speech dominates the stories. The narrative portions provide particular settings for the extended speeches by the Assyrian general, Hezekiah, and Isaiah quoting the Lord. (Most translations print 37:22–29 and 38:10–20 in poetic form.) The four chapters are a transition from the first part of the book to the second and, to some extent, repeat the double vision of destruction and restoration in chapters 34–35.

The first two chapters are a war of words with the final victory going to the words of Isaiah and the Lord.[4] The enemy is Assyria, whose defeat, but not annihilation, is forecast in 37:29–35 and then narrated in verses 36–38. The army stops at the walls of Jerusalem, the flood reaches only to the neck, and the remnant is left (37:31–32). In the crisis, Hezekiah proves himself to be a king more reliant on the Lord than Ahaz was in chapter 7.

As in chapters 1–12, the stories refer to named individuals, for example, Sennacherib of Assyria, Eliakim, Shebna (see 22:15–25 for the last two), Joah, Tirhakah of Egypt, and Esarhaddon of Assyria; and to places, for example, Lachish, Libnah, and Nineveh. This contrasts with the remainder of the book, which uses traditional names and is much less specific in its references to people and places.

Hezekiah's illness and recovery in chapter 38 are a story of faithfulness and reward, but the reward is limited since Hezekiah is granted only fifteen more years of life. This is analogous to Jerusalem's fate. The city is saved from Sennacherib and then destroyed by Babylon about a century later. The Assyrian army may stop at the walls of Jerusalem, but the invading cosmic army of 5:26–30 and 13:1–16 keeps coming. Chapter 39, the arrival in Jerusalem of messengers from Merodach-baladan of Babylon, marks the transition from Assyria to Babylon as the enemy, even though we already know Babylon's ultimate fate from chapters 13–14 and 21.

7. 40:1–49:13

The section opens with the call to comfort the Lord's people and closes with a short hymn celebrating the comforting. (The fact that the break is made in the middle of a chapter indicates that chapters do not have to be taken as the only way to separate the material into meaningful parts.) With the rest of chapters 40–66, the section shares a style distinct from that in most of chapters 1–39. Large parts of the latter look to the events of the last third of the eighth century as significant for developing patterns and images central to Isaiah's vision. Chapters 1–23 and 36–39 include a large number of specific names of individuals and places, all of which can be located in that early setting. With the exception of the names and titles for God, Israel, and Zion-Jerusalem, chapters 40–66 use few names of other people and places. The chapters are similar to 24–27 and 34–35.

Most of the speeches in chapters 40–66 are comparatively long and coherent. Many, if not most, of them sound like one side of an ongoing conversation and argument in which we can reconstruct only part of what the other side is saying. The feature is clear in 40:1–49:13 in the use of questions, usually with answers provided (e.g., 40:12–31; 41:2–4; 45:9–13; 48:14–16).

> Who has measured the waters in the hollow of his hand?
> Who has marked off the heavens with his hand? . . .
> Do you not know? Have you not heard? Has it not been
>   told to you from the very start?
> Have you not understood from the time the earth was founded?
> It is he who sits above the earth's horizon, whose inhabitants
>   look like grasshoppers;
> It is he who stretches out the heavens like a curtain,
>   who pitches them like a tent to sit in.
>   (40:12, 21–22)

The conversational quality is also evident in the calls to assemble for a debate or a trial (e.g., 41:1; 43:9; 44:7–8; 45:20–21) and in the declarations that others, mainly idols, have no answers or are unable to answer (e.g., 41:28–29; 46:1–7).

> Set forth your case! says the Lord. Lay out your arguments!
>   says the King of Jacob.
> Let them lay them out and tell us what will happen.
> Tell us about the past, what it was, so that we may consider it. . . .
> Tell us about the future so that we may know that you are gods.
> Do something good or evil so that we may be terrified of you.
> But you are less than nothing and your work is less than zero;
>   any who choose you are an abomination.
>   (41:21–24)

In part the debate is with other nations and their idols, but this is a backdrop to the main debate with Israel/Jacob. On the one hand, Israel is in despair and doubts the Lord's ability to save them.

> Why do you say, O Jacob, and assert, O Israel,
>   "My way is hidden from the Lord, and my claim
>   for justice passes by my God"?
>
>   (40:27)

To counter the despair both God and prophet assert and reassert the divine power obvious in God's creation of the world.

> Do you not know? Have you not heard?
> An everlasting God is the Lord, the Creator of the ends of the earth.
>   (40:28)

On the other hand, Israel resists the message of hope because it involves Cyrus, a foreign king, who is referred to as the Lord's shepherd and even the anointed, the messiah (44:28–45:1; see p. 154). These are terms used elsewhere in the Hebrew Bible mainly for a Davidic king. There is a twofold thrust to the argument. God is able to save and saves in the way God chooses.

> Woe to whoever quarrels with the one who fashions him. . . .
> Thus says the Lord, the Holy One of Israel,
>   the one who fashions him:
> Will you question me about the future, about my children?
> Will you give me orders about the work of my hands?
> I, I[5] made the earth, and I created humanity upon it;
> I, my own hands stretched out the heavens,
>   and all their hosts I give orders to;
> I, I aroused him [Cyrus] in righteousness,
>   and I straighten out all his ways;
> He, he will rebuild my city, and my exiles he will set free.
>   (45:9–13)

Cyrus, the one called from the east and from the north, is a human manifestation of the powerful force whose first appearance was at the end of chapter 5. The force took on cosmic and divine proportions in chapter 13. Assyria was the first human manifestation and Babylon the second. Assyria swept through the land but stopped at the walls of Jerusalem. The city symbolizes the remnant. Babylon came next and took people into exile, leaving Jerusalem and the land in ruins. The remnant in chapters 40–66 is the people in exile and those left in the land; deserted Jerusalem symbolizes both groups. The time of exile ends with the message of comfort for the remnant surviving the onslaughts.

> Speak to Jerusalem's heart and proclaim to her
> That she has served her sentence, that her penalty is paid,
> That she has received from the Lord a punishment double
>   what her sins deserved.
>
> (40:2)

God is the approaching force: "Look! The Lord God comes with strength, his arm rules for him" (40:10). The human form is Cyrus, who shares some of the characteristics of the army of 5:26–30:

> He gives nations to him [Cyrus] and their kings he tramples;
> He treats them like dust with his sword,
>   like windblown straw with his bow;
> He pursues them—he passes by safely,
>   and his feet do not touch the road.
>
> (41:2–3)

The divine-human force now comes for Israel's benefit. "Cyrus [is] my shepherd, and he will carry out all that I want," including rebuilding Jerusalem and the temple (44:28). The final end for Babylon is announced in chapter 47, and it is mentioned for the last time in 48:20.

Amid the talk of hope and of divine power for creation and redemption, there are strong echoes of previous parts of Isaiah and their message that it is human evil and sin, particularly those of Israel, that have brought disaster upon them. Chapters 40–42 are repeated assertions both of comfort and return for Israel-Jerusalem, indeed for all poor and needy, and of the divine ability to perform this. But this is still the people of old who have eyes and ears but who do not see and hear what matters (42:20); this is the deaf and blind people of Isaiah 6. They have been plundered and are locked in prison, but

> Who surrendered Jacob to spoilers and Israel to robbers?
> Is it not the Lord whom we have sinned against?
> They were not willing to walk in his ways,
>   and they would not obey his teaching.
> He poured his heated rage upon him, the fury of war.
>
> (42:24–25)

8. 49:14–54:17

Speeches contrasting Zion-Jerusalem's despair with assurances that the Lord can and will restore them open the section. We hear no more of Cyrus or of the arguments that God as Creator has the power and right to call Cyrus.

> Zion says, "The Lord has forsaken me, my Lord has forgotten me."
> Does a woman forget her infant, showing no compassion
>   for the child of her womb?
> Even if these could forget, I, I will not forget you.
>
> (49:14–15)

The Lord's servant both speaks (49:4–9) and is described (52:13–53:12) in the midst of these proclamations to Zion-Jerusalem. I deal with the servant in more detail in chapter 5 (see pp. 186–200). These two poems on the servant in Isaiah 49 and 52–53 contrast misery and salvation. Citing 49:4–9, which is part of 40:1–49:13, shows that the division into sections is helpful but not a hard-and-fast separation of the material.

In chapter 54 the poet assures a barren and abandoned woman that she will be restored and will have abundant children: "The children of the desolate woman will be more than those of the married woman" (54:1). The woman is both Jerusalem and any abandoned woman in need. The chapter closes with a declaration about the servants of the Lord, not the individuals Zion-Jerusalem and the Lord's servant: "This is the heritage of the Lord's servants and what they have a right to expect from me" (54:17). The remainder of the book concerns these servants, God's people, and focuses on their relation to Israel and, in chapters 60–62, to Jerusalem.

9. Chapters 55–59

Chapter 55 is transitional. It opens with the motif of thirst that is frequent in chapters 40–54: "Ho! All that thirst come to the waters" (v. 1). Choice is central in chapters 56–66: "Seek the Lord while he is to be found; call to him while he is near" (v. 6). Joy closes the chapter: "Indeed, you go out in joy, and in peace you are brought back" (v. 12).

Chapters 56–59 stress the related themes of choice and decision that underlie the division of the people into the righteous, the Lord's servants, and the wicked, "those who know nothing, all who turn to their own way, their own gain" (56:11). The servants include foreigners and eunuchs, two normally excluded groups (56:2–8). The wicked, the violent, and the unknowing include many in Israel. The deciding factors are the attitude toward God and the matching behavior.

> Maintain justice, and do what is right.
> (56:1)

> All who maintain the Sabbath by not profaning it,
>   and who hold fast to my covenant—
> I bring them to my holy mountain, and I make them happy
>   in my house of prayer.
>
> (56:6–7)

> If you do not trample on the Sabbath by pursuing
>   your own business on my holy day;
> If you call the Sabbath a delight and the Lord's holy day an honor, . . .
> Then you may delight in the Lord, and I will make you ride
>   on the heights of the land.
>
> (58:13–14)

In many ways the depictions of the people here and in chapters 63–66 recall those in 1–12 and 28–33. Isaiah comes full circle, and the remnant of chapters 40–54 finds itself struggling with many of the same problems and issues as the Israel of old. Chapter 59 is a lengthy list of the people's sins and violence. The Lord reacts, for "it is evil in his eyes" (v. 15). God repays enemies with wrath (v. 18), but "he comes to Zion as redeemer, to those in Jacob who turn from rebellion" (v. 20). This is the first mention of Zion-Jerusalem by name since 52:1–9, and it forms a fitting introduction to chapters 60–62.

10. Chapters 60–62

This is a keystone in chapters 55–66. Chapters 60–62 are filled with images of brilliance, joy, and abundance, while the surrounding chapters describe divine wrath and the pleas of the people for mercy and forgiveness. In chapter 60 the poet addresses a woman—each "you" is feminine singular—who is called City of the Lord, Zion of the Holy One of Israel (v. 14). She is bathed in light and her children, her inhabitants, return to her.

Arise! Shine! For your light comes, and the glory of the Lord
   rises upon you. . . .
Lift your eyes and look around: they all gather, they come to you,
Your sons come from far away and your daughters,
   at their nurses' side.

(vv. 1–4)

In chapter 61 an unidentified person proclaims that she or he has been anointed by the Lord to release all prisoners, particularly Zion's children. Once released, "they rebuild the ancient ruins, the old desolate sites they restore" (v. 4). A person, perhaps the prophet, rejoices in the Lord, "for he has clothed me in garments of salvation, and with a robe of righteousness he has wrapped me" (v. 10).

There will be no rest for anyone until Zion is restored in accord with the image of chapter 60.

For Zion's sake I will not keep silent, and for Jerusalem's sake
   I will not rest,
Until her righteousness goes forth as a bright light
   and her salvation burns like a torch.

(62:1)

The three chapters close with a renewed call to build the highway for both people and city.

They are called "The Holy People," "The Redeemed of the Lord,"
And you are called "Sought Out," "A City Unforsaken."

(v. 12)

11. Chapters 63–66

Isaiah closes with divine wrath, human pleas for mercy, and a sharp distinction between those with and those against the Lord.

I trample peoples in my anger, and I make them drunk in my wrath,
   and I pour their lifeblood on the ground.

(63:6)

Look! The Lord comes in fire, and like a whirlwind his chariots,
To repay with his wrathful anger and to rebuke with flames of fire.

Yes, by fire—by his sword—the Lord judges all flesh;
   and many are those slain by the Lord.

(66:15–16)

   The people plead for divine help. They describe God's past mercy and their present misery. God was forgiving despite their rebellion, especially during the exodus.

O that you would rend the heavens and descend . . .
O make your name known to your enemies so that
   the nations will tremble before you. . . .
Be not exceedingly angry, O Lord, and do not remember sin forever.

(64:1–2, 9)[6]

There is a distinction between those with and those against the Lord; the Lord speaks to the latter.

My chosen inherit [the land], and my servants dwell there. . . .
But you who forsake the Lord, who forget my holy mountain, . . .
I destine you to the sword, and all of you crumble
   before the slaughter.
Look! My servants eat but you are hungry.
Look! My servants drink but you are thirsty.

(65:9–13)

   The poet stresses positive images and themes in the creation of new heavens and a new earth and with the fertility and joy of Jerusalem.

Be glad for Jerusalem, sing with her, all you who love her!
Rejoice, rejoice with her, all you who have mourned for her. . . .
For I am extending to her peace like a river and,
   like a flooding stream, the wealth of nations. . . .
And it is known that the hand of the Lord is with his servants,
   and his rage with his enemies.

(66:10–14)

Isaiah closes with a mixed image. All are forever in the Lord's presence and bowed in worship. But they can go forth and "see the bodies of the people who rebel against me, for their worm does not die, and their fire cannot be quenched" (vv. 22–24).

Endnotes to Chapter 1

1. Aram is roughly equivalent to modern-day Syria.
2. See my *Isaiah 34–35: A Nightmare/A Dream* (Journal for the Study of the Old Testament Supplement 281; Sheffield: Sheffield Academic Press, 1999).
3. Translations resolve the ambiguity by using Edom in the translation of v. 9 or by including a footnote indicating that Edom is meant (TNK). NJB employs a neuter pronoun: "its streams will turn into pitch."
4. I take the phrase "war of words" from Danna Fewell's study of the matching narrative in 2 Kings: "Sennacherib's Defeat: Words at War in 2 Kings 18:13–19:37," *Journal for the Study of the Old Testament* 34 (1986): 79–90.
5. In Hebrew the verb form indicates both person and number; "I made" is one word. To use the separate pronoun with the verb emphasizes the subject. I mark this by repeating the pronoun: "I, I" and "he, he." There is a similar emphasis in the repetition, "I, my hands." Translations differ in how they treat these pronouns. They may indicate the pronoun with a phrase such as "I myself" (NJB), "It was I" (TNK, NAB), or "I alone" (REB, GNB); or they may not indicate it at all: "He shall rebuild my city" (v. 13: NRSV, NAB).
6. See pp. 20–21 for discussion of the one-verse difference between the Hebrew and most English translations.

Chapter 2

What Does Isaiah Think?

Evil and Good

Themes are the abstract concepts that we use to talk about the meaning of Isaiah, what Isaiah thinks and says; images are concrete, imaginative ways of expressing these themes. Although the focus of this chapter is on themes, it is impossible to discuss them without presenting the imagery that accompanies them. Further, because themes in Isaiah are closely interconnected, discussion of one theme will include others so that the chapter cannot be divided into self-contained sections that deal with just one theme. I reiterate my earlier comment that since I am reading Isaiah as a grand, unified poem, I freely compare and contrast passages from throughout the book often without giving attention to their context (see pp. 4–5). The passages are connected by similar thematic content. I start with the twin themes of human evil and human good and then move into other thematic aspects of Isaiah.

Human evil and sin take a variety of forms. Sin is often presented against a background of divine care and good, that is, a reason is provided why certain human attitudes and actions are wrong and sinful. "Children I raise, but they rebel against me" (1:2).

> I am the Lord your God who teaches you how to prosper,
> Who leads you on the road you should walk on.
> Oh, if only you had paid attention to my commandments!
> Then your prosperity would be like a river
> and your success like the waves of the sea.
>
> (48:17–18)

Sin is rebellion against authority, a refusal to do what one should: "If you refuse and rebel . . ." (1:20). The authority may be that of a parent or of a ruler who has presented laws and statutes for the people to follow. In Isaiah this background of divine authority, this expectation that humans should do some things and not do others, is briefly stated or alluded to more than it is expressly argued for. The ultimate basis is God the Creator, who brings the world into being and who provides a moral order for the created realm. Creation and its creatures, both animal and human, should act in certain ways. "The ox knows its owner, but Israel does not know" (1:3). Goodness is to live and act in accord with this order; wickedness is to transgress and violate it. It is Israel's sins, whether those of the people as a whole or those of the leaders, that are most frequently detailed.

Against the large-scale backdrop of creation and human morality, Isaiah presents the particular relationship between God and the people Israel.

> You, Israel, my servant; Jacob, whom I have chosen;
>   children of Abraham whom I love;
> Whom I brought with strength from the ends of the earth,
>   and called from its farthest reaches.
>
> (41:8–9)

The relationship is not unique or exclusive. What holds for humanity and the other nations in general holds for Israel in particular and vice versa. Israel's story mirrors the story and destiny of humanity and of any part of humanity, as does the story of humanity or of any nation mirror that of Israel. There is tension and play between the general (humanity) and the particular (Israel) in Isaiah.

Sin is rejection of the Lord: "They have forsaken the Lord; they have despised the Holy One of Israel" (1:4; also 5:24). "You have forgotten the God who saves you, and the Rock who provides you refuge you have not remembered" (17:10). Or it is the doing of unspecified evil: "You did what was evil in my sight, and that which I do not delight in you chose" (65:12; also 1:16–17). They are "a rebellious people who walk in the way that is not good, who pursue their own desires" (65:2). The majority of accusations are such categorical and unspecified statements. Righteousness and goodness are to trust and hope in the Lord, to choose God's ways: "If you are willing and listen . . ." (1:19). "Let us walk in the light of the Lord" (2:5). "You know that I am the Lord; whoever hopes in me will not be put to shame" (49:23). "Seek the Lord while he is to be found; call to him while he is near" (55:6).

What is sin and what is good are usually opposed images of each other. For example, sin is not doing what is good and should be done: "You have forgotten the God who saves you" (17:10). To remember is to praise God (12:1; 25:1), to walk in the divine paths and to wait on the Lord.

> The road of the righteous is level; O Just One,
>   you level the path of the righteous.
> Indeed, O Lord, we wait for you in the road of your
>   decisions [judgments]; your name and your memory
>   are our very desire.
>
> (26:7–8)

"The righteous" is translated "the just" (NAB), "the upright" (NJB), and "the good" (GNB). The wicked are sinful and God punishes them because "you did what was evil in my sight and that which I do not delight in you chose" (65:12). The good are rewarded and are happy; they are those who "choose that in which I delight, holding fast to my covenant" (56:4).

In contrast to these general accusations of moral evil, Isaiah specifies many forms of social corruption and exploitation.

> Everyone loves a bribe and pursues gifts;
>   They do not deal justly with the orphan, nor does
>   the widow's plea come to them.
>
> (1:23)

> Woe! Those who legislate evil legislation
>   and write oppressive written laws[1]
> So that they can block the needy from justice
>   and rob my people's poor of their rights,
> So that widows can be their spoil and they can plunder orphans!
>
> (10:1–2)

> No one brings suit righteously; no one seeks justice truthfully;
>   They trust in empty pleas; they speak lies; they conceive mischief
>   and they beget depravity.
>
> (59:4)

Justice is at the other moral pole; it is to uphold and maintain the social order and to protect the weak. I will speak at greater length about justice and righteousness in a separate section (see pp. 51–54).

> Cease to do evil. Learn to do good.
> Seek justice: rescue the oppressed,
> Deal justly with the orphan, plead for the widow.
>   (1:16–17)

> Is not this the kind of fasting I choose:
> Loosen unjust bonds; cut the ropes of the yoke;
> Set the oppressed free; break every yoke?
> Is not it to share your bread with the hungry
>   and to bring the homeless poor into your home?
> When you see the naked, cover them; do not hide yourself
>   from your own people.
>   (58:6–7)

Other accusations of the prophet concern violations of Israel's cultic practices, often in concert with forms of social injustice. "You plant plants for the Pleasant One [a title for a fertility god] and set out shoots for a strange god" (17:10). "You fast only in your own interests and to oppress your workers" (58:3). There are "those who sanctify and purify themselves to go into gardens . . . and eat the flesh of swine, vermin, and mice" (66:17). Proper cultic behavior is important even for other nations. "The Egyptians will know the Lord at that time; they will offer sacrifices and fulfill the vows they make" (19:21).

> Foreigners who are joined to the Lord to minister to him,
>   to love his name and to be his servants—
> All who keep the Sabbath by not profaning it
>   and hold fast to my covenant—
> I will bring them to my holy mountain and make them happy
>   in my house of prayer.
>   (56:6–7)

The above citation from 58:6–7 stresses that cultic actions are important but not primary. Even the temple can be overemphasized.

> The heavens are my throne and the earth my footstool.
> What, then, is this house you are building for me?
> This place, then, is it to be my resting place?

My hand made all these things, and they are all mine—
    says the Lord.
This is the one I look upon—the poor and broken in spirit,
    the one who trembles at my word.
               (66:1–2; also 1:10–17)

Lack of knowledge, ignorance, is another broad category of sin. It can be combined with blindness and deafness, both physical and spiritual: "Listen carefully but do not understand; look closely but do not know" (6:9). "The princes of Zoan are complete fools; Pharaoh's wise counselors give stupid counsel" (19:11). Lady Babylon does not see her place in God's plan: "You did not take these things to heart; you did not remember their final outcome" (47:7; also 42:25). The parody of the idol maker in 44:9–20 plays on the ignorance of both the idol and its maker; the picture fits that of Israel in other parts of Isaiah.

They [both idols and makers] do not know; they do not understand,
    for their eyes are too smeared for them to see and their minds
    for them to comprehend. They do not take it to heart;
    there is neither knowledge nor understanding.
               (44:18)

On the other hand, knowledge of the Lord and the divine ways is a central virtue.

They do neither evil nor corruption on my holy mountain
For the earth is filled with the knowledge of the Lord
    as the waters cover the sea.
               (11:9)

The goal of God's actions is often to generate knowledge in humans.

So that all together may see and know, may consider and understand
That the hand of the Lord has done this, that the Holy One
    of Israel has created it.
               (41:20)

God brings Cyrus

so that you [Cyrus] may know that I the Lord am he
    who calls you by name. . . .

So that they [humanity] may know, from where the sun rises
to where it sets, that there is not another besides me;
I am the Lord and there is no other.

(45:3, 6)

Having or regaining sight and hearing are part of the process of
acquiring knowledge of the Lord.

On that day the deaf will hear the words of a scroll,
And from a deep darkness the eyes of the blind will see.
The poor will continually rejoice in the Lord, and the neediest
will delight in the Holy One of Israel.

(29:18–19)

Pride and arrogance are the final category of sin that I look at in
this section; they are prevalent in Isaiah. They are usually connected
with imagery of height, for example, mountains and trees (see
2:12–16). Pride is to think that one is God's equal. The king of Babylon sets his throne in heaven and says, "I am like the Most High"
(14:13–14), and Lady Babylon says, "I am and there is no other" (47:8,
10; see 45:6 cited above). To be proud is to go against God's ways and
to regard one's accomplishments as one's own. Assyria goes beyond
God's express mission and regards its victory as its own work. "With
the strength of my hand I have done it; with my wisdom, yes, my
understanding" (10:5–14).[2] Israel may know that God is against them
and has smashed their buildings.

But Ephraim and the Samaritans say in their pride and arrogance,
"Bricks have fallen, but we will rebuild with fine stone;
Sycamores have been cut down, but we will replace
them with cedars."

(9:9–10)

Height is not always arrogance. The Lord can be on high and
exalted: "I saw the Lord on a throne, high and lifted up" (6:1). Humans
should be humble, lowly, broken.

Thus says he who is high and lifted up, who dwells in eternity,
whose name is Holy.
"In a high and holy place I dwell and also with one broken
and of humble spirit,

So that I can revive the spirit of the humble and revive the heart
of the broken."

(57:15)

Isaiah can switch this valuation of high and low, however, since
humans who are righteous are set on high and are not considered
proud or arrogant. Note the rejection of social corruption:

Those who walk righteously and speak honestly,
    who despise getting profit from oppression,
Who hold their hands back from taking a bribe, who close their
    ears to proposals of bloodshed, and who shut their eyes
    to sights of evil—
They will dwell on heights; their refuge will be rock fortresses.

(33:15–16; also 58:14)

Disaster and Punishment

The presence of human sin and the absence of human good are usually followed or accompanied by disasters that are inflicted by God as
punishment and judgment[3] or that are the natural and logical outcome
of the behavior. The disaster may be military invasion and its resultant woes.

Your country is desolate, your cities burned with fire;
    right in front of you aliens devour your land—
        it is desolate as overthrown by aliens.
And daughter Zion is left . . . like a besieged city.

(1:7–8)

In the fourteenth year of King Hezekiah, Sennacherib,
    king of Assyria, attacked all the fortified cities of Judah
    and captured them.

(36:1)

Your holy cities have become a wilderness; Zion has become
    a wilderness; Jerusalem is desolate.
Our holy and beautiful house, where our fathers praised you,
Has been burned with fire, and all our pleasant sites
    have become a desert.

(64:10–11)

It can be social disorder and chaos when "everyone oppresses every-one else, and the youth insults the elder" (3:5).

> I stir up Egyptian against Egyptian; they fight within
>   their own families, neighbor against neighbor,
> City against city, kingdom against kingdom.
>   (19:2)

Priest and prophet reel with beer; they are confused because of wine;
    they stagger with beer.
They wander in vision and stumble in their actions.
                                                    (28:7)

> The dogs [leaders] have a powerful appetite;
>   they do not know what being full is.
> The shepherds know absolutely nothing.
> They all turn to their own way, each and every one to
>   their own gain.
> "Come on, let us get some wine; let us get drunk on beer."
>   (56:11–12)

Finally, there are the scenes of devastated nature, of empty land, of dry and infertile land. We will discuss the scenes and their imagery further in the next chapter.

And now I make known to you what I am about to do to my vineyard.
I take away its hedge, and it is devoured; I break down its wall,
    and it is trampled ground.
I make it a waste; it is not pruned and it is not hoed;
    and it is overgrown with briers and thorns.
And I command the clouds that they rain no rain upon it.
                                          (5:5–6; also 7:23–25)

> The Light of Israel will become a fire, and his Holy One a flame.
> It will burn and devour his thorns and briers in one day.
> It will consume the glory of his forest and his farmland,
>   both breath and flesh; and it will be as the wasting away of one.
> The remnant of the trees of his forest will be so few that a child
>   could write them down.
>   (10:17–19)

Damascus ceases to be a city; she has become a heap of ruins;
  the cities of Aroer are deserted.
They are for flocks who can lie down, and no one will disturb them.
                                                                (17:1–2)

The waters of the Nile dry up; the river is parched and arid;
  Its canals stink; the rivers of Egypt are shrunken and parched.
Reed and rush rot.

                                                                (19:5–6)

Justice and Righteousness

On the positive side are descriptions of a just and peaceful society, social order, and a fertile land. "Justice" and "righteousness" are a frequent pair in Isaiah. The Lord expected both in his vineyard (5:7). This is the standard translation of the underlying Hebrew words, and I note that the Hebrew terms mean something different than their English translations. The Hebrew concept of "justice," in many of its biblical uses, is fairly close to our English concept and refers to a society that values fairness, especially impartiality in court, and a society in which all share in the bounty of God, land, and produce. Justice is both social, of the people as a whole, and individual, as in the just person. Justice includes social justice, in our sense of the phrase, and personal behavior and morality.

"Righteousness," particularly when paired with "justice," is similar to the latter in meaning and can often carry a more explicit religious connotation. Righteousness is both social and individual. The righteous person is just and also a good, moral, and religious person who maintains "the law" (more will be said of this later) in what we would categorize as social, personal, and religious (including cultic) spheres of life.

The pair "justice" and "righteousness" expresses what is the best of a society. Justice and righteousness are both what people, especially those in power, should do and the essential characteristics of the good society. The pair is both means and end. The justice and righteousness of the people and of God produce the just and righteous society. "Zion is redeemed by justice, and those who return to her, by righteousness" (1:27; see 5:16). To put it simply, if one lives righteously, then one is righteous and therefore saved, delivered; all three aspects are expressed in Hebrew with the same terms. "Salvation" and "deliverance," which are often the preferred translations of the Hebrew words for "justice" and "righteousness," are denotations seldom, if ever, found in the use of the English terms "justice" and "righteousness."

As examples of the range of meaning of the Hebrew terms, NRSV translates 56:1, "Maintain justice, and do what is right." TNK has "justice and equity," NJB, "judgement and uprightness," and GNB, "what is right and justice."[4] The term for "righteousness" is translated in NRSV "victorious" in 41:10, "success" in 48:18, and "vindication" in 54:17. I render the last occurrence as "what they have a right to expect from me" (see p. 38). In 46:12–13 NRSV translates the term twice with "deliverance":

> Listen to me, you stubborn of heart,
>   You who are far from deliverance:
> I bring near my deliverance, it is not far off,
>   And my salvation will not tarry;
> I will put my salvation in Zion, for Israel my glory.

TNK translates "deliverance" and "salvation" with "victory" and "triumph." (Other translations show a similar range.)

Members of society have the right to fair and just treatment in court (see 1:23 and 10:1–2). Israel expects justice from the Lord. "Why do you say, O Jacob . . . 'My way is hidden from the Lord, and *my claim for justice* passes by my God'?" (40:27). The italicized phrase translates the Hebrew term for "justice"; others render it with "right" (NRSV) or "cause" (REB). GNB renders the verse freely but accurately:

> Israel, why then do you complain
> that the LORD does not know your troubles
> or care if you suffer injustice?

Other characteristics can be added to this basic pair to expand the depiction of the proper life and the good society. The description of the shoot in 11:1–5 is a catalog of positive terms to be added to the pair "justice" and "righteousness."

> The spirit of the Lord rests upon it [the shoot], a spirit of wisdom
>   and understanding,

a spirit of counsel and strength, a spirit of knowledge and fear
of the Lord. . . .
He does not judge by what his eyes see, nor does he decide
by what his ears hear,
But he judges the poor in righteousness, and he decides
with fairness for the weak of the land. . . .
Righteousness is a belt around his waist, and truthfulness
[or faithfulness] a belt on his hips.

Isaiah 11:6–9 presents the vision of the peaceable kingdom, in
which "the wolf dwells with the lamb, and the leopard lies down with
the kid," and "the earth is filled with the knowledge of the Lord." The
more familiar "lion laying down with the lamb" is not literally in the
Isaiah text but represents a dramatic interpretation of the passage by
opposing the powerful lion with the innocent, helpless lamb. Edward
Hicks (1780–1849) painted more than fifty versions of the scene from
Isaiah 11; he depicted the animals and the child, often with more animals than in the text, and generally used *The Peaceable Kingdom* in the
different titles of his paintings.

A group of terms similar to those in 11:1–9 occur in chapter 32,
which includes a brief glimpse of the surrounding desolation. The
close of the chapter emphasizes peace.

When you see a king reigning in righteousness
and princes ruling in justice:
Each of them is like a shelter from the wind, a refuge
from the storm. . . .
The palace is deserted, the noisy city abandoned;
Both hill and tower are now dens forever, the joy of asses,
pasture for flocks,
Until a spirit is poured out on us from on high,
And the wilderness becomes farmland, and farmland
is thought of as a forest.
Justice dwells in the wilderness, and righteousness lives
in the farmland.
The work of righteousness is peace, and the effect
of righteousness is unending calm and security.
My people live in a peaceful pasture, in secure dwellings
and quiet resting places.

(32:1, 14–18)

My final example is from 33:5–6.

> The Lord is exalted; indeed, he dwells on high.
> He fills Zion with justice and righteousness . . .
> Abundant salvation, wisdom, and knowledge;
>   the fear of the Lord is his treasure.

"Fear of the Lord" is religious awe and respect, not just abject fear. It is one of the spirits resting on the shoot and, indeed, is his inspiration and delight (11:2–3; see pp. 180–82).

The Remaining Few

The devastation, whether military or natural, is not total; there is a remnant: "Daughter Zion is left like a booth in a vineyard" (1:8). One of Isaiah's sons has the symbolic name Shear-jashub, "a remnant returns" or "a remnant will return" (7:3; 10:21). In the descriptions of destruction in chapters 1–39, something, however small, remains. "The power of Moab is crushed despite its great multitude, and its remnant is very small and weak" (16:14). The terrible flood that is Assyria reaches only to the neck (8:8), and the attack of Sennacherib turns back at the walls of Jerusalem (chaps. 36–37).

> The remaining survivors of Judah will again strike root downward and bear fruit upward, for a remnant will go forth from Jerusalem and survivors from Mount Zion. (37:31–32)

"Remnant" is associated with images of cleansing, refining, and separating the wheat from the chaff. "Remnant" welds the theme, the concept, to the image, what is pictured.

> I turn my hand against you; I smelt away, as with lye, your dross,
>   and I remove all your alloy.
> And I return your judges as at the beginning,
>   and your counselors as at the first.
>
> (1:25–26)

> Whoever is left in Zion and remains in Jerusalem will be called Holy—everyone who is recorded for life in Jerusalem—once the Lord has washed away the vomit of the daughters of Zion, and

the bloodstains of Jerusalem he has cleansed from her midst by a
spirit of judgment and by a spirit of burning. (4:3–4)

The Lord will thresh from the Euphrates to the river of Egypt,
and you, O Israelites, will be gleaned one at a time. (27:12)

Remnant is not the same explicit theme in chapters 40–66, since
these chapters present the fortunes and the destiny of the remnant
whose return is proclaimed in 1–39. The chapters develop at greater
length the themes of return, restoration, and rebuilding that are
glimpsed in 1–39. Central to return is the image of the road, the way,
which we will examine in the next chapter. Return is followed by
restoration and rebuilding of both land and city, even though the land
lies desolate. The cities are all burned (1:7); "cities are laid waste without inhabitant; houses with no one in them" (6:11).

[I am the Lord] who says to Jerusalem, "She is to be inhabited,"
  and to the cities of Judah,
"They are to be rebuilt, and I will raise up their ruins."

(44:26)

They rebuild the ancient ruins; the old desolate sites they restore;
They reestablish the ruined cities, the desolate sites from long ago.

(61:4)

Restoration includes repopulation, which is often portrayed as children returning to their mother, Zion-Jerusalem. In the initial image in
the following passage, God has drawn a picture of the city on his hand.

Look, I [the Lord] have inscribed you [Zion] on my palms;
  your walls are always before me.
Your builders move faster than your destroyers,
  and those who ruined you leave you.
Lift your eyes about you and look: they all gather, they come to you.
By my life, says the Lord, you will wear them all like jewelry;
  you will bind them on like a bride. . . .
The children of your time of bereavement will yet say
  in your hearing:
"This place is too cramped for me; make room for me so that
  I may live here."

(49:16–20)

Justice and Mercy

This thematic pair marks an important contrast and even contradiction within Isaiah. The pair "justice" and "mercy" is mine and does not refer to an actual Isaianic pair like "justice" and "righteousness." Justice, in the sense that I use it here, adds another layer of meaning to the above discussion of justice and righteousness. Justice is the principle that reward (restoration and prosperity) and punishment (disaster and destruction) follow respectively and irrevocably from good and evil. To put it in familiar terms, the good prosper and the wicked suffer.

If you are willing and you listen, the good of the land you will eat;
But if you refuse and rebel, by a sword you will be eaten,
  for the mouth of the Lord speaks.

(1:19–20)

This is retributive justice and it permeates the vision of Isaiah. Disasters and human suffering are explained as the inevitable result of human sin and ignorance, whereas peace and human prosperity flow from humans trusting in the Lord and walking in the divine ways. Retributive justice relates to social justice in the sense that if the latter is not present in a society, such as Israel's, then that society will be justly punished.

A large part of Isaiah's vision proclaims, threatens, or promises a good or a disastrous outcome, dependent on human actions. The image of refining and cleansing implies that the wicked are burned away (punished) and the good restored to their former purity: "I have refined you but not with silver; I have chosen you through the ordeal of a furnace" (48:10). Israel must cleanse themselves: "Your hands are full of blood. Wash! Clean! Remove the evil of your doings from before my eyes" (1:15–16).

Mercy, however, disrupts the automatic and irrevocable connection between action and result. In its main sense, mercy stops, or at least mitigates, the punishment that should follow upon crime or sin. For example, the people do refuse God's way and rebel, but they are not always eaten by the sword (1:20), because God forgives them.

Mercy and forgiveness are offered by God and by the prophet based on a change in behavior, on repentance. Repentance is the concept and the image of changing one's present sinful attitude and actions and returning to ways that are in accord with God's desires. The theme of repentance fits with images of return journeys, of restoration, and of throwing away the past.

In that day humans will cast forth their idols of silver
   and their idols of gold,
That they made for themselves to worship, to the moles
   and to the bats,
To enter the caverns of the rocks and the clefts of the cliffs,
From before the terror of the Lord, and from the glory
   of his majesty,
When he rises to terrify the earth.

(2:20–21)

Mercy, based on repentance, shares much with retributive justice, since one must change (i.e., do what is good) to be forgiven (i.e., be rewarded). If one does not change when offered the opportunity, then there is no forgiveness.

I am ready to be consulted by those who do not ask;
   I am ready to be found by those who do not seek me.
I say, "Here I am! Here I am!" to a nation that does not call
   on my name.
I spread out my hands all day long to a rebellious people
Who continue to walk in the way that is not good,
   following their own plans. . . .
Yes, I place right in their laps full repayment for their sins
   and the sins of their ancestors.

(65:1–2, 6–7)

This is the mercy that Hezekiah seeks when he faces his natural death. The illness and threat of death are not a punishment; Hezekiah simply does not want to die at this time. He bases his plea on his good life, and God responds positively.

Hezekiah prayed to the Lord: "O Lord, I beg you, remember how I have walked before you in faithfulness and total commitment, how I have done only that which is good in your sight." And Hezekiah wept bitterly. . . . Thus says the Lord, . . . "I hear your prayer; I see your tears; and now I am adding fifteen years to your life." (38:2–5; also 33:2)

The people's lengthy plea to the Lord for attention and help in 63:7–64:12 is based not on the goodness of those praying but on their need and on the existing relationship with the Lord. The prayer rehearses, in 63:7–14, the divine choice of Israel, their rebellion, and God's continuing presence with them.

> I cause all to remember the *kindnesses* of the Lord,
>   the Lord's acts for which he is praised,
> Because of all that the Lord has done for us and the great good
>   for the house of Israel,
> That he has done for them in his *compassion*,
>   in his great *kindnesses*. . . .
> In his love and in his compassion he redeemed them;
>   he lifted them and carried them all the days of old.
>
> (vv. 7, 9)

The italicized terms are NIV's rendering of key Hebrew words for the concept of mercy. Although the first and third words are the same in Hebrew, NRSV offers this translation of the three: "gracious deeds," "mercy," and "steadfast love." REB has yet another series: "unfailing love," "tenderness," and "faithful love." GNB, NAB, NJB, and TNK offer the same terms as these except that TNK has "kind acts" for the first term and NAB, "favors"; GNB uses "constant love" for the third term.

The varied English words taken together represent the basic range of meaning of mercy: God has initiated something with the people without any prior actions or attitudes on their part. This is outside the system of justice, for it is a first act, a creation without a preceding situation that motivates it; therefore, it is described using terms such as "love" and "kindness." The very first divine act of mercy is the creation of the entire world.

> Thus says God, the Lord,
> Who creates the heavens, who stretches them out,
>   who spreads the earth and what springs from it,
> Who gives breath to the people on it, and spirit to those
>   who walk in it.
>
> (42:5)

The cosmic creation is followed by God's creation and choice of a people, whether this refers to a specific time in the past such as the exodus from Egypt or to any subsequent time when God creates or re-creates a chosen people or person.

> I, the Lord, have called you in righteousness;
>   I have taken you by the hand;

I have guarded you; I have given you as a covenant of people,
  as a light of nations,
To open eyes that are blind, to bring the prisoner from the dungeon.
                                                                    (42:6–7)

As we will see later, the one addressed can be the prophet, the servant introduced in 42:1, Israel as a whole, or Cyrus (see pp. 186–89). In any case, the one addressed is called to act; the call looks to the future and the person's reaction. The person or group is not called because they deserve the call and the divine protection; the call does not look to the past. Such a call is part of divine action conveyed in the images of God as parent, teacher, and creator, and it brings us to the human response to the divine initiative. Once created, they, whether humanity as a whole or Israel in particular, enter into a realm of justice. They must respond to this act of creation and to this Creator, and their future fate depends on this response. "Children I raise, but they rebel against me" (1:2). "They revolted and tormented his holy spirit. And he became an enemy to them; he fought against them" (63:10).

But this does not have to be the end of the story. God can put aside retributive justice, that is, sin and punishment, by another act of divine mercy reminiscent of the past. "He [the Lord] remembered the days of old, of Moses and his people." These were the olden times when God led the people through water and desert "to make for himself an everlasting name . . . a glorious name" (63:11–14). Despite their rebellions, the Lord stayed with the people, but in chapter 63 they feel that they are abandoned for good.

Where are your zeal, your strength, the churning of your heart? . . .
You, O Lord, are our father, Our Redeemer is your ancient name.
Why, O Lord, do you make us wander from your ways;
  why do you harden our heart so that we cannot fear you?
Return for the sake of your servants, the tribes of your heritage.
For a brief time your holy people had possession [of the heritage];
  now our enemies have trampled your holy place.
                                                                    (63:15–18)

As in chapter 59, the people employ powerful imagery to confess their sins and to ask God to save them in their distress.

We all are like one who is unclean; all our righteous deeds
  are like a filthy rag;

> We all are withered like a leaf; our sins carry us away
>   like the wind. . . .
> Do not be exceedingly angry, O Lord! Do not remember
>   sin forever!
> But now, consider! We all are your people!
> Your holy cities are a wilderness; Zion is a wilderness,
>   Jerusalem a desolation. . . .
> Faced with this, will you restrain yourself, O Lord?
>   Will you be silent and afflict us so horribly?
>
> (64:6, 9–10, 12)

At times Isaiah mixes and alternates themes of justice and mercy. In the following passage, in parts a, c, and d justice dominates, while in b and e, mercy does.

a. You [Israel] have burdened me with your sins;
    you have worn me out with your iniquities.
b. I, I am he who wipes away your rebellions for my own sake,
    and your sins I do not remember.
c. Make me remember; let us go to trial;
    tell me so that you may be found innocent.
d. Your first father sinned and your leaders rebelled against me;
    I disgraced the holy princes, and I handed Jacob over
    to utter destruction and Israel to condemnation.
e. And now hear, O Jacob, my servant; O Israel, whom I have chosen!
    Thus says the Lord who makes you, who fashions you in the
    womb—he will help you:
    Do not fear, O my servant, O Jacob! O Jeshurun, whom I have chosen!
    For I pour water on the thirsty ground and streams on the dry;
    I pour my spirit on your offspring and my blessing on those
    who spring from you.

(43:24–44:3)

Isaiah's Vision: The Real and the Ideal, the One and the Many

The tension between justice and mercy is central to Isaiah and is a powerful part of the vision. The vision hovers between a real world and an ideal world, between a waking world and a world of dreams. The vision is anchored in reality. Isaiah reviews the historical times of ancient Israel, which are recognizable in the particular names, places, and events even when expressed in poetic terms and images. And he presents the human world in which both the ancients and we moderns live. This is a world of both good and evil, of both peace and violence, and a world in which events at times follow one another in a just and fair manner and at other times defy any logic. In defying any logic, events in human history can turn out far better or far worse than anticipated. Isaiah imagines equally dreams and nightmares.

For Isaiah God's creation of the world defies explanation as does the subsequent choice of Israel. God may create a world or people for the sake of the divine glory and name, but this tells us nothing about why God created this particular world or people. Divine motivation is the realm of mercy, grace, kindness, love, and compassion. Once created, the world and its people enter the realm of justice and must follow a moral order. If they sin or rebel, if they ignore or despise the Creator, if they think themselves God's equal, then they are punished and experience hardship or disaster. However, the punishment can be lessened or even totally stopped by mercy and forgiveness, whether or not the people repent and change. God can always create and choose anew.

> Yes, the former troubles are forgotten,
>   for they are hidden from my eyes.
> See! I am creating new heavens and a new earth
> And the former things are not remembered;
>   they do not come to mind.
>
> (65:16–17)

A perfectly just world is as much an ideal, dream world as is a world in which God assures peace and prosperity for all and forever. The latter would be a perfect world in which there would be no need for retributive justice, for reward or punishment. Isaiah envisions both worlds of perfect justice and of perfect peace at different points in the vision but always holds them up against the world in which we live where things do not work out perfectly regardless of what principles or patterns we expect life to follow. Yet the vision is there to inspire us, to draw us into it and give us other ways of seeing our world, and to call us to wait, hope, and trust in God. The world may not be just, but we can still passionately strive for justice.

Countering the just, peaceful, and prosperous societies is the far grimmer side of Isaiah. I refer to the dark, nightmarish scenes of ferocious armies, devastating invasions, and the desolate lands left behind.

This is when events go far worse than expected and when a drive to violence and destruction seizes all, including God. For a modern reader, these nightmares are some of the most difficult passages in Isaiah and in the Hebrew Bible. This is the realm of vengeance, wrath, rage, and slaughter—a realm all too familiar to us who have lived in the twentieth century.

> Go into the rock caves and into hollows in the dust—
> From the terror of the Lord and from his dread majesty
>   when he rises to terrorize the earth.
>
> (2:19)

> Therefore the anger of the Lord was kindled against his people,
>   and he stretched out his hand against them and he struck them;
> The mountains quaked, and their corpses were like refuse
>   in the middle of the streets.
> For all this his anger has not turned away,
>   and his hand is stretched out still.
> He raises a signal for nations from afar, and he whistles for him
>   from the end of the earth;
> Look! Hastily, swiftly he comes!
> None is weary, not one stumbles; no one slumbers
>   and no one sleeps.
>
> (5:25–27)

> Why are your robes red, and your clothes like those of one
>   who treads the winepress?
> I have trodden the wine vat alone, and there was not one
>   from the peoples with me.
> I trod on them in my anger and trampled them in my rage.
> Their juice spattered on my clothes, and all my robes are stained.
> Yes! A day of vengeance is in my mind, and the year
>   for me to redeem has come. . . .
> I trampled peoples in my anger; I made them drunk with my rage;
>   I poured out their lifeblood [juice] on the ground.
>
> (63:2–4, 6)

Scenes of violence and gore dominate chapters 13–14, 24, and 34 and are found at many points throughout the book. The destruction results in a desolate and empty land that is inhabited by desert animals and demonic creatures.

Until cities are wastes without inhabitant, and houses without people,
and the land is totally desolate.
And the Lord sends all people afar, and a vast barrenness is
in the midst of the land.

(6:11–12)

She [Babylon] will never be lived in, and she will not be dwelt in
for all times;
No Arab will tent there, and shepherds will not rest their flocks there.
Demons will rest there, and howling creatures will fill their houses;
Ostriches will dwell there and hairy-demons will cavort there.

(13:20–21)

The earth is shattered in pieces; the earth is torn to shreds;
the earth is shaken to its depths.
The earth staggers like a drunk and sways like a hut.
Its sin lies heavy upon it; it falls and cannot rise again.

(24:19–20)

Isaiah's vision is a panorama of the entire cosmos. It encompasses God, the entire world, and its inhabitants; and, in both the form and content of the book, it attempts to be all-inclusive. The vision includes dreams and nightmares, peace and violence, good and evil. And the prophet alternates and intertwines, sometimes in rapid sequence, the many aspects, possibilities, and alternatives that are presented for any topic. Isaiah does not reserve separate parts of the book for each topic; they are mixed together throughout the book, often in bewildering fashion. Although I approach Isaiah according to different topics, the examples cited for any one topic are relevant for other topics. This is another reason for my practice of drawing examples from different parts of the book.

Isaiah intones the worldwide scope of his vision in the initial and closing references to heavens and earth, indeed new heavens and a new earth (1:2; 65:17; 66:2; also 13:5). God is the creator of the entire world and all that lives within it. All humanity is addressed at points (2:9–11; 11:1–10); at others it is "all flesh," perhaps even including animals: "The glory of the Lord is revealed, and all flesh sees it together" (40:5). "All flesh comes to bow down before me" (66:23). "This is the plan planned for the whole earth, and this is the hand stretched out over all the nations" (14:26).

Within humanity, Isaiah distinguishes between Israel and the nations. When "the mountain of the Lord's house rises above all the mountains, . . . all nations stream to it; many peoples come" (2:2–3). "On that day the root of Jesse will stand as a signal for peoples; nations will come to him to inquire" (11:10). In these passages and others, the nations are at peace with Israel and indeed seek God's will through them or with them. God's plan is for the peace and prosperity, the salvation, of all. The one called in 42:5–9 is "a covenant of people, a light of nations" (also 49:8).

> They [the nations] bring all your kin from all nations as an offer-
> ing to the Lord . . . on my holy mountain Jerusalem, says the
> Lord, just as the Israelites bring the offering, in clean vessels, to
> the house of the Lord. And I even take from them [nations and
> Israelites] some to be priests and Levites. (66:20–21)

The vision of peace reaches a high point at the close of chapter 19. From one view, the nations are punished and then forgiven; from another, even with the nations, God can again, in love and kindness, create and choose.

> The Lord strikes Egypt, striking and healing; they return to the
> Lord; he hears their prayers and heals them. On that day there is
> a highway from Egypt to Assyria, and Assyria goes to Egypt and
> Egypt to Assyria. Egypt worships with Assyria. On that day Israel
> is a third with Egypt and Assyria, a blessing in the midst of the
> earth, whom the Lord of Hosts has blessed, "Blessed is my peo-
> ple Egypt; the work of my hands Assyria; and my heritage Israel."
> (19:22–25)

This returns us to the contrast between the glowing part of Isaiah's vision of God, nations, and Israel, and the dark side. The latter is the grim part in which the nations are foes invading and destroying Israel and who are in turn defeated and destroyed. On the one hand, their forbidding fate is their just deserts.

> The Lord broke the rod of the wicked, the club of rulers,
> That beat peoples in fury, beating without cease,
> That ruled nations in anger, persecuting them without end.
> (14:5–6)

Your adversaries I contend with, and your children I save.
I make your oppressors eat their own flesh, and they are drunk
   with their own blood as with wine.

(49:25–26)

At other points, the nations are caught up in the cosmic cataclysm, the outburst of divine rage that sweeps over the world. Many of the nations, whose doom is pronounced and even lamented in chapters 13–23, are mainly in the way of these larger forces, whether they are the unnamed army of 5:26–30 and 13:1–16, Assyria, or Babylon. The nations caught in the cataclysm are not accused of the violence and pride that the last two are. At times it is simply a matter of another nation understanding what is actually happening; the Philistines are admonished: "Do not rejoice . . . because the rod that beat you is broken. From the root of the snake comes forth a serpent, and a fiery asp branches out from it" (14:29).

Even mighty Egypt and its rulers are accused solely of foolishness in thinking that they can escape the onslaughts of Assyria and then of Babylon (19:1–15; chap. 20). Egyptians do not exalt themselves against the Lord in the way Assyria and Babylon do. Egypt is a symbol of what is powerless and unreliable, a type of idol. Egypt's king is "the staff made of a broken reed which, when someone leans on it, pierces their hand. Such is Pharaoh, king of Egypt, for all who trust in him" (36:6).

To summarize, Isaiah, dealing with both Israel and the nations, develops the possible relationships that can exist between them, for example, peaceful and hostile, helping and hindering, and equal and dominant. All can play the different roles so that either Israel or a nation can be the attacking foe or the dominant power that rules over the other. "They [Israel] will hold captive those who held them captive and they will rule over those who oppressed them" (14:2; also 51:21–23).

Isaiah displays the different relationships that exist between God and humanity, even when the latter is divided into Israel and the nations. Isaiah's multisided presentations continue. God is creator, supporter, parent, and savior of all, especially of Israel. God is judge, punisher, and destroyer of the rebellious, sinful, arrogant, and violent. God appears in these various roles with individuals or smaller groups, mainly within Israel, or with whole nations. God is against the proud whether it is Shebna (22:15–19), the king of Babylon (14:4–21), or all humanity (2:9–22; 3:11). The Lord is for the righteous whether it is

Hezekiah (chap. 38), the servants (65:8–16), or any human (3:10). On the other hand, the Lord can call someone without regard for their moral or religious standing. Cyrus is called and supported even though he does not know who the Lord is (45:4).

Such thematic diversity, which is the subject of this chapter, is an essential part of Isaiah's all-inclusiveness, an integral part of the vision. Isaiah does not present his vision of the world as a simple morality play in which good always wins and evil always loses or in which there are clearly defined good guys and bad guys. Israel and the nations, or various nations, play both of the latter roles and experience both justice and mercy. This is an important part of the tension and the play that exist between the general (humanity) and the particular (e.g., Israel and Assyria) in Isaiah. Further, as we will see with characters, there is considerable overlap between the different nations and groups, whether they are portrayed as righteous or doomed. From the perspective of actors on the stage of the vision, Isaiah is not a simple drama in which Israel stands separate and distinct from all the other peoples in the book.

The thematic diversity and all-inclusiveness are combined with their formal counterpart. Isaiah speaks of the thematic possibilities, the content, in as many ways as possible; this is the book's form, how it is written. Isaiah's poetry, whether we look at parallelism, figurative language, imagery, and so on, is characterized by diversity. In Isaiah form and content are inextricably bound; I separate them only for purposes of analysis.

The poet envisions a world in which all is related and intertwined— God and humanity, Israel and the nations, good and evil, justice and mercy, the nation and the individual. To match the vision, Isaiah writes a book that mixes and presents all of these different aspects in a constantly shifting style. To put it simply, when reading Isaiah, one can easily react by asking the prophet and even God to make up their mind.

I call this diversity Isaiah's encyclopedic quality. When Isaiah treats a topic, he looks at it from many sides and considers a variety of the connotations and implications of these many sides. This is the case with the treatment of judgment and mercy and of Israel and the nations and all the complicated variations in their relationships. Another example is the richness of Isaiah's vocabulary, which I discuss briefly since it is more obvious in the Hebrew text than in English translation.

Isaiah employs a basic set of words that he repeats throughout the book, for example, the words for "sin," "iniquity," and "rebellion" and the words for "good," "righteous," and "knowing the Lord." These form large sets of synonyms and near-synonyms. Other examples are the sizable number of words for the parts of the body, plants, and animals. Isaiah mentions most parts of the body: outside and inside (head and heart: 1:5); top to bottom (from the sole of the foot to the head: 1:6); eyes, ears, mouth, jaws, lips, and tongue (1:20; 6:5, 10; 30:27–28); hand, palm, fingers, arm, and legs (1:15; 2:8; 47:2; 49:16; 52:10).

Isaiah employs this rich basic vocabulary throughout the book and adds to it a considerable number of words that occur a limited number of times in the book, sometimes only once or twice. For example, the word translated "dross" in most translations of 1:22 and 25 occurs only in these two places in Isaiah. In the last verse of the book the word that is translated "abhorrent," "horror," "loathsome," or "disgusting" in the different Bibles occurs only there in the book. Isaiah uses about ninety words each for plants and their parts and for animals, and about one-half of each group are used only one or two times. Isaiah requires a translator to frequently consult both Hebrew and English dictionaries and perhaps a thesaurus. It is a challenge to the translator to reflect this diversity of terms without forcing the reader of the translation to frequently consult a dictionary, and the translations meet the challenge differently. The rendering of the one term in the book's final verse is an example of the range of English synonyms that can be used. The previous discussion of the terms for God's mercy in 63:7 is another (see pp. 56–58).

Endnotes to Chapter 2

1. The translation reflects the Hebrew in which the verbs and the nouns have the same basic meaning.
2. See pp. 144–48 for more on Assyria and on pride.
3. In biblical studies, "judgment" usually refers first to the punishment that is pronounced and only second to the process that leads to the pronouncement.
4. The two Hebrew nouns have related forms that are nouns, adjectives, and verbs. Isaiah uses all of the terms in different settings and with varied meanings, but it is impossible to do more than note this since to try to represent it in English would produce strange translations or would require elaborate notation of the Hebrew words being translated. The other translations of the Bible vary greatly in how they render these terms, either as a pair or singly; at times I will note variations in some of the translations to indicate the range of meaning.

Chapter 3

What Does Isaiah Imagine?

An image appeals to the senses. It is a concrete object that we visualize and imaginatively hear, touch, taste, and even smell. An image is sensual and a theme is intellectual. We see an ox and we think, dumb. An image can be of a particular object or group, for example, the cedars of Lebanon and the oaks of Bashan (2:13), or of a larger grouping such as trees in general. "His heart and the heart of his people shook as the trees of the forest shake before the wind" (7:2).

Imagery occurs throughout the book of Isaiah, and repeated images help to hold the disparate parts and themes together. Perhaps even more than in other chapters, here I will draw examples of an image from widely separated parts of the book. My main interest is not the contexts themselves or the sequential ordering of the passages cited, but how Isaiah deploys and varies an image in different contexts.

Imagery is a fine illustration of the vision's drive to be all-inclusive. Isaiah does not offer just individual, separate images in one chapter and then others in the next chapters. Rather he develops an image throughout his book by looking at different aspects of it, by giving many examples, and by using the image in a variety of settings so that it can have different and even opposed meanings. Isaiah employs a large number of words for plants and for the parts of a plant, for example, roots, branches, and foliage (see p. 67). He often employs the same image with opposed themes and values. A tree can be an image of misery—"I am a dry tree" (56:3)—and of life—"the days of my people will be like the days of a tree" (65:22).

Birds are an image with multiple uses in Isaiah. They are those defenseless before the king of Assyria.

My hand has found the wealth of peoples like one finds a nest,
And as one gathers abandoned eggs,
   so I have gathered the entire earth.

>   There was not one that flapped its wings, opened its mouth,
>   or even chirped.
>
>   (10:14)

This is similar to the Moabite women on their way to Zion; they are "like flapping birds, like abandoned nestlings" (16:2). People in distress, such as Hezekiah, moan like a dove (38:14; see 59:11). On the other hand, the Lord protects Jerusalem like hovering birds (31:5) that form a shield over the city. Finally, "those who wait for the Lord will renew their strength; they will soar with wings like eagles" (40:31), and Jerusalem's children return flying like doves (60:8).

Within imagery, there is great flexibility in how large or small we make a grouping of images and in how we subdivide that grouping. In this chapter I employ large groupings (e.g., rural-pastoral imagery) with loose subdivisions (e.g., domestic and wild, and plants and animals); this works well, but I am not presenting this as the only way to approach Isaianic imagery. The discussion is necessarily selective. Readers can begin with this and then develop their own ways of dealing with the imagery and indeed with the other aspects of Isaiah.

We will look at some major sets of imagery in Isaiah with examples from all parts of the book, but I am not presenting every type of imagery. Nor am I going to develop all the meanings and nuances that are attached to a given image. To do so would require us to discuss virtually every passage in Isaiah in detail. I again leave it to my readers to unfold and elaborate for themselves the richness and the relevance of Isaiah. Finally, for the sake of simplicity and referencing, although the translation of each passage is mine, I use the NRSV's translation of the specific terms for trees, plants, animals, and such, and I note variations in other translations.

The Teaching and the Way

"The way" is an integral image in Isaiah. For example, it is a metaphor for proper moral and religious behavior, the Lord's ways and paths (2:3); a reference to the highway, whether of the exodus or of return from exile (11:15–16; 35:8–10; 40:3–4); and a metaphor for moral and spiritual change, repentance (62:10–12). "The teaching," the divine word, relates closely to the moral and religious meanings of the way. The pair, the teaching and the way, is a central part of the themes and accompanying imagery of good and evil, righteousness and sin, and divine mercy and justice. The passages that we will discuss are excellent examples of the inextricable ties of imagery and themes; we cannot speak of the image of the way without also speaking of the themes of God's teaching and word.

Finally, my discussion of many of the passages dealing with the pair or one of its parts will deal with what the passage in question says with only occasional reference to its immediate context. This accords with the focus of my book and, at the same time, with my overall view of Isaiah as a vision of the variety of ways in which the relations of God's ways and human ways can display themselves across time and across cultures. How God and humans relate, positively or negatively, can change with time and with place, but Isaiah does not depict any simple processes of progress or regress. The final chapters of the book of Isaiah continue to display the same themes and images (regularity) but add new aspects and presentations (variety).

Divine teaching occurs in the prophet's initial call to Israel.

> Hear the word of the Lord, you rulers of Sodom!
> Give ear to the teaching of our God, you people of Gomorrah!
> (1:10)

But the people do not heed this call.

> They have rejected the teaching of the Lord of Hosts,
> And the word of the Holy One of Israel they have despised.
> (5:24; see 30:9)

Torah is the Hebrew word for "teaching," which is the translation in 1:10 in NRSV, NJB, and REB; NAB and TNK use "instruction" and KJV and NIV, "law." All three renderings are possible, and one translation of the Bible can employ all three with different occurrences of *torah*. For example, NRSV renders it "instruction" in 5:24, "laws" in 24:5, "teaching" in 42:4, and "law" in 42:24.[1] I prefer "teaching" and "instruction" in most of my translation—24:5 and 42:24 are exceptions—because this is the primary meaning of *torah*. Through *torah*, the Lord teaches and shows the proper way to live life (see 28:29); *torah* is not a set of written laws, similar to a modern-day law code, that prescribes and controls life. I use "law" a minimal number of times because it carries connotations of rigidity and finality not present in the Hebrew term.

In Isaiah the divine teaching parallels the Lord's "word" (1:10; 2:3; 5:24), "ways" (42:24), "justice" (42:4; 51:4), and "righteousness" (51:7). One example is 2:2b–3.

> All the nations flow to it, many peoples come and say,
> "Come, let us go up to the mountain of the Lord,
>   to the house of the God of Jacob,
> That he may teach[2] us his ways and that we may walk in his paths,
> For teaching comes forth from Zion, and the word of the Lord
>   from Jerusalem."

Movement dominates the passage: flowing, going up, walking, coming forth, ways, and paths. They go up because the word goes forth. The nations emphasize the Lord's ways, teaching, and word that they want to live by and to walk in. This is central to the vision: the demand that humans live in certain ways and not in others. We have seen and will continue to see the diverse terms and images Isaiah uses to express this demand. At this point I focus on the imagery of the way, the road, and examine the varied meanings it has in different contexts.

The Lord's way and word encompass all areas of human life: personal, family, social, and religious, and the realm of national and international politics. But Isaiah does not reduce the Lord's word to a set of rules or laws. Maintaining a just society, trusting in the Lord, keeping a balance between religious and social practices are central demands that are not spelled out in detailed lists of dos and don'ts. This accords with the overall tenor of Isaiah's vision as we explored it in the previous chapter. God requires goodness, justice, and righteousness, but even at the close of the vision readers, ancient and modern, are left to discern and to work out the relevance and implications of the requirements and of the vision for their lives, for their attempts to walk in the paths of the Lord.

The image of the way is analogous to the theme of justice and righteousness (see pp. 51–54). The way is a demand, an expectation, and it is at the same time the result that follows from meeting that expectation. To put it redundantly, if one walks (acts) in the Lord's ways, then one walks (lives) in the Lord's ways. The Lord's ways are equally a moral code and a spiritual goal. The nations go to the Lord's mountain to learn how to live on that mountain. We read Isaiah's vision literally and symbolically; it is anchored in this world and at the same time points to other spiritual and visionary possibilities. The mountain is

Jerusalem and the land of Israel, and it is a symbol for life lived with the Lord (38:20–21). We will look later at a fuller picture of this life; for now we focus on the way.

In chapter 11 the poet connects the image of the road with the themes of remnant and of return; the return is a type of the exodus that allows us to speak of a new exodus that is most apparent in chapters 35 and 40–55. The highway is the way back.

> The Lord will extend his hand again to gather the remnant
>   of his people that remains from Assyria and Egypt. . . .
> He will raise a signal to the nations, and he will collect
>   the outcasts of Israel;
> The dispersed of Judah he will gather from
>   the four corners of the earth. . . .
> And there will be a highway for the remnant of his people
>   who remain from Assyria,
> As there was for Israel when they came up from the land of Egypt.
>   (11:11–12, 16; see 19:23)

The exodus motif is obvious in the following.

> Thus says the Lord, who makes a road through the sea
>   and a path in powerful waters,
> Who leads out chariot and horse with an army
>   of powerful warriors.
>   (43:16–17; see 51:10)

The road for the remnant is in the wilderness, and God provides for the people on their way home. The highway is the way back that takes on characteristics of the goal: it is holy (4:3), and only the redeemed go there.

> Indeed, waters break forth in the wilderness. . . . The burning sand
>   is a swamp. . . .
> There emerges there a highway, yes, a way; it is called the Holy Way.
> The unclean do not pass over it; it is for those who walk in the way;
>   fools do not wander there. . . .
> But they walk there, the redeemed, yes, the ransomed of the Lord,
>   they return;
> They come to Zion with song, yes, everlasting joy on their heads.
>   (35:6–10; see 43:19)

Chapter 40 opens with the well-known command:

> In the wilderness prepare the way of the Lord,
> Make straight in the desert a highway for our God.
> (40:3; see 57:14; 62:10)

The highway is for God to approach the people and subsequently for the people to return to Jerusalem.

The Lord guides the released prisoners and the blind "on a road they do not know; on paths they do not know I guide them" (42:16; see 49:8–12). The Lord is their redeemer and their teacher. "I am the Lord your God who teaches you how to prosper, who leads you on the road you should walk on" (48:17). The highway, the road, is at one and the same time all of these: the moral and religious way of life, the dry path through the sea, the journey through the wilderness on the way back from Egypt (exodus) or from Assyria and Babylon (exile and dispersion), and the spiritual journey back to life in the Lord's house, life on the holy mountain.

Many are "not willing to walk in his roads; they will not hear his teaching" (42:24). Those who might help the woman in chapter 47 cannot, for "they all wander in their own way" (v. 15; see 53:6). The people's leaders "know absolutely nothing; they all turn to their own way" (56:11; see 57:17). Israel, at one point, confesses that they wander from the Lord's ways, that their hearts are too hard (63:17). God continually pleads with "a rebellious people who continue to walk in the way that is not good, following their own thoughts" (65:2; see 66:3). The last phrase alludes to a central declaration by the Lord.

> Let the wicked forsake their *way* and the worthless their *thoughts*. . . .
> Indeed, my *thoughts* are not your *thoughts*, nor are your *ways*
>   my *ways*—says the Lord.
> For as the heavens are higher than the earth, so are my *ways*
>   higher than your *ways* and my *thoughts* than your *thoughts*.
> (55:7–9)

> Because of such refusals to walk in the proper paths,
>   the people's ways are corrupted.
> Their feet run to evil, and they rush to shed innocent blood;
> Their thoughts are thoughts of depravity; desolation
>   and destruction are in their highways.
> The way of peace they do not know, and there is no justice
>   in their paths.

Their roads they have made crooked; whoever walks in them
does not know peace.

(59:7–8)

Finally, the corruption produces deserted ways.

Highways are deserted; travelers have ceased.
A covenant is broken; cities rejected; humanity disregarded.

(33:8)

Imagery of Field, Forest, and Farm

Isaiah opens his vision with an image that fits this category: "The
ox knows its owner, and the ass its master's crib." These are domestic
animals matched by the sacrificial animals of 1:11: rams, bulls, lambs,
and goats. Wild animals appear in the depiction of the onrushing
army: "Their roaring is like that of a lion; they roar like young lions"
(5:29). The domestic comprises pastures and their corresponding animals, and tilled fields, gardens, and vineyards and their plants and
crops. The wild comprises forests and fields and their corresponding
animals or beasts and plants, especially trees and briers.

The wild includes not just beasts but small, repulsive creatures.
People throw their idols "to the moles and to the bats" (2:20); those
who reject the Lord go into gardens where they eat "the flesh of pigs,
vermin, and rodents" (66:17). In his grave the king of Babylon has
maggots for a bed and worms for a blanket (14:11). Humans look like
grasshoppers to the Creator (40:22; see 33:4). Israel should not fear
their enemies, "for the moth will eat them like clothing, the worm will
eat them like wool" (51:8).

In their apostasy Israel has engaged in fertility worship that turns
against them. Characteristic of Isaiah's multiple use and valuation of a
given image, gardens here, as in 65:3 and 66:17, are not a positive image.

You are certainly ashamed of the oaks in which you delighted;
You blush for the gardens that you have chosen.
For you are like an oak whose leaf withers,
And like a garden that has no water.

(1:29–30)

Plant and garden images can summarize the full process of planting, growth, and (attempted) harvesting. Expanding the image in this
way illustrates Isaiah's desire to be inclusive.

> Although you plant plants for the Pleasant One [a fertility god]
>   and set out slips for a strange god,
> Although you make them grow on the day you plant them
>   and make them blossom on the very morning you sow them,
> The harvest disappears in a day of disease and incredible pain.
> (17:10–11)

The full process of plant growth occurs in the following depiction of abundance. I comment later on the violent closing statement (see p. 83).

> He will provide rain for your seed with which you sow the ground and for the grain,[3] the produce of the ground, which will be rich and nourishing. Your cattle will feed on that day in broad pastures; the oxen and the donkeys that till the ground will eat salted fodder that has been winnowed with shovel and fork. On every high mountain and on every lofty hill brooks of water will flow on the day of heavy slaughter when towers fall. (30:23–25)

Isaiah and the Lord provide Hezekiah a positive sign that he will be delivered from the Assyrians.

> This is the sign for you: This year eat what grows by itself and next year what springs from that. In the third year sow and harvest; plant vineyards and eat their fruit. The remaining survivors of Judah will again send roots downward and bear fruit upward. A remnant will certainly go forth from Jerusalem and survivors from Mount Zion. (37:30–32; see 45:8 and 55:10)

The parable of the farmer in 28:23–29 is a developed pastoral image. It refers to more than just proper harvesting techniques, since the Lord does not beat or thresh forever with his rod and club, Assyria (10:5, 24–26).

> Give ear and hear my voice; pay attention and hear my words.
> Does the plowman plow all day to sow, constantly opening
>   and harrowing his ground?
> Once he has leveled its surface, does not he scatter dill[4]
>   and strew cummin[5]?
> Does he not place wheat in rows, barley in its place,
>   and spelt[6] as its border?

For his God teaches him the proper way; he instructs him.
In the same way, dill is not threshed with a heavy sledge,
    and a cartwheel is not rolled over cummin.
Rather dill is beaten with a club and cummin with a rod;
Grain is crushed, but not for too long or too finely;
He may drive the cartwheel and horses over it,
    but he does not pulverize it.
This too comes from the Lord of Hosts:
He renders counsel wonderful and wisdom magnificent.

The Song of the Vineyard provides my final example of the process of preparation and planting.

Let me sing for my beloved my love song concerning his vineyard:
My beloved had a vineyard on a very fertile hill.
He dug it and cleared it of stones, and planted it with choice vines;
He built a watchtower in its midst, and also hewed out a wine vat for it;
He expected it to yield grapes, but it yielded wild grapes.

$$(5:1–2)^7$$

The "beloved" is the Lord, and "the vineyard of the Lord of Hosts is the house of Israel" (v. 7). The beloved's response to Israel's transgression, yielding wild grapes, is to return the vineyard to its wild state.

And now I make known to you what I am about to do to my vineyard.
I remove its hedge, and it will be devoured; I break down its wall,
    and it will be trampled ground.
I make it a waste; it is not pruned and it is not hoed;
    and it is overgrown with briers and thorns.
And I command the clouds that they rain no rain upon it.

$$(5:5–6; see 27:2–5)$$

Chapter 7 closes with the fulfillment of this threat and adds insects to the desolate scene.

On that day the Lord will whistle for the fly at the sources of the rivers of Egypt and for the bee in the land of Assyria. They will all come and settle in the steep ravines, in the caves in the rocks, on all the thorn bushes, and in all the pastures. . . .

On that day each will raise a young cow and two sheep and will eat curds made from the abundance of milk they give; indeed, everyone left in the midst of the land will eat curds and honey.[8] On that day every place where there had been a thousand vines worth a thousand pieces of silver will become briers and thorns; people will go there only with bows and arrows, for briers and thorns will cover all the land. For fear of briers and thorns, you will not go to any of the hills that had been hoed; they will be a place to let cattle loose and to let sheep trample.[9] (7:18–25; see 32:13)

Memorable scenes of the return to the wild and even to the demonic come at the end of chapter 13 with the devastation of Babylon and in chapter 34 with the conversion of the land into a home for owls, howling creatures, and goat demons. These were cited previously to exemplify the content and themes of the book (see pp. 29 and 32–33). Chapter 35, the second half of the poem in 34–35, is a countering scene of joy and restoration; verses 6–10 were cited to exemplify the image of the way (see p. 33).

At points in his vision, the prophet declares return and restoration by personifying wild nature and by replacing the thorn and the brier with flourishing trees.

> Surely you go out in joy, and in peace you are brought back.
> The mountains and the hills burst forth in song before you,
>   and all the trees of the land clap their hands.
> Instead of the thorn there comes up the cypress;
>   instead of the brier there comes up the myrtle.
> And for the Lord this is a memorial and an everlasting sign
>   that will not be cut off.
>
> (55:12–13)

The Lord, the Forester

The Lord is both gardener and forester. God prepares the ground and sows the seed. The opening verses of the Song of the Vineyard capture the image. Harvesting is part of the role and is frequently an image of punishment and destruction. In the Song of the Vineyard, the Lord destroys the vineyard because it does not produce a crop fit to harvest. The next excerpt moves from the domestic to the untamed; the Lord prunes the vines to prevent a harvestable crop.

For thus the Lord says to me:
"I quietly gaze from my dwelling like the glowing heat of the sun,
  like a cloud of dew in harvest heat."
For, before the harvest, when the flowering is over and the blossom
  becomes a ripening grape,
he cuts the shoots with pruning knives and lops off the new branches.
All the plants are then abandoned to the birds of prey from
  the mountains and to the animals of the land;
The birds of prey will summer in them, and the animals of the land
  will winter under them.

(18:4–6)

The poet uses tree imagery negatively and positively to portray the Lord, the violent forester, and the remnant, the sign of hope, that is left amid the devastation. I omit the chapter break in the following to strengthen the image's impact. Tall trees symbolize pride.

Now look! the Sovereign,[10] the Lord of Hosts,
  is violently lopping off the boughs;
The tallest trees are cut down; the lofty crash down.
He hacks down the thickets of the forest with an ax,
  and the Lebanon, in its majesty, topples.
A shoot goes forth from the stump of Jesse,
  and a branch grows out from its roots.

(10:33–11:1)

Gleaning is the process of gathering the grain and fruit that are left by the harvesters, and it readily represents a remnant. Flesh wasting away is an image of the diseased or violated body (1:5–6; 10:18).

On that day Jacob's glory will fade, and his ample flesh waste away. It will be as when the reaper gathers standing grain and harvests the ears with his arm, and as when one gleans the ears in the Valley of Rephaim—only gleanings are left, as when one shakes an olive tree: only two or three berries on the highest bough, four or five on its fruitful branches. (17:4–6; see 24:13)

In another context, the Lord totally destroys princes and the rulers of the world with no remnant left.

Scarcely are they planted; scarcely are they sown;
  scarcely has their stem taken root in the earth,

> When he blows on them and they dry up,
>> and a storm carries them off like stubble.
>>> (40:24; see 41:2)

To counter this, transformation and replanting portray restoration and hope. "Is it not just a little while before Lebanon becomes farmland, and farmland is thought of as a forest?" (29:17). Transformation reverses the Lord's fiery destruction of thorns and briers and of "the glory of his [Assyria's and Israel's] forest and his farmland" (10:17–18). The latter action results in a tiny remainder: "The remnant of the trees of his forest will be so few that a child could write them down" (10:19). To write down means to count, to number. But the time of desolation is limited; the poet combines pastoral imagery with themes of justice and peace.

> The palace is deserted, the noisy city abandoned;
> Both hill and tower are now dens forever, the joy of wild asses,
>> pasture for flocks,
> Until a spirit is poured out on us from on high,
> And the wilderness becomes farmland,
>> and farmland is thought of as a forest.
> Justice dwells in the wilderness, and righteousness lives
>> in the farmland.
> The work of righteousness is peace, and the effect
>> of righteousness is unending calm and security.
> My people live in a peaceful pasture, in secure dwellings
>> and quiet resting places. . . .
> Happy are you who sow wherever there is water,
>> who let the ox and the donkey roam free.
>>> (32:14–20)

Pastoral imagery and the theme of justice mix in the following:

> For as the earth sends forth its sprouts,
>> and as a garden makes the sown sprout,
> So the Sovereign, the Lord, makes righteousness
>> and praise sprout before all the nations.
>>> (61:11)

The Lord, the grand gardener and forester, answers the pleas for help of all in need.

The poor and the needy are seeking water and there is none;
   their tongue is parched with thirst.
I the Lord answer them; I the God of Israel do not forsake them.
I open rivers on the bare hills; fountains in the middle of valleys.
I turn the wilderness into ponds and the dry land into springs of water.
In the wilderness I place the cedar, the acacia, the myrtle, and the olive;
In the desert I put the cypress, the plane, and the pine as well.

(41:17–19; see 60:13)

God aids Israel specifically by providing water and nourishment. Water and spirit are nourishing and life-giving. The spirit rests on the shoot (11:1–2) and the servant (42:1; 61:1), and is poured out on the people (32:15).

I pour water on the thirsty ground and showers on the dry land;
I pour my spirit on your descendants and my blessing
   on your offspring.[11]
They will sprout like a green tamarisk,[12]
   like willows by flowing streams.

(44:3–4)

Jerusalem and Israel are transformed into gardens that are akin
   to the garden of Eden.
The Lord indeed comforts Zion; he comforts all her ruins;
He makes her wilderness like Eden, her desert like the garden
   of the Lord.
Rejoicing and joy are found in her, thanksgiving songs
   and the sound of music.

(51:3)

The Lord will always guide you and fill your needs
   in the scorched land;
He will strengthen your bones, and you will be like a
   watered garden, like a spring whose waters never fail.

(58:11; see 60:21)

The Israelites are called The Righteous Oaks, The Lord's Planting (61:3), reminiscent of Jerusalem, The Righteous City (1:26).

Finally, God and prophet employ pastoral imagery to proclaim the new event. The Lord has fulfilled the past word, mainly a promise of judgment and destruction, and now there is a new word, mainly a promise of mercy and return. The past is put aside, and people should focus on the new that is about to happen. The new thing is compared to a plant that is just sprouting forth from the ground and whose future shape is not yet clear.

See, things once predicted have come to be; new things I now foretell.
Before they sprout I announce them to you.

(42:9)

The new thing is a radical transformation of nature, and both wild animals and the chosen people should praise the Lord for it.

Do not remember what happened before; do not consider what
    happened of old.
I am doing something new: right now it is sprouting,
    do you not perceive it?
I am putting a road in the wilderness, rivers in the desert.
Wild animals honor me, jackals and ostriches,
Because I place water in the wilderness, rivers in the desert,
To give drink to my chosen people, the people I formed for myself,
that they might declare my praise.

(43:18–21)

The Lord's powerful word accomplishes this.

Just as the rain and snow come down from the heavens
And do not return there without watering the earth—
Rather they make it fertile and they make it sprout
so that it provides seed for the sower and bread for the eater—
So does my word that comes from my mouth:
    it does not return to me unfulfilled—
Rather it does what pleases me and accomplishes
    what I sent it to do.

(55:10–11)

Images and More Images

Even though the above passages focus on rural and pastoral imagery, there is a mixture with other imagery; the mixture intensifies and expands if we take the passages in their larger contexts.

The following discussion explores how Isaiah thoroughly mixes the presentation of themes, characters, and images and how it is impossible to offer a passage that exemplifies only one theme or one image.

For example, military and pastoral imagery combine. In 5:29 it is the Lord's invading army that roars like a lion; in 7:18–19 the Lord whistles for Egypt and Assyria, who are an immediate manifestation of that divine army; the agricultural abundance of 30:23–25 is linked, in its closing comment, with slaughter and the destruction of towers (see p. 76); the remnant promised Hezekiah in agricultural terms in 37:30–32 are those who survive the Assyrian siege of Jerusalem. The people once in darkness now rejoice before the Lord "as they rejoice at the harvest, as they shout when dividing plunder" (9:3). Perhaps the best-known example of the military and the pastoral is the enduring image of beating swords and spears into plows and pruning tools (2:4).

The combination of the rural and the military first occurs in the depiction of isolated Zion; the scene links the urban (the city), the rural (the vineyard), and the military (the siege). The link was implied in 37:30–32, which focused on the fate of the besieged city Zion-Jerusalem.

> And daughter Zion is left like a booth in a vineyard,
> Like a lodge in a cucumber field, like a besieged city.
> (1:8; see 32:14)

And it is the city Zion that the Lord is to make like Eden, the garden of the Lord (51:3). However, we should not turn the distinction between the urban and the rural, the city and the country, into a sharp contrast. In the ancient Near Eastern world they were not as separate as in today's industrialized societies. One had only to go outside the city walls to encounter fields, vineyards, and flocks.

In the parable in 28:23–29, the farmer tramples and crushes grain to prepare it for winnowing and the process of turning it into flour (see pp. 76–77). This is one type of trampling; there are others. The Lord tears down the vineyard's hedge and animals trample it (5:5; 7:25). The meaningless rituals and sacrifices are part of Israel's sin; they enter the sanctuary not in awe but to trample the Lord's courts (1:11). To put it simply, because they trample on what is the Lord's, they are in turn trampled on: "Now our enemies have trampled your sanctuary" (63:18). Assyria, the Lord's weapon, is called to despoil the people and to turn them into trampled or trodden ground "like mud in the streets" (10:6; see 5:25). The poetic justice that repaid Israel's trampling applies also to Assyria.

> The Lord of Hosts has sworn:
> "As I have planned it so will it be, and as I have designed it
>   so will it happen:
> I will break Assyria in my land, and I will trample upon him
>   on my mountains."
> (14:24–25)

The king of Babylon ends up like a trampled corpse (14:19). This fate applies to all who are arrogant, symbolized by the lofty city:

> He brings it [the city] down to earth, he lays it in the dust,
> A foot tramples it, the feet of the poor, the soles of the needy.
> (26:5–6)

Cyrus crushes all in his way. "He [Cyrus] tramples rulers like mud, like a potter treading clay" (41:25).

The strongest image of trampling occurs in 63:1–6. The Lord's bloodstained garments are like those of one who has been treading grapes in a winepress (see 16:10).

> Who is this coming from Edom, in crimsoned garments,
>   from Bozrah?
> This one, splendidly attired, striding in his great might?
> It is I, speaking victoriously, great enough to save!
> Why is your attire red and your clothes like those of one
>   who treads the winepress?
> I have trodden the winepress alone, and there was not one
>   from the peoples with me.
> I trod on them in my anger and trampled them in my rage.
> Their lifeblood spattered on my clothes,
>   and all my robes are stained.
> (63:1–3)

The brief digression on trampling offers passages that exemplify how Isaiah's richness can be plumbed by examining the usage of one image and one set of terms combined by the sense of trampling.

Light and Darkness

This is a rich and complicated set of images that span the range of Isaiah's vision from the depths of sin and violent destruction to the heights of salvation and glorious restoration, and includes much of the ordinary, everyday aspects of these images. I begin my investigation with an exclamation in its immediate context and then in its relation to the rest of the book of Isaiah. I explore how one phrase, one image, develops and expands into a complicated imagery. The exclamation occurs immediately after the grand vision of the elevated mountain of the house of the Lord. Translation in the present tense emphasizes that the speaker is reacting to what is being seen and not to a description of a future event.

> All the nations flow to it, many peoples come and say,
> "Come, let us go up to the mountain of the Lord . . .
> That we may walk in his paths
> For teaching comes forth from Zion. . . ."
> Nation does not lift a sword against nation,
>   and they no longer learn war.
> "O house of Jacob, come, let us walk in the light of the Lord!"
>
> (2:2–5)

Previously we focused on the imagery of movement in the passage and will later explore the peace that results from pilgrimage to the mountain (see pp. 72 and 174–75). The exhortation to the house of Jacob is uttered by personified Israel or by the prophet speaking on behalf of the people. The speaker, apparently shamed by the other nations' resolve to seek the Lord's ways, turns their statement to his own purposes. Their "Come, let us go up . . . that we may walk in his paths" becomes "Come, let us walk in the light of the Lord." The nations speak of Zion-Jerusalem as "the house of the God of Jacob"; our speaker refers to the people Israel, who should be at home on that mountain, since they are the house of Jacob. But in the time of this speaker, they are not on the mountain, they are not walking in the Lord's paths. "The light of the Lord" refers both to Jerusalem and to the Lord's teaching, word, and ways. If they follow and live by the latter, then they can dwell peacefully and securely in Jerusalem, God's holy mountain, the house of prayer (33:13–16; 56:6–8). Jerusalem is thus both the actual city, the site of the temple, and a symbol for being right with God, for walking in the proper ways and living in the divine presence. The exhortation, then, is a central theme of the entire book of Isaiah: Let us—ancient Israel and modern readers—walk in the Lord's light!

"Light" parallels "good" in a woe pronounced against those who have perverted reality. A speech or saying introduced by "Woe" is both a lament mourning the doom of those who act this way and a threat warning others to avoid this way.

> Woe! You who say to evil, good, and to good, evil.
> Who put darkness for light and light for darkness,
> Who put bitter for sweet and sweet for bitter!
>   (5:20)

Chapter 5 closes with the rapid advance of the army called by God. Its arrival results in "only darkness and distress; and the light grows dark with clouds" (v. 30). The dour image is expanded in chapter 13.

> Indeed, the stars of the heavens and their constellations
>   do not gleam with their light;
> The sun is dark when it rises, and the moon does not shine
>   with its light.
>   (13:10; see 24:23)

The close of chapter 8 and the opening of chapter 9 are uncertain in the Hebrew; but, like the close of chapter 5, they portray a time and place of distress and misery, darkness and gloom, as a prelude to the transformation announced in 9:2.[13]

> The people walking in darkness see a great light;
> Those dwelling in a land of deep darkness—light shines on them.

In these examples the opposition of light and dark matches the opposition of good and evil. Darkness is paired with bitterness, distress, and death. "Deep darkness" reflects the Hebrew term sometimes understood as a phrase, "the shadow of death" (KJV, NIV). Even though this is a word, not a phrase, which means darkness or gloom, the word as it stands in Hebrew still contains a pun on, a verbal allusion to, "the shadow of death." NJB attempts to capture the pun in "shadow dark as death" and REB with "dark as death."

Isaiah does not maintain these matching oppositions — light:good::
darkness:evil—throughout the book; they can be reversed. After the
condemnation of Assyria, there is a denunciation of both the king of
Assyria and Israel in 10:15–19.

> Therefore the Sovereign, the Lord of Hosts,
>   sends a wasting disease among his stout warriors,
> And instead of his glory, there is a burning that burns like
>   the burning of fire.
> The Light of Israel becomes a fire, and his Holy One a flame.
> It burns and devours his thorns and briers in one day.
>
> (10:16–17)

Light is a destructive fire that is like a horrid disease. In 1:5–7 the
poet links in a similar manner a battered body with desolation, fire,
and devouring.

> On what can you be beaten further that you continue to rebel?
> The whole head is sick, and the whole heart faint.
> From the sole of the foot even to the head,
> There is no soundness in it: Bruises and sores and bleeding wounds;
> They have not been drained, and they have not been bound up,
>   and they have not been softened with oil.
> Your country is a desolation; your cities are burnings in fire;
> Your land, in your very presence aliens eat it,
> A desolation, as overthrown by aliens.

These destructive burnings are like the fire that has no one to quench
it (1:31; 66:24). Walking in the light of the Lord turns out to be a more
fearsome undertaking than we would have thought in our first reading of 2:5.

> Sinners in Zion are frightened; trembling has seized the godless:
> "Who of us can live with a devouring fire?
> Who of us can live with an everlasting blaze?"
>
> (33:14)

This is the Lord: "his fire is in Zion and his furnace in Jerusalem"
(31:9). Destructive fire occurs at several other key points in the opening chapters of Isaiah, where it is combined with plant imagery.

Therefore, as a tongue of fire devours stubble,
  and as dry grass sinks down in the flame,
So their root will be a stench, and their blossom go up like dust.
                                    (5:24; see 6:13)

The act of devouring holds the next passage together. Fire leads to cannibalism as human devours human.

Wickedness indeed burns like fire; it devours briers and thorns;
It kindles the thickets of the forest; they billow up
  in a column of smoke.
Through the fury of the Lord of Hosts the land was scorched[14]
  and the people became like fuel for the fire. . . .
They gorge on the right and are still hungry;
They devour on the left and are not filled;
They devour the flesh of their own kin.
                                      (9:18–20)

Fire, on the other hand, can be cleansing, as in the process of smelting; refining is a double-edged image, positive for what remains and negative for what is removed. Jerusalem's silver is fouled with dross, and the punishment accords with this condition: "I turn my hand against you; I smelt away, as with lye, your dross, and I remove your entire alloy" (1:25; see 48:10).[15] In another cleansing process the Lord washes the daughters of Zion and removes bloodstains from Jerusalem "with a just spirit and a fiery spirit" (4:4; see 1:15–16). The ensuing proclamation combines creation with exodus imagery of the divine presence, symbolized by the tabernacle (Exod. 25–31, 35–40).

The Lord will create over the whole site and over the assemblies of Mount Zion a cloud for the day and the brilliance of a flaming fire for the night. Indeed, over all the glory there is a canopy. It serves as a pavilion, a shade by day from the heat, and a refuge and a shelter from the storm and rain. (Isa. 4:5–6)

This is a decided shift in the opposition of light and dark since here darkness is shade that protects from the heat (i.e., the sun). Light, in the form of the desiccating sun, is destructive and evil: "They [released prisoners] neither hunger nor thirst, and neither wind nor sun batters them" (49:10).

Zion is exhorted to help the refugees from Moab: "Make your shade like night even though it is high noon" (16:3). Egypt's shade is a false protection and is Israel's shame (30:2–3). In contrast, the Lord is a secure refuge.

> You are a fortress for the poor, a fortress for the needy
>   in their distress,
> A shelter from the storm, shade from the heat.
>
> (25:4)

And so are princes who rule justly.

> Each of them is like a shelter from the wind, a refuge
>   from the storm.
> Like streams of water on dry ground, like the shade
>   of a massive rock in a thirsty land.
>
> (32:2)

To put in darkness, then, can be protection, as when the Lord hides one rescued "in the shadow of my hand" (51:16; see 49:2). On the other hand, placing in darkness can be an attempt to hide something from others. This does not work in the case of hidden wealth, since God gives it to Cyrus: "I give you treasure concealed in the dark and secret hoards" (45:3). Israel wants to hide their deeds.

> Woe to those who would hide their plans too deep for the Lord,
> Whose deeds are done in the dark, and who say,
> "Who sees us? Who knows us?"
> You pervert everything as though the clay could be thought
>   equal to the potter.
>
> (29:15–16)

Blindness and Sight

To hide in the dark can have the effect of rendering blind those who are hiding. The above woe against those hiding their actions is followed in chapter 29 by the proclamation that a miraculous transformation is to occur in "just a little while." The transformation includes healing and joy.

> On that day the deaf will hear the words of a scroll, while from gloom
>   and from darkness the eyes of the blind will see;

> The poor will continually rejoice in the Lord, while the needy
>   of humanity will celebrate in the Holy One of Israel.
>
> (29:18–19)

Divine concern for the poor is manifest throughout Isaiah; God trans-
forms the wilderness to provide water and shelter for the needy
(41:17–19; see p. 81). Isaiah often links the deaf with the blind. Blindness and deafness are both physical and spiritual. The Lord sends the
prophet to tell the people:

> Listen carefully but do not understand; look closely but do not know.
> Deaden the mind[16] of this people; stop up their ears; seal their eyes—
> Lest they see with their eyes, hear with their ears, understand with
>   their minds, and then repent and be healed.
>
> (6:9–10)

The condition of being totally closed to anything outside oneself,
human or divine, persists for both Israel and for many parts of humanity, and appears at different points in the book. The above passage
from chapter 29 is the first proclamation in Isaiah that the condition
can be reversed. It is followed in a subsequent chapter by a description of just rulers who provide shelter for their subjects, including a
beneficial darkness that is

> Like the shade of a massive rock in a thirsty land.
> And the eyes of those who see will not be sealed;
> The ears of those who hear will pay attention;
> The minds of the thoughtless will gain understanding
>   and knowledge;
> The tongues of stammerers will speak fluently.
>
> (32:2–4)

To the body imagery we have already encountered, we can add
tongues to the trio of eyes, ears, and minds/hearts. Healing is part of
the grand transformation announced in the second part of chapters
34–35; healing restores the diseased and battered bodies imaged, for
example, in 1:5–6 (see p. 87). Hands and knees join the list of body
imagery.

> Strengthen weak hands, and faltering knees firm up;
> Say to trembling hearts: Be strong! Do not fear! . . .

> Then are opened the eyes of the blind,
> and the ears of the deaf are opened;
> Then the lame leap like deer, and the tongue
> of the speechless sings.
>
> (35:3–6a)

Previously we looked at the agricultural abundance described in 30:23–25 (see p. 86); the passage continues with a proclamation that combines light and healing.

> The light of the moon will be like the light of the sun, and the light of the sun will be seven times brighter, like the light of seven days, when the Lord binds up his people's wounds and heals the injuries left by his blows. (30:26; see 1:5–6)

True to the all-inclusive aspect of the vision and the style of juxtaposing different and even contradictory statements, the scene shifts abruptly and harshly in the next two verses. (Assyria is a flood in 8:7–8.) We can add lips, jaws, and neck to the list of body parts named in Isaiah.

> See, the name of the Lord comes from afar: his anger is blazing
> and his threat is deadly;[17]
> His lips are filled with fury, and his tongue is like a devouring fire;
> His breath is like a flooding torrent—reaching up to the neck!—
> That will sift nations with a destructive sieve,[18] and place a
> misleading bridle on the jaws of peoples.
>
> (30:27–28)

In a positive use of the image of light, the Lord calls the servant to be "a light to nations" (42:6; see 49:6). The phrase has several meanings including showing the light, the teaching, and the ways of the Lord to the nations. To reveal the Lord's word to others is "to open eyes that are blind, to bring the prisoner from the dungeon, from the prison those who sit in darkness" (42:7). Once those in darkness are released, God proclaims:

> I lead the blind on a road they do not know;
> on paths they do not know I guide them.
> The darkness before them I turn into light,
> the rough places into level ground.
>
> (42:16)

This exploration of blindness and sight and the connection with imagery of darkness and light includes a variety of cited examples that themselves include a variety of imagery. They are all illustrations of how Isaiah mixes themes and images. The image of the body and its parts is consistently touched upon in these texts, especially when the body has been beaten or seriously impaired. Salvation is then portrayed as healing wounds and removing the physical handicaps.

In terms of the body, there is insight into the psychological process of gaining understanding through the use of the senses of sight and hearing whether or not the process is depicted as successful: "So that they may see and [as a result] know" (41:20), or "Look closely but do not know" (6:9). In this context, salvation is enlightenment and insight. "Erring spirits will know how to understand, and those who find fault will learn how to accept instruction" (29:24).

Isaiah employs pastoral and rural imagery in some of the texts— "the lame leap like deer" (35:6)—and in their immediate contexts (e.g., 30:23–25). In addition, the poet weaves the image of the road with other images; this was investigated at length at the beginning of this chapter. Finally, the cited texts combine and contrast themes of judgment and salvation. The Lord's blazing and destructive anger in 30:27–28 contrasts with the binding of wounds and the healing compassion in 30:26.

The transition from chapter 42 to 43 presents a contrast in the use of fire imagery for divine justice and mercy. The second image combines an ordeal by fire with an ordeal by water. My omission of chapter and verse numbers heightens the contrast.

> They [Israel] were not willing to walk in his roads;
>> they would not hear his teaching.
> And he poured upon him [Israel] wrath, anger, and the fury of war;
> It blazed all about him, but he did not know;
>> it burned him, but he did not take it to heart.
> And now, thus says the Lord, who created you,
>> O Jacob, and who formed you, O Israel.
> "Do not fear, for I have redeemed you; I have called you
>> by my name: You are mine!
> When you pass through the waters, I am with you,
>> and through the rivers, they do not overwhelm you.
> When you walk in the midst of fire, you are not scorched,
>> and in the midst of flame, it does not burn you."
>
>   (42:24–43:2)

The image of the shattered potter's vase provides a distinctive combination of fire and water to match that in 43:2: "Among the smashed pieces there is not found a fragment to scoop fire from an oven or to dip water from a cistern" (30:14; see 64:2).

The Lord's lengthy announcement of the call and commissioning of Cyrus in 44:24–45:7 juxtaposes judgment and salvation.

> I am the Lord and there is no other.
> I form light and I create darkness.
> I make peace and I create evil.
> I the Lord make all these things.
> (45:6–7)

"I create evil" is a shocking statement that is usually softened in translations, except for KJV. Instead of "peace" and "evil," NAB, NRSV, and TNK contrast "weal" or "well-being" and "woe"; GNB, "blessing" and "disaster"; NIV, "prosperity" and "disaster"; and NJB, "well-being" and "disaster." The terseness of the statement increases its impact.

Fire, Water, and a Garden

Trees and fire are central to the domestic scene of the idol maker in 44:9–20.

> [The idol maker] plants a cedar and the rain makes it grow. When it is large enough to burn, he takes part of it and warms himself. He starts a fire and bakes bread. But he also makes a god and worships it; he makes an idol and bows to it. Half of it he burns in fire, and over this half he roasts meat, eats, and is full. He also warms himself and says, "Good, I am getting warm as I watch the fire."[19] He makes the remainder into a god, his idol; he bows down and worships it. (vv. 14–17)

The scene contrasts with that at the close of chapter 47. The condemned woman looks to sorcerers and astrologers to save her.

> But look, they are like stubble, fire burns them;
> They cannot save even themselves from the power of the flame.
> This is neither a coal to warm oneself by nor a fire to sit before!

> Such to you are they with whom you have exhaustively traded
> from your youth—
> All wander on their own way—there is none to save you!
>
> (47:14–15; see 50:10–11)

In chapter 58 the prophet and the Lord concentrate on the question of proper religious observance, exemplified by fasting in verses 1–9a. A ritual is the lesser part of worship of the Lord, since proper worship requires a faithful attitude toward God and the corresponding compassionate behavior toward others. In the imagery of chapter 58, true worship is not to turn in on oneself, to have one's head perpetually bent "like a bulrush." It is not to fight with others "with a vicious fist." Rather it is to go out from oneself to others to free them and to share one's food with them. One commentator refers to this as "the exodus in place" in which the image and movement of exodus, going out, are used to speak of a change in one's relation to other people and things. This is a moral and spiritual change, not an actual physical move from one locale to another.[20] If such worship and care of others is performed,

> Then your light will break forth like the dawn,
>   and your healing will sprout quickly;
> Your vindicator[21] goes before you;
>   the Lord's glory is your rear guard.
>
> (58:8)

The prophet combines light and healing as in 35:3–6a (see pp. 90–91) and continues with the assertion:

> Indeed, water breaks forth in the wilderness and streams
>   in the desert.
> And the burning sand is a swamp, and the thirsty ground,
>   springs of water.
>
> (35:6b–7)

Water and light are paralleled; they break forth in chapters 35 and 58 as a sign that people have gone forth to others and that they all, helper and helped, experience restoration and salvation.

In 58:9b–12 the prophet repeats the lesson about proper worship and reinforces the connection with pastoral imagery, including the garden (see pp. 80–81). Strengthening bones is one more image for bodily healing.

> If you remove the yoke from your midst . . .
>   if you share yourself with the hungry,
> Then your light will rise in the darkness
>   and your gloom will be like noontime.
> The Lord will always guide you and fill your needs
>   in the scorched land;
> He will strengthen your bones and you will be like
>   a watered garden, like a spring whose waters never fail.
>   (vv. 9b-11)

In 58:13–14 the prophet and God repeat the lesson yet a third time and close with the people riding "on the heights of the land" and feeding on "the heritage of your forefather Jacob."

We have discussed parts of chapter 59 in terms of its themes of sin and justice and its varied imagery (see pp. 19 and 74–75). The prophet denounces the people's sins in verses 1–8 and they affirm them in verses 9–15a. They are spiritually blind.

> Therefore justice is far from us, and righteousness does not reach us;
> We wait for light, and lo! darkness; and for brightness,
>   but in gloom we walk.
> We grope like the blind along a wall, like those
>   who have no eyes we grope;
> We stumble at noon as in the twilight, among the vigorous
>   as though we were dead.
> We all growl like bears; like doves we moan mournfully.
> We wait for justice, but there is none; for salvation,
>   but it is far from us.
>   (vv. 9–11)

The Lord responds to the people's blatant sin with fury and violence, but still "a Redeemer comes to Zion, for those who turn from transgression in Jacob" (v. 20; see 1:27).

In chapters 58 and 59 the poet focuses on sin, violence, and darkness and on the countering promises of life and light. The speeches and scenes form the backdrop for the brilliance witnessed by Zion in chapter 60.

Arise! Shine! For your light comes, and the glory
　of the Lord rises upon you.
Darkness certainly still covers the earth,
　and thick darkness peoples,[22]
But the Lord rises upon you, and his glory appears over you.
Nations come to your light and kings to the brightness
　of your dawn.

(vv. 1–3; see 62:1–2)

The poet depicts, with striking images, the abundance of Zion: the return of her sons and daughters and the gathering of the wealth of the nations (vv. 4–5). There will no longer be violence or destruction within her. In the following we move quickly from light to plant imagery as we did in the above excerpts from chapter 58.

The sun will no longer be your light for day,
　nor will the bright moon provide you light for night;
Rather the Lord will be your light everlasting,
　and your God your splendor.
Your sun will not again set or your moon withdraw,
　for the Lord will be your light everlasting.
Your days of mourning are at an end.
Your people, all of them righteous, will possess the land forever.
They are the sprout I planted, the work of my hands
　that glorify me.

(vv. 19–21; see 30:23–26)

Chapters 58–60 tell a story of and depict scenes of sin, confession, and devastation that are succeeded by those of restoration and prosperity. The poet depicts the scenes and their themes with his usual rich imagery and terminology. We can read them in sequence or separately. The brilliance of chapter 60 is not the end of the story, not a closing and concluding vision, since Isaiah's final images of fire and light are not pleasant ones like these but are reminders of the violence of the world and of God.

Look! The Lord comes in fire, and like a whirlwind his chariots,
To repay with his wrathful anger and to rebuke with flames of fire.
Yes, by fire, with his sword, the Lord judges all flesh;
　and many are those slain by the Lord.

(66:15–16)

They go out and see the bodies of the people who rebel against me.
Their worm will never die; *their fire will never be quenched*;
  they will be a horror for all flesh.

(66:24)

Water and Dryness

This is another rich and varied imagery that we have come upon in
preceding examples. Water first appears in Isaiah as an impurity akin
to dross in pure silver: "Your [Jerusalem's] silver has become dross;
your wine is mixed with water" (1:22). The negative valuation of water
occurs throughout Isaiah.

Chapter 1 closes with dryness, the absence of water. The people are
withered and set aflame by a mere spark.

They are certainly ashamed of the oaks in which you delighted;[23]
You blush for the gardens that you have chosen.
For you are like an oak whose leaf withers,
  and like a garden that has no water.
The strong will become like tinder, and their work like a spark;
They will burn, the two of them together,
  and there will be no one to quench them.

(1:29–31; see 15:6)

This is a natural development, since what is dry is susceptible
to being burned, to being turned to mere dust, and to being easily
blown away. Isaiah employs these aspects of the dry in a variety
of settings, usually in combination with other rural and pastoral
imagery.

Therefore, as a tongue of fire devours stubble,
  and as dry grass sinks down in the flame,
So their root will be a stench, and their blossom go up like dust;
For they have rejected the teaching of the Lord of Hosts,
  and the word of the Holy One of Israel they have despised.

(5:24)

Egypt is the land of the Nile, a land dependent on the annual floods
of the river; the vision of its desolation is appropriately a detailed scene
of a parched land. Workers dependent on the river, whether for fish
or flax, are despondent.

Waters disappear from the sea; the Nile is parched and dry.
Canals stink; the branches of Egypt's Nile are totally parched;
    reed and rush rot.
There are bare places by the Nile, on the very edge of the Nile.
All that is sown by the Nile dries up, is blown away,
    and is totally gone.
Fishermen mourn and groan; all who cast a hook into the Nile
    and all who spread a net on the water—all lose heart.
Those who prepare flax are ashamed along with carders and weavers.
Her spinners are dismayed, and all her artisans are sick at heart.

                                                                (19:5–10)

After the prophet denounces Jerusalem for fertility worship (17:10–
11), the people express their conviction that God is ultimately for
them. They contrast the power of water with the nothingness of dust.
Their exclamation contrasts the repeated roaring and raging of the
nations with the Lord's single shout.

Ah, the roar of many peoples, they roar like the roaring of the seas.
Ah, the rage of the nations, they rage like the raging
    of mighty waters.
The nations rage like the raging of mighty waters.
He shouts at them and they flee afar,
Driven by the wind like chaff from the mountains,
    like whirling dust[24] before a storm.
At evening, lo, terror; before morning, it is gone.
This is the fate of those who despoil us, the lot of those
    who plunder us.

                                                                (17:12–14)

The exalted Lord contrasts with those who produce dust (see
26:16–18 for a similar claim using birth imagery).

"Now I arise," says the Lord, "now I exalt myself;
    now I lift myself up.
You conceive chaff, you bear stubble; your breath is a fire
    that devours you.[25]
Peoples will be heaps of white ash, cut thorns burning in fire."

                                                                (33:10–12)

To God all nations are like dust (40:15); the mightiest are nothing:

"He blows on them and they dry up, and a storm carries them off like stubble" (40:24).

The cloud by day and the fire night in Isaiah 4 are an exodus image. Exodus imagery includes the dry road through the sea, and the poet employs and expands the image to portray the remnant returning from exile.

> The Lord will totally destroy the tongue of the Egyptian sea;
> He will wave his hand over the River[26] with his mighty wind;
> He will split it into seven streams and allow people to cross it
>   in sandals.
> Thus there will be a highway for the remnant of his people
>   that remains from Assyria
> As there was for Israel when he came up from the land of Egypt.
>
> (11:15–16)

In the midst of the hymn of chapter 12, which immediately follows this passage, we are informed: "while rejoicing you will draw water from the wells of salvation."[27] In context this refers to God's sustenance of the people as they travel through the wilderness, a theme found in several of the passages already cited.

The poet connects the exodus with the departure from Babylon. The Lord's enemies, pictured as fire, are "quenched like a wick," unlike the servant in 42:3 and the eternal fire in 1:31 and 66:24.

> Thus says the Lord, your Redeemer, the Holy One of Israel,
> For your sakes I send to Babylon and I bring down
>   all her bars. . . .[28]
> I am the Lord, your Holy One, the creator of Israel,
>   your king.
> Thus says the Lord, who makes a road through the sea
>   and a path in powerful waters,
> Who leads out chariot and horse with an army
>   of powerful warriors.
> They lie down, they do not rise, they are extinguished,
>   quenched like a wick.
>
> (43:14–17)

In their prayer to the Lord, the people recall the days of old.

> Where is he who brought them up out of the sea
>   with the shepherd[29] of his flock?
> Where is he who put his holy spirit in their midst?
> Who made his glorious arm march at Moses' right hand?
> Who split the waters before them to make for himself
>   an everlasting name?
>
> (63:11–12)

Besides this specific exodus tradition of the crossing of the sea on dry ground, Isaiah reflects the general tradition of the Lord's power to transform nature by drying up water. The transformation benefits the needy and the blind (see 41:17–19 on p. 81).

> I lay waste mountains and hills, and all their greenery I dry up;
> I turn rivers into islands, and pools I dry up.
> I lead the blind on a road they do not know;
>   on paths they do not know I guide them.
>
> (42:15–16)

> Is my hand too short to redeem; do I not have the power to deliver?
> By my mere shout I dry up the sea, I turn rivers into wilderness;
> Their fish stink from lack of water, they lie dead from thirst.
> I clothe the heavens with blackness and cover them with sackcloth.
>
> (50:2–3)

The first question is answered in 59:1–2. "See, the Lord's hand is not too short to save. . . . Rather, your iniquities have been barriers between you and your God." The odor of rotting fish recalls the denunciation of Egypt (19:5–10; see p. 98). The final image alludes to the ninth plague, darkness (Exod. 10:21–29).

In the Song of the Arm of the Lord in Isa. 51:9–11, the poet asserts, against the questioning of divine power in 50:2, the power of the Lord's arm. The arm is personified and addressed as "you." In the brief poem, the poet combines images and themes of creation, flood, exodus, exile and wilderness, return, and the defeat of evil forces whether mythic or human. He concludes as all the redeemed, past, present, and future enter into Zion. The last verse, 51:11, repeats 35:10 and alludes to the power and imagery of that entire poem, Isaiah 34–35.

> Awake, awake, clothe yourself with might, O Arm of the Lord!
> Awake, as in days of old, the ages of long ago!

> Was it not you who hacked Rahab in pieces,
>   who pierced the Dragon?
> Was it not you who dried Sea, the waters of the Great Deep,
> Who turns the abysses of Sea into a road for the redeemed
>   to cross on?
> The ransomed of the Lord return; they come to Zion singing,
>   with everlasting joy on their heads.
> Rejoicing and joy reach out, while grief and sighing flee.
>   (51:9–11)

The short poem is an allusion to, a poetic version of, the ancient Near Eastern myth of creation as a battle between the creator god and the powers of chaos, frequently in the form of a sea monster or dragon. In short, the creator god would defeat and slay the monster and then create the world and humanity out of the corpse. In Canaanite versions of the myth the monster is called Leviathan, Rahab, or Sea. This version of creation is excluded from Genesis 1, the first depiction of creation we encounter in the Hebrew Bible, but is reflected elsewhere.[30]

The "Great Deep" and the "abysses of Sea" refer to the watery realms that underlie the world; the watery realms that lie above the heavens match them (Gen. 1:1–8). The flood is imagined as the inrushing of waters when the Great Deep breaks forth and the windows of heaven open (Gen. 7:11; see Isa. 54:9). A similar scene is in Isaiah 24: "The windows of heaven are open and the foundations of the earth tremble" (v. 18). When he summons Cyrus to rebuild Jerusalem, the Lord commands the Deep, "Dry up! I make your rivers run dry" (44:27).

I bring this section to an end with one final example of how Isaiah does not confine himself to using an image in only one setting with only one meaning: "The wicked are like the tossing sea that cannot rest: its waters toss up mire and mud" (57:20). At another point, the Lord declares his power in a different use of this image: "I am the Lord your God who stirs up the sea into crashing waves" (51:15).

Waters Flow in the Wilderness

In a reversal of drying up the sea, Isaiah depicts the Lord turning the dry into the wet, providing water in the desert. We have already seen this in many of our cited passages, for example, the saving wells of 12:3 and the just princes in 32:2. The latter are "like streams of water on dry ground, like the shade of a massive rock in a thirsty land." The great restoration of Isaiah 34–35 is pictured in these terms.

Yes, waters break forth in the wilderness and streams in the desert.
The burning sand is a swamp, and the thirsty ground, springs of water.
(35:6–7)

This is imagery for both the exodus from Egypt and the return from Babylon. The Lord provided water for the Israelites at Marah (Exod. 15:22–26), Rephidim (17:1–7), and Meribah (Num. 20:2–13).[31]

Leave Babylon! Flee Chaldea! . . .
"The Lord has redeemed his servant Jacob."
They do not thirst when he leads them through the wastes;
He makes water flow from the rock for them;
He split the rock and water gushed out!
(Isa. 48:20–21)

The Lord cares for the thirsty poor by providing water and by planting trees; I cited the full passage as an example of rural-pastoral imagery (see p. 81):

I open rivers on the bare hills; fountains in the middle of valleys.
I turn the wilderness into ponds and the dry land
into springs of water.
(41:18; see 44:3–4)

This correlates with the provision of water and food and its opposite, the removal or denial of nourishment; I present the theme and imagery of nourishment only as it touches upon wetness and water. God removes "support and staff, all support of bread and all support of water" (3:1). The following passage blends matching and contrasting images. The people suffer from three lacks: ignorance, hunger, and thirst. Sheol, which is the underworld and a symbol of death, is hungry and swallows the people; they go down Sheol's throat. Indeed, all humanity goes down, while the Lord is raised up. What is left are small cattle and aliens feeding, unlike the hungry Jerusalemites.

Therefore my people go into exile without knowledge;
their nobles are dying of hunger, and their multitude
  is parched with thirst.
Therefore Sheol has enlarged her throat and opened her mouth
  without measure;
Her [Jerusalem's and/or Sheol's] honored and her multitude
  go down, her throng and all who exult in her.
Humanity is bowed down, everyone is brought low,
  and the eyes of the exalted are humbled.
And the Lord of Hosts is exalted by justice, and the Holy God
  shows himself holy by righteousness.
And the lambs graze as in their pasture, and among the ruins
  fatlings and aliens feed.

(5:13–17; see p. 6 for the final verse)

If people, particularly Israelites, provide water for themselves during a time of siege, this shows a lack of trust in the Lord. This is analogous to a human striving for the heights in contrast to the Lord placing them there; the first is pride, the latter a proper reward (see pp. 48–49). "The conduit of the upper pool" (7:3; 36:2) is a water supply for Jerusalem that was crucial during the siege of the city by Aram and Israel and by Sennacherib. At the time of siege, the Israelites armed and fortified themselves.

And you stored the waters of the Lower Pool . . . but you did not
look to him who was doing this, and you had no regard for him
who was shaping this from long ago. (22:9–11)

The Lord calls the Jerusalemites to mourn. The negative valuation of food continues.

But instead: rejoicing and joy; killing oxen and slaughtering sheep;
  eating meat and drinking wine.
"Eat and Drink! For tomorrow we die!"

(22:13; see 21:5)

Drunkenness is a frequent complaint of Isaiah: "Woe! Heroes in drinking wine and warriors at mixing drink" (5:22; see 5:11–12). The leaders of Ephraim are overcome with wine (28:1). "They are muddled by wine and they stagger with strong drink" (v. 7). Zion is "drunk but not from wine" (51:21). She has instead drunk from the cup of staggering and of wrath, but now the Lord takes the cup from her hands and places it in the hands of her tormentors (vv. 22–23).

The Rabshakeh refers to eating and drinking in both repulsive and attractive terms. He speaks in Judahite so that the people of the city will hear that they are doomed "to eat their own dung and to drink their own urine" (36:12). But if they surrender to the Assyrian king, then "they will eat from their own vines and fig trees and drink from their own cisterns" (v. 16). The Lord employs an even more repulsive image: "I make your [Zion's] oppressors eat their own flesh, and they are drunk with their own blood as with wine" (49:26). The poet offsets these grim images.

> Ho! All that thirst, come to the waters. You who have no money,
>   come! Buy! Eat!
> Come, buy wine and milk without money and without cost.
> Why spend your money for that which is not food
>   and your earnings for that which does not satisfy?
> Listen closely so that you may eat what is good
>   and delight yourselves in rich food.
>
>   (55:1–2)

I close with two contrasting images of a river. The first is the strict "if . . . then" of justice, while the second declares divine mercy.

> Oh, if only you had paid attention to my commandments!
> Then your prosperity would be like a river,
>   and your success like the waves of the sea,
> Your descendants like the sand, and your offspring like its grains.
> Their name would never be cut off or obliterated from before me.
>
>   (48:18–19)

> For thus says the Lord:
> "I am now extending to her peace like a river and,
>   like a flooding stream, the wealth of nations."
>
>   (66:12)

The Human Body and Its Emotions

The human body and the course of human life is another set of imagery that we can trace in the book of Isaiah. I limit myself to a few comments. We have seen an image of the whole body, especially when it is diseased or impaired and in some instances subsequently restored and healed. The span of human life is material for metaphor and image: from conception: the Lord "who fashions you in the womb" (44:2), to birth: "As soon as Zion was in labor, she delivered her children" (66:8; see 23:4), through infancy, childhood, and adult life to death: "An infant plays over the asp's hole" (11:8); "One who dies at a hundred years is but a youth" (65:20).

Emotions are part of the human body, and Isaiah's use of emotional language cuts across all of our categories: poetry, themes, imagery, and characterization. It occurs in almost all, if not all, of our cited examples. I draw attention to this facet of Isaiah's vision, but do not deal with it in detail. The great emotional range is yet another aspect of Isaiah's all-inclusive, encyclopedic quality. Isaiah spans the full range of human emotions, the emotions both of the human speakers and characters present in his vision and of his readers.

His use of repetition and figurative language has a powerful emotional effect attached to it. (My use of "powerful" has an emotive appeal of its own.) Saying something two or more times, using synonyms and parallels, quickly moves beyond a simple statement of fact. In his opening denunciation, the poet hammers home his point with repetition and "strong words."

> Woe! Sinful nation,
> Iniquitous people,
> Offspring of evildoers,
> Children who act corruptly!
> They have forsaken the Lord;
> They have despised the Holy One of Israel;
> They have turned back.
>
> (1:4)

Instead of focusing on the poetic use of repetition (parallelism) or on the depiction of the people in the passage, I focus on the emotions of the speaker and on the intended emotional impact on the audience, both those within the vision and those reading it at a later time. The latter includes us, the contemporary readers. Isaiah expresses not just the state of the people, but in addition his and God's disgust and frustration with them.

The Lord calls the people "stubborn of heart" (46:12 NRSV, etc.). The phrase is literally something like "mighty" or "strong of heart"

or even "bulls in heart." (The word for "strong" or "bull" occurs in
10:13 and 34:7 and is applied to God in 1:24 and 60:16, the Mighty
One.) The image, the figure "stubborn of heart," expresses the divine
frustration with this obstinate people: "Listen to me, you who have
hearts of bulls, who are so far from deliverance." God depicts the
people's obstinacy and stubbornness in another striking image: "An
iron sinew is your neck, your forehead bronze" (48:4).

Isaiah's emotional range includes the descriptions of the Lord's
wrath, anger, fury, and vengeance that occur throughout the book from
the first (1:24) to the final chapter (66:15–16). God does not react to
the evil and rebellion of Israel or of any other human dispassionately,
and Isaiah does not want his readers to react dispassionately. Divine justice is not a matter of bare principle applied logically or mechanically.

The poet counters the negative emotions with expressions and
descriptions of joy and happiness. The people of darkness now see
light.

> You have made great their *joy*;
> They *rejoice* before you with the *joy* of harvest
> As people *celebrate* while dividing plunder.
>
> (9:3)

In Hebrew as in English, "rejoice" is a verb related to the noun "joy."

> Sing, O heavens! and celebrate, O earth! O mountains,
>   break into song!
> For the Lord has comforted his people and on his
>   suffering ones has compassion.
>
> (49:13)

Repetition strengthens the positive impact: comfort and compassion,
God's people and those who are suffering.

In the next passage, the poet depicts the messenger's approach with
the image of his physical feet; he then speaks of the message in general but emphatic terms.

> How beautiful on the mountains are the feet of the herald,
> Announcing peace, heralding good, announcing victory.
>
> (52:7)

Joy is the reaction.

Break into song all together, you desolate ruins, O Jerusalem!
For the Lord has comforted his people, he has redeemed Jerusalem.

(52:9)

Those addressed within the vision and all subsequent readers of the book of Isaiah are to share in the exultation.

Even though the preceding discussion offered many rich examples, it is still a selective treatment. This derives in part from my commitment to present ways of reading Isaiah rather than a focused, developed interpretation of the entire book. I looked at different images combined in the same passage with examples drawn from throughout Isaiah and commented on the connections between a given image and a particular theme or character. I noted some of the connections in the previous chapter on themes and will note others in the following chapters. My goal is to lead my readers into the vision and world of Isaiah, to give them initial directions on what to look for and how to treat it, and then leave it to them to explore this world and to turn it into their own.

Endnotes to Chapter 3

1. *Torah* occurs in Isa. 1:10; 2:3; 5:24; 8:16, 20; 24:5; 30:9; 42:4, 21, 24; 51:4, 7.
2. This is the verb related to the noun "teaching." The correspondence is obscured in NRSV and REB, which use "teach" and "instruction," and in KJV, NIV, and NJB, which use "teach" and "law."
3. Literally the term means "bread" (NJB, TNK) or "food" (NIV).
4. This is a plant whose seeds are used as a seasoning; translations vary. GNB and REB agree with NRSV. KJV has the obsolete "fitches," i.e., vetch; NAB, the rare "gith," a type of fennel; NJB, "fennel"; NIV, "caraway"; and TNK, "black cumin."
5. This is a secondary spelling for the more frequent cumin, another plant whose seeds are used for seasoning.
6. This is a type of wheat. KJV uses "rye"; TNK, "emmer," which is a wheat; REB, "vetches"; and GNB sidesteps precise identification by using "other grain."
7. To be understood as bitter, rather than the expected sweet, grapes.
8. Eating curds and honey can be a royal delicacy or a sign that that is all there is to eat.
9. TNK translates the last sentence: "But the perils of thornbush and thistle shall not spread to any of the hills that could only be tilled with a hoe; and here cattle shall be let loose, and sheep and goats shall tramp about." The translators comment that this refers to "marginal farm land, too rocky for the plow" and even for briers and thorns. They note that the Hebrew term for sheep also means goats, and therefore they render "sheep and goats."
10. This is the way that both NRSV and TNK render the Hebrew term *'adon*, which means "lord" in a generic sense. Others, e.g., KJV and REB, use "Lord" in contrast to "LORD" for Yahweh.

11. There is a pun in Hebrew, since the terms for descendants and offspring refer to agricultural "seed" and "what comes forth" (42:5). God cares for humans and plants.

12. This is NRSV and REB; the other translations are similar to NJB's "among the grass."

13. See pp. 20–21 for discussion of the verse differences between the Hebrew text and most translations in chaps. 9 and 64.

14. To be "scorched," "burned," or "set on fire" is the usual translation of this rare Hebrew word; the translation is based on the context. NAB and TNK render the verb as "quakes" and "quaked," referring to the mountains shaking in 5:25.

15. Along with impure silver, Jerusalem's "wine is mixed with water" (1:22), but since the water cannot be removed from the wine, such "dewatering" is not part of the punishment.

16. The Hebrew term is "heart," as in NAB, NIV, and NJB. In biblical psychology the heart is associated with one's entire inner being, and it is just as much the seat of reason and intelligence as of emotion; therefore it can be translated "mind" in contexts such as chaps. 6 and 32.

17. The Hebrew for the last phrase is uncertain and translations vary. For example, NRSV renders: "burning with his anger, and in thick rising smoke"; TNK: "in blazing wrath, with a heavy burden"; and NAB: "in burning wrath, with lowering clouds."

18. This phrase is uncertain in Hebrew. My translation is similar to NIV, NJB, and NRSV. REB, "to load the nations with an evil yoke," is similar to TNK, "to set a misguiding yoke upon nations."

19. This translation is similar to GNB, NIV, NJB, and REB. Others take "watch" as a metaphor for feel or experience and translate like NRSV, "I can feel the fire."

20. See Rémi Lack, *La symbolique du livre d'Isaïe* (Analecta Biblica, 59; Rome: Biblical Institute Press, 1973), 129–36.

21. The Hebrew word means righteousness (REB), justice (NJB), victory (GNB; see 41:2), vindication, and vindicator (NAB, NRSV, TNK); see above, pp. 51–54.

22. NJB captures the image of night and dawn: "Look! though night still covers the earth and darkness the peoples, on you Yahweh is rising."

23. "They" is the reading in the MT. Most translations follow some other Hebrew manuscripts and one other ancient version and change it to read "you." I take the shift from "they" to "you" as the transition from the third-person denunciation of sinners in v. 28, "they," to the direct accusation of the people, "you," in this verse.

24. The Hebrew term refers to something whirling, rolling, or tumbling: tumbleweed (NAB, NIV, TNK) or thistledown (REB).

25. This is a literal translation as in NIV and NRSV. Others change "your" to "my" and translate similar to TNK: "My breath will devour you like fire." The Hebrew word for "breath" means spirit or wind. These meanings underlie REB, "a wind like fire will devour you," and NAB, "my spirit shall consume you like fire."

26. This is the Euphrates, as in 8:7, but it alludes to the Nile in this context.

27. This is NRSV. TNK renders "fountains of triumph." The phrase could be "wells gained in victory" (see pp. 51–54 and 134–35).

28. The Hebrew of the omitted phrase is uncertain. NRSV renders, "and the shouting of the Chaldeans will be turned to lamentation," and TNK, "and the Chaldeans shall raise their voice in lamentation."

29. The Hebrew has the plural, "shepherds" (NRSV), referring to all the leaders; the

Greek has the singular, "shepherd" (e.g., NIV, REB, TNK), referring to Moses. NJB capitalizes the noun, "the Shepherd of his flock."

30. For Leviathan see Isa. 27:1; Pss. 74:12–14; 104:25–26; and Job 41:1. For Rahab see Isa. 30:7 (not translated as such in KJV and TNK) and Ps. 89:9–11. Like TNK, I translate "Sea," a proper name paralleling Rahab. The other translations render it "the sea."

31. All three stories revolve around the people's grumbling against Moses and the Lord; the last story indeed ends with the Lord barring Moses from entering the promised land, because he failed to reveal the Lord's holiness.

Chapter 4

Who Speaks
and Who Acts in Isaiah?

Isaiah comprises mostly poetic speeches in which someone, an individual or a group, speaks about themselves or, more often, about others. By comparing and contrasting these speeches, we can develop a sense of the major speakers (e.g., the poet-prophet and the Lord) and of the main ones spoken about (e.g., Israel and Assyria). The dramatic characters of the vision of Isaiah are personages who can be described in terms of their attitudes, motivations, and actions. I use "character" in a broad sense since, first, some of these dramatic characters (e.g., Israel, Jerusalem, and Babylon) also appear at points as the people, the geographical area, or city that they were in ancient times. Even though Isaiah's vision extends into the realms of dreams and nightmares, it is anchored in this world. Babylon is mainly a symbol of overweening pride and the usurper of God's throne, but in one chapter it is simply the ancient city (see 39:1).

Second, some of the speakers are only voices without a name; the servant in chapters 42 and 49 is a fine example. Corresponding to this are speeches that mention another without giving the latter a name or other specific designation; the servant spoken of in chapter 53 and the woman in chapter 54 are examples.

Third, we are dealing with a grand poetic vision, and our reading must be sensitive to the metaphorical and symbolic possibilities of the particular text and of the characters that we meet in it. In chapter 39 Merodach-baladan, king of Babylon, sends envoys to Hezekiah to congratulate him on his recovery. This is a straightforward narrative and equally an anticipation and symbol of the future destruction of Jerusalem and the exile of the people.

In tracing Isaiah's depictions of the major characters, I pay more attention to context and to the sequential ordering of parts of the book than I have in my other analyses, but I am not offering a developed reading of the book only in its present order. I still pursue my reading practice of comparing and contrasting texts from throughout the book of Isaiah. As with images and themes, in Isaiah's vision there is change and movement but there are also enduring principles of good and evil and enduring patterns of human behavior. When we trace characters' portrayals in given passages, large or small, we will pay attention to them as they are in the passage and will, at the same time, note how they fit general patterns in Isaiah.

I start with a passage from Genesis, 25:27–33, a prose narrative that will lead us into the complexities of speeches and speakers in Isaiah.

> When the boys grew up, Esau was a skillful hunter, an outdoorsman, while Jacob was a quiet man who stayed in camp. Isaac loved Esau, for he had a taste for wild game, and Rebekah loved Jacob. At one time when Jacob had cooked a stew, Esau came in from outdoors and he was famished. Esau said to Jacob, "Give me a little of that red stuff, for I am famished." . . . Jacob said, "First sell me your birthright." And Esau said, "I am at death's door; of what use is a birthright to me?" Jacob said, "Swear to me first." And he swore to him, and he sold his birthright to Jacob.

The narrator introduces the characters by name and notes significant aspects of their personalities. The brief story of the stew and the birthright illustrates the differences between the impetuous hunter and the crafty homebody. Esau and Jacob demonstrate these traits in various ways in other stories in Genesis. In this story, actual dialogue is brief and to the point; the narrator sets the scene and then provides the conclusion.

Hezekiah and the Rabshakeh

In these chapters, although the story has a similar structure of setting, dialogue, and outcome, the dialogue is anything but brief and to the point. The narrator describes the initial setting with detail but says nothing about the personalities involved beyond their names and titles.

> In Hezekiah's fourteenth year, Sennacherib, king of Assyria, attacked the fortified cities of Judah and captured them. The king of Assyria sent the Rabshakeh [an Assyrian title for general or commander] from Lachish to Jerusalem to King Hezekiah with

a great army. He stood by the conduit of the Upper Pool by the highway to the Fuller's Field. Eliakim, son of Hilkiah, chief of the palace, and Shebna the secretary, and Joah, son of Asaph, the recorder came out to meet him.

The Rabshakeh said to them, "Tell Hezekiah, 'Thus says the great king, the king of Assyria: "What makes you so confident?"'" (36:1–4)

The fourteenth year of Hezekiah is 701 B.C.E., and the Assyrian army that began its onrush over thirty years before with Ahaz during the Syro-Ephraimite War has now reached the walls of Jerusalem (see p. 24). In the meantime both Damascus (Aram) and Samaria (Israel) have been swept away (see 17:1–3 and 28:1–4). As I noted in the description of the book of Isaiah, chapters 36–37 are part of the transition in 36–39, a transition that looks back to the characters, images, and themes of 1–35 and ahead to those of 40–66. Chapters 36–37 signal parts of the transition. Hezekiah has succeeded his father Ahaz on the throne, and Assyria will depart the scene at the close of the two chapters. Indeed, the prophet has already described the central scene of the two chapters in vivid imagery. "Your country is a desolation, your cities are burning in fire; your land: right in front of you aliens eat it. . . . And daughter Zion is left . . . like a besieged city" (1:7–8). Again we have the Isaianic tension and balance of movement in time and permanence of image.

The site of the conduit is the same place where Isaiah and his son, A Remnant Returns (Shear-jashub), met Ahaz when he faced the attack of Aram and Israel. Isaiah told Ahaz, "Be careful! Be calm! Do not fear! Do not lose your resolve because of these two smoking stubs of burning sticks!" (7:3–4). But Ahaz could not trust. He would not even ask for a sign that this promise was sure because to do so would mean that he trusted God and not his own military preparations. Preparations for a siege include weapons, fortifications, and water.

On that day you looked to the weaponry of the House of the Forest.[1] You saw that there were many breaches in the city of David, and you stored the waters of the Lower Pool. You counted the houses of Jerusalem and tore them down to fortify the wall. You built a reservoir between the walls for the water of the Old Pool. But you did not look to him who was doing this, and you had no regard for him who was shaping this from long ago. (22:8–11)

Ahaz, king of Judah and member of the house, the dynasty, of David, is a type of the fearful person, the one who cannot trust in God even when given many assurances of God's reliability. Therefore this passage from chapter 22 can be applied to Ahaz even though it does not explicitly or grammatically—"you" is masculine plural and refers to the rulers in Jerusalem—concern him in its context. In chapters 7 and 22 both Ahaz and the Jerusalemites typify fear and self-reliance, and both display this at the time of the siege of Jerusalem by Aram and Israel.

In chapters 36–37 Hezekiah faces a siege by the Assyrian king Sennacherib and his general the Rabshakeh. We can compare and contrast his reactions with those of Ahaz and the Jerusalemites. In chapter 36 the three men who come out to meet the Rabshakeh play a small role in the story despite the detail of their introduction (see vv. 3 and 22). From 22:15–25 we know that both Shebna and Eliakim are doomed figures whose success will be short-lived (see p. 30); they cast a pall over this story in chapters 36–37. Joah, the recorder, appears only here in Isaiah. Once the three men are on the scene, the Rabshakeh speaks and we encounter the complexities of speeches in Isaiah's vision.

First, there are several lengthy and short exchanges in chapters 36–37 with varying speakers before the outcome is narrated in 37:36–38. The dialogue between the initial setting and the final outcome is much longer than that in the Genesis story. "Dialogue" may not be the best term to use for the exchanges, since dialogue implies a give-and-take that is not evident here.

Second, we are dealing with speeches within speeches, indicated by the use of several sets of quotation marks in my translations. (Other translations restrict their use of quotation marks, especially within a quotation, to lessen this confusing use of double or even triple sets of marks. I use them to highlight the complexity.) The king of Assyria sends his general as a messenger to relay a message to King Hezekiah through his three officials, who are thereby messengers. The two kings never speak to each other directly. The use of messengers who quote others who may in their turn quote even others can often leave us, as readers, wondering exactly who is speaking to whom. (I will return to this topic of messengers and speeches within speeches in my later discussion of the prophet.)

The Rabshakeh challenges three bases for Hezekiah's confidence: Egypt's help (vv. 5–6), the Lord (vv. 7 and 10), and military might (vv.

8–9). In his first challenge of the Lord, the Rabshakeh quotes the people ("we") and Hezekiah; he speaks to both the people and to Hezekiah.

> And if you say[2] to me, "It is in the Lord our God that we trust," is it not his high places [cultic sites] and altars that Hezekiah removed announcing to Judah and Jerusalem, "Before this altar alone [the Jerusalem temple], you will worship"? (v. 7)

At the close of his threat, the Rabshakeh quotes the Lord.

> Is it indeed without the Lord that I have attacked this land to destroy it? The Lord said to me, "Attack this land and destroy it." (v. 10)

This recalls the Lord's use of Assyria as a tool, a razor (7:20) or a rod (10:5), to punish the people; to this extent the Rabshakeh is quoting accurately. The Rabshakeh's statement also recalls the Assyrian's vaunted claims to be doing all of this solely because of his own abilities and power (10:5–14). But, akin to Shebna and Eliakim, his day in the sun is limited, for once God is done with Assyria as an instrument, "I will punish the grandiose thoughts of the king of Assyria and his overbearing and arrogant looks" (10:12). The passages are bound by their reference to a common character, Assyria.

In chapter 36 Eliakim, Shebna, and Joah, like Ahaz, react with fear and wish to limit the audience of this challenge. They request the general to speak in Aramaic, an international language of the times used by diplomats but not by the common people, and not to "speak in Judean in the hearing of the people on the wall" (36:11).

The Rabshakeh speaks directly to the people in Judean because they are the ones who will be immediately and brutally affected if the king captures Jerusalem. The declaration in verses 13–20 quotes the king of Assyria and repeats much of the first challenge, focusing again on the unreliability of God.

> Hear the words of the great king, the king of Assyria. Thus says the king, "Do not let Hezekiah deceive you, for he is not able to deliver you; and do not let Hezekiah make you rely on the Lord when he says, 'The Lord will certainly deliver us; this city will not be given into the hand of the king of Assyria'. . . . Do not let

> Hezekiah mislead you when he says, 'The Lord will deliver us.'
> Have any of the gods of the nations delivered their land from the
> hand of the king of Assyria?" (vv. 13–15, 18)

The three officials formally report the challenge to Hezekiah, and he
responds by sending his own messengers.

> When King Hezekiah heard this, he tore his clothes, put on sack-
> cloth, and went into the house of the Lord. He sent Eliakim chief
> of the palace, Shebna the secretary, and the elder priests, all wear-
> ing sackcloth, to Isaiah the prophet, the son of Amoz. They said
> to him, "Thus says Hezekiah, 'This day is a day of distress, of
> rebuke, and of rejection. . . . Perhaps the Lord your God has
> heard the Rabshakeh's words, whom the king of Assyria his mas-
> ter sent to defy the living God, and the Lord will rebuke the
> words that the Lord your God has heard. Offer a prayer for the
> remnant that is left.'" (37:1–4)

Isaiah responds with a message from the Lord similar to the one delivered to Ahaz over thirty years before; we again have speeches within
speeches.

> When the servants of King Hezekiah came to Isaiah, Isaiah said
> to them, "Thus you will say to your master, 'Thus says the Lord,
> "Do not fear because of the words that you have heard. . . . I will
> cause him to fall by the sword in his land."'" (vv. 5–7)

The fall does not occur until after another exchange. The Rabshakeh's next message, written on a scroll and containing a group of
speeches within speeches, repeats his defiance by negating God's own
words; it is as though he overheard the Lord's message to Hezekiah.

> He sent messengers to Hezekiah, "Thus you will say to Hezekiah
> king of Judah, 'Do not let your God in whom you trust deceive
> you when he says, "Jerusalem will not be given into the hand of
> the king of Assyria."'" (vv. 9–10)

Hezekiah spreads the scroll out in the temple and prays to God; this
is the only time in these chapters that someone speaks directly to the
one who is to receive the message. Hezekiah asks that God, "who
made heaven and earth," pay attention to the mocking and defiant

words of Sennacherib. He acknowledges that the Assyrians have devastated all the other lands and

> have thrown their gods into the fire, for they are not gods but only the product of human hands—wood and stone—and they destroyed them. But now, O Lord our God, save us from his hand so that all the kingdoms of the earth may know that you are the Lord, you alone. (vv. 19–20)

Isaiah sends a divine response to Hezekiah without being explicitly bidden to by God; and, to complicate matters further, the response is addressed to Sennacherib and denounces him for his defiance, violence, and pride. God and prophet negate the Assyrian's words just as he negated God's words in the scroll. The ultimate contest is between God and the king of Assyria, not between Hezekiah and Sennacherib; the immediate contest is for the loyalty or surrender of Hezekiah. He is the one who must act on his trust or his fear.

> Isaiah son of Amoz sent to Hezekiah, "Thus says the Lord, the God of Israel, 'Because you prayed to me about Sennacherib, the king of Assyria, this is the word that the Lord speaks against him:
>
> "She despises you, she mocks you, the virgin daughter Zion!
> Behind you she tosses her head, daughter Jerusalem! . . .
> Because you have raged against me and your noise has
>   come to my ears,
> I am putting my hook in your nose and my bit in your mouth;
> I am turning you back on the road by which you came."'"
> (vv. 21–22, 29)

The prophet repeats the divine assurances that "a remnant will leave Jerusalem" and that the king of Assyria "will not come into this city," and then the conclusion is narrated:

> The angel of the Lord went and struck 185,000 in the Assyrian camp. . . . Sennacherib, king of Assyria, returned home and dwelt in Nineveh. When he was worshiping in the house of Nisrok, his god, Adrammelek and Sharezer, his sons, killed him with a sword. They fled into the land of Ararat. Esarhaddon his son reigned after him. (vv. 36–38)

Speeches in the Vision of Isaiah

The discussion illustrates the problems and issues we encounter in reading any speech in Isaiah. First are their length and their repetitive nature. In part the length is due to the large number of issues and themes presented in the narrative and in the dialogue. The major themes in chapters 36–37 are the trio of trust, reliance, and confidence in God and their opposite, fear and trust in one's own devices; the promised deliverance and salvation by God, the survival of the remnant, are the basis for the trust. The power and the defiant arrogance of the king of Assyria are the object of the fear. This is part of the tension between justice and mercy. Assyria is punished for raging against God and for incredible violence (justice), but Hezekiah and Jerusalem are to be saved because the Lord has promised it (mercy). "The zeal of the Lord of Hosts is doing this. . . . I am shielding the city to save it for my own sake and that of David my servant" (37:32, 35). Two minor themes are idols and knowledge (37:20). Most speeches in Isaiah, especially those of any length, will have several major themes accompanied by other minor themes; speakers in Isaiah do not limit themselves to only one point.

Further, the demands of rhetoric and poetry are stronger than the demands for succinctness and clarity. The Assyrian, Hezekiah, Isaiah, and the Lord are not just saying something about trust and deliverance, or their lack, but are saying it in ways that will be most impressive and therefore persuasive. They want to convince and motivate their hearers, not just give them information. The hearers, mainly Hezekiah and the Jerusalemites, are to act on the messages whether that action is surrender to Sennacherib or trust in the Lord and refusal to surrender. The number of themes and issues and the variations on them are part of this persuasive rhetoric; the hearer may be moved by the rhetoric just as much as convinced by the content of the argument. Terminology, style, and imagery that appeal to the emotions are an integral part of persuasive rhetoric (see pp. 104–07).

Other speeches in the book of Isaiah share these features of length and repetition. They are trying to impress and persuade just as much as to impart information. Most of the passages cited to this point are examples of these features. Persuasive rhetoric consistently employs emotive terms and imagery, because it appeals to the emotions and the imagination just as much as, if not more than, to the intellect.

At the level of the entire book, Isaiah, the poet and visionary author, wants to convince and motivate his readers. He wants to convince his readers to trust in and to wait on the Lord in ways akin to those of Hezekiah and not to waver in fear in ways akin to those of Ahaz. Thus for the whole book the demands of rhetoric and poetry are stronger than the demands for succinctness and clarity. Isaiah presents a vision of God and humanity, of Israel's special place within the world, and of how Israel and all humans are to live in that world and respond to God's words and teachings. The positive side of the vision is countered by the descriptions of all the evils and violence that wrack this world. Each aspect and stage in this vision is displayed with fullness and detail; Isaiah both tells us and shows us what the vision is. Since the vision is of the entire world and of all humanity and since it seeks to be all-inclusive of that world and of human experience, Isaiah unfolds this vision of God and a near boundless world with ample detail and repetition.

Second is the complexity of the speeches. They are often messages delivered by another than the main speaker and are speeches within speeches. And a given speech may be addressed to more than one person. The Lord, in 37:22–29, speaks to Hezekiah although the speech is addressed literally to Sennacherib. In chapters 36–37 these matters can be sorted out because this is a narrative in which the speakers, the audience, the subject matter, and the beginnings and closures of the speeches are clearly indicated.

In much of Isaiah we do not have such clarity about who is speaking to whom and what is the extent of a given speech, especially when the Lord or the prophet is speaking. I previously discussed this using 1:2–4 as an example (see pp. 15–16). There my focus was on issues posed for a translator in deciding whether and where to use quotation marks and breaks on the printed page to indicate whether the Lord or Isaiah is speaking. Translators differ in their use of such marks and breaks because the Hebrew text itself is ambiguous on these points and allows several ways of understanding where a given speech begins and ends and when there is a change of speaker.

Isaiah addresses the heavens and earth in a general declaration to all hearers in heaven and on earth: "Hear, O heavens! Give ear, O earth!" In such a declaration, the prophet speaks to his hearers and readers in a different way from that of other statements. When God or the prophet addresses another, for example, Israel or a nation, we as readers overhear the exchange. The general addresses are spoken openly, and readers can easily feel that they are being directly addressed. "Hear, you who are far, what I have done; know, you who are near, my might" (33:13). The open style includes the declarations by prophet and God of what is or will be. They speak directly to the readers.

> In future times the mountain of the house of the Lord will be established as the highest of the mountains and raised above the hills. (2:2)

> Look! The Sovereign, the Lord of hosts, is removing
> from Jerusalem and from Judah support and staff,
> all support of food and all support of water.
> (3:1)

> Look! The Lord is stripping the earth bare and emptying it;
> he twists its surface and scatters its inhabitants.
> (24:1)

> The poor and the needy are seeking water and there is none;
> their tongue is parched with thirst. I the Lord answer them;
> I the God of Israel do not forsake them.
> (41:17)

> Thus says the Lord, "Maintain justice and do what is right,
> for my victory is soon to come and my deliverance to be revealed."
> (56:1)

> The spirit of the Lord is upon me because the Lord has anointed me;
> he has sent me to announce good news to the poor,
> to bind up the brokenhearted.
> (61:1)

These include the frequent comments in the first half of the book about what it will be like "on that day."

> On that day the Lord will remove the fine anklets, the hair bands, and the crescents. (3:18)

> On that day the Lord's planting will be for beauty and glory, and the fruit of the land for the pride and splendor of the remnant of Israel. (4:2)

On that day the Lord will punish, with his harsh and powerful sword, Leviathan, the fleeing serpent, Leviathan, the twisting serpent. (27:1)

The Lord and the Prophet Speak

God and prophet are the most frequent speakers in the book. I use "prophet" in the inclusive sense of the poet and do not restrict it to only the eighth-century prophet, Isaiah, son of Amoz. As a speaker, God is often subordinate to the prophet to the extent that the divine speeches are quotations. As I will soon discuss, this is not simple quotation because of the consistent overlapping of divine and prophetic speech. There are different quotation phrases used in the Hebrew text, and the translations differ on how they render them. The phrases are placed at the beginning, middle, or end of a divine statement. The following examples illustrate some of the variations in form and placement:

> *The Lord speaks*: Children I raise and bring up.
>   (1:2; also 8:5)

Hear *the word of the Lord*, you rulers of Sodom!
Give ear to *the teaching of our God*, you people of Gomorrah!
What to me is the multitude of your sacrifices? *says the Lord*.
I have had enough of burnt offerings of rams and the fat of fed beasts.
                                    (1:10–11)[3]

Come now, let us argue it out, *says the Lord*:
Though your sins are like scarlet, they can be as white as snow;
though they are red like crimson, they can be like wool.
If you are willing and you listen, the good of the land you will eat;
but if you refuse and rebel, by a sword you will be eaten, for *the mouth of the Lord speaks*. (1:18–20; for the last phrase see 40:5; 58:14)

For *thus says the Lord*, "I am extending peace to her like a river."
                                    (66:12)[4]

At times God speaks directly without introduction. God interrupts the poet in the midst of the Song of the Vineyard.

He dug it and cleared it of stones, and planted it with choice vines;
He built a watchtower in the midst of it, and also a wine vat
    he hewed out in it;

He expected it to yield grapes, but it yielded wild grapes.
And now, inhabitants of Jerusalem and people of Judah,
Judge between me and my vineyard.
What more was there to do for my vineyard that I have not done in it?
Why, when I expected it to yield good grapes, did it yield wild grapes?

(5:3–5)

The first speech against Assyria follows immediately upon the prophet's denunciation of Israel's rulers.

To whom will you flee for help? Where will you leave your wealth?
So that you will not crouch among the prisoners
    and fall amid the slain?
For all this his [the Lord's] anger has not turned away,
    and his hand is stretched out still.
Woe, O Assyria, rod of my anger—the club in their hands is my fury.
Against a godless nation I send him; against the people
    of my wrath I commission him.

(10:3–5)

Direct divine speech is more prevalent after chapter 40, but it is not confined to that part of the book, and in that part God is frequently quoted. Chapter 40 opens, " 'Comfort, comfort my people,' says your God," and the prophet closes the book using "says the Lord" four times in the last five verses.

At the transition from chapter 40 to 41, the prophet is describing the rewards that come to those who wait for the Lord, when the Lord breaks in with a strong demand.

Those who wait for the Lord renew their strength;
    they soar on wings like eagles; they run and do not faint;
    they walk and do not become weary.
Be silent before me, O coastlands! Let the peoples renew
    their strength!
Let them draw near, then let them speak. Let us come together
    to settle this.
Who has roused a victor from the east, called him to his service? . . .
Who has done and achieved this? It is the one who announces
    the flow of history from the very first.
It is I, the Lord, the first and the last, I am the one.

(40:31–41:4)

God directly calls Israel and the servant whether the latter is named Israel or not.

> But you, O Israel, my servant; Jacob, I have chosen you.
>
> (41:8)

> Here is my servant whom I uphold, my chosen in whom I delight.
>
> (42:1)

Hear me, O house of Jacob, all the remnant of the house of Israel,
Who have been carried since birth and borne since leaving the womb:
"Even when you grow old, I am he; even when you turn gray,
   I, I will carry.
I, I made and I, I will bear; I, I will carry and I will deliver."

> (46:3–4)

God announces a new creation.

> Certainly the former troubles are forgotten; certainly they are
>   hidden from my eyes.
> See! I am creating a new heavens and a new earth,
> And the former things will not be remembered; they will not
>   come to mind.
>
> (65:16–17)

This is the last direct divine declaration in Isaiah's vision, and even it closes, several verses later, with "says the Lord."

> The wolf and the lamb feed together; the lion eats straw like the ox;
>   the serpent: dust is its food![5]
> They do neither evil nor corruption on my holy mountain—
>   says the Lord.
>
> (65:25)

The speeches of the Lord and of the prophet usually overlap. I discussed the opening verses of Isaiah earlier from a translator's point of view and the concern with whether and where to use quotation marks and spaces between verses (see pp. 15–16).

> 1:2. Hear, O heavens! and give ear, O earth!
> For the Lord speaks:

Children I rear and bring up, but they rebel against me.
3. The ox knows its owner, and the donkey the crib of its master;
Israel does not know, my people do not understand.
4. Woe! Sinful nation, iniquitous people,
Offspring of evildoers, children who act corruptly!
They have forsaken the Lord; they have despised
    the Holy One of Israel; they have turned back.

The prophet speaks first and quotes the Lord. The Lord's speech obviously extends at least through verse 3 ("*my* people"). The quotation may continue into verse 4, although it ends referring to the Lord in the third person, and most consider this a sign that the prophet is now speaking. Translators show this with the use of quotation marks around verses 2–3 and an added space between verses 3 and 4. We can, on the other hand, assume here and at other points in the book that the Lord is still speaking and refers to himself in the third person. This would heighten the distance between God and people. "Woe! Sinful nation. . . . They have forsaken the Lord" is more emphatic than "They have forsaken *me*."

To summarize, verses 2–3 clearly distinguish divine and prophetic speech. The ambiguity, the overlapping, occurs in verse 4, which can be regarded as either divine or prophetic speech or as both. The ambiguity continues in verses 5–7. The prophet or the Lord addresses the people as "you";[6] there is no explicit indication as to who is speaking: "On what can you be beaten further that you continue to rebel? . . . Your country is a desolation, your cities are burning in fire; your land, in your very presence aliens eat it." In verse 8 the prophet or God shifts from the personal "you" to the third person: "And daughter Zion is left like a booth in a vineyard, like a lodge in a cucumber field, like a besieged city." Verses 4–8 are characterized by ambiguity of speaker.

"We" speak in verse 9: "If the Lord of Hosts had not left us a few survivors, we would have become like Sodom, we would have resembled Gomorrah." "We" are the people, the remnant, declaring, with similes, gratitude for the close escape; they are not like Sodom and Gomorrah, which were totally annihilated. The prophet responds in verse 10 with metaphor; they are Sodom and Gomorrah because of their wickedness (see p. 13). "Our God" is an unambiguous sign that the prophet speaks to the people as one of them.

Hear the word of the Lord, you rulers of Sodom!
Give ear to the teaching of our God, you people of Gomorrah!

In verses 11–20 the prophet quotes the Lord, with reminders in verses 11, 18, and 20 that this is a quotation.

"What to me is the multitude of your sacrifices?" *says the Lord* . . .
Come now, let us argue it out, *says the Lord*:
Though your sins are like scarlet, they can be as white as snow;
    though they are red like crimson, they can be like wool.
If you are willing and you listen, the good of the land you will eat;
    but if you refuse and rebel, by a sword you will be eaten,
    for *the mouth of the Lord speaks*.

The intertwining and overlapping of divine and prophetic speech continue in the chapter and throughout the book. Verses 21–26 are an accusation, an announcement of punishment, and a proclamation of restoration. In verses 21–23 the speaker denounces Jerusalem and its rulers.

How she has become a whore! The Capital Faithful!
She was full of justice, righteousness lodged in her—
    but now murderers!
Your silver had become dross. . . .
Your princes are rebels and friends of thieves.

The Lord is introduced in formal style in verse 24a and quoted in verses 24b–26.

Therefore says the Sovereign, the Lord of Hosts,
    the Mighty One of Israel:
"Woe! I am comforted concerning my enemies,
    and I am avenged concerning my foes!
I turn my hand against you; I smelt away, as with lye, your dross,
    and I remove all your alloy. . . .
Afterward you will be called The City of Righteousness,
    The Capital Faithful."

It seems clear that the prophet speaks directly in verses 21–24a and quotes the Lord in verses 24b–26. Yet we could see the Lord as the speaker who denounces the city, employs an elaborate formula that stresses divine majesty, and then proclaims cleansing and restoration. The metaphor of impure silver in the denunciation is repeated in the punishment (see p. 88); the faithful city, righteousness, and the rulers appear in the denunciation and in the proclamation of restoration. Even if we posit different speakers for verses 21–24a and 24b–26, the repetitions tightly bind the two parts.

I could apply this detailed analysis to many other speeches in Isaiah, but this would introduce issues and complexities that are beyond the intended scope of my book. Suffice it to say that the Lord's and the prophet's declarations blend into each other and that it is often difficult, if not impossible, to say exactly where each begins or ends. I emphasize the ambiguity, the blending, over attempts to state definitively that God or prophet is the sole speaker.

I consider this intertwining and overlapping of divine and prophetic speech, this ambiguity, as an integral part of Isaiah's vision and not as a problem that blocks our reading and interpretation. Isaiah shows us and indeed lets us hear the mutual relationship between God and prophet. To put it simply, if the prophet does not have a word of God to proclaim, then he is not a prophet; but if God does not have a prophet to put the divine word into human language, then the divine word is never spoken to humans. For Isaiah, God and prophet need each other, and therefore what they say intertwines and blends. The frequent difficulty or impossibility of deciding whether the Lord or the prophet is speaking is a significant part of Isaiah's understanding of what a prophet is, of what prophecy is.

A prophet is a messenger who reports the Lord's message to humans, in particular Israel, but a prophet is like an ambassador who has the authority to explain the message and to put it in words relevant to the audience and its situation. For example, in Isaiah 36 the Rabshakeh is an ambassador who delivers the gist of the king's message (Surrender!), but states it in ways fitting the actual situation at the walls of Jerusalem. In the Hebrew Bible a messenger, especially one with a message delivered orally, is commissioned with a two-part order: to go (to be sent) and to say.

> Jacob *sent* messengers to his brother Esau . . . *instructing them,*
> "*Thus you will say* to my lord Esau, 'Thus says your servant Jacob,
> "I've been staying with Laban. . . ."'" (Gen. 32:3–4)

This results in the speeches within speeches that we encountered in Isaiah 36–37.

During the vision of the Lord in the temple, the prophet reports the two-part commission:

> I heard the voice of the Lord asking, "Whom can I send? Who will go for us?" I said, "I am here! Send me!" And he said, *"Go and say to this people. . . ."* (6:8–9)

At a later point Zion-Jerusalem herself appears in the role of messenger; she is told to go and speak to others. God and/or the prophet may be exhorting her.

> *Get up* on a high mountain, O Zion, herald of good news;
> *Raise your voice* in a loud shout, O Jerusalem, herald of good
>   news;
> Raise it; fear not;
> *Say* to the cities of Judah, "Here is your God!"
>
> (40:8–9)

For Isaiah, prophecy is intimately involved with God's word: both receiving it and transmitting it. The messenger, the prophet, is not a mere mouthpiece who only reports the message word-for-word. The messenger is a translator and interpreter. The prophet recasts the divine speeches in his own words and imagery, and the distinctions between prophetic and divine speech blur as God's words and human words merge. For Isaiah, prophecy is this mixing and blending of divine and human speech.

The Prophet, the Poet, Isaiah

Isaiah is named in the titles in 1:1; 2:1; and 13:1 and appears as a named character only in chapters 7, 20, and 37–39. When the prophet speaks in the first person, "I," in chapters 6 and 8, he does not name himself. The appearance of the individual named Isaiah in chapters 7, 20, and 37–39 is part of the makeup of the book that concentrates particular named individuals in chapters 1–39. The prophet-poet who speaks in the remainder of the book, in both chapters 1–39 and 40–66, is unnamed.

The anonymity is significant to the vision, which is far more about prophecy in general than it is about the eighth-century prophet Isaiah, son of Amoz, even though Isaiah's name is given to the book. God created the world and remains an active agent in it. God reveals divine actions and intentions through human messengers, prophets, who report and interpret the divine message to the human audience, whether Israel or all humanity. Another prophet set in the eighth century states it well: "The Lord God certainly does not do something without revealing the plan to his servants the prophets" (Amos 3:7).

As with the other particular events and people of the eighth and sixth centuries, the author of the book of Isaiah uses the named prophet Isaiah as an anchor for the more extended investigation of what prophet and prophecy entail. To be a prophet like eighth-century Isaiah is to be a messenger and an envoy for God. It is to present God's message and words in ways that will inspire people, the hearers and readers of the prophetic words, whether oral or written, to trust in the Lord and to live their lives, in this world of wonder and of violence, in accord with this trust and hope. The book of Isaiah is more concerned with what it is to be a prophet, with how anyone can fill a prophetic role, than with any one individual who filled that role at one point in history.

The book is about prophecy and divine speech and, at the same time, it is itself prophetic words. For the author of the book, to be a prophet is to write the vision of Isaiah; it is to be both prophet and poet. In this vision we encounter one prophet named Isaiah who is an exemplar of the mission of reporting and interpreting the divine word, but who in many ways is supplanted by other notions of what a prophet is.

A countering force is people's resistance to and even rejection of the prophet and of God. Many of the passages we have discussed to this point reflect this in references to the people's rebellion, sin, ignorance, and so on. In chapters 6 and 8, the prophet, using autobiographical "I," narrates his commissioning as prophet, his rejection by the people, and his hope in the future acts of God. For him there is no hope for change in the present.

> Bind up the message, seal the teaching with my disciples. As for me, I wait for the Lord, who is hiding his face from the house of Jacob, and I hope in him. Here am I and the children that the Lord has given me as signs and portents in Israel that come from the Lord of Hosts, who dwells on Mount Zion. (8:16–18)

At a subsequent point in the vision, the message is still sealed.

The vision of all this has become to you like the words of a sealed scroll. If they give it to someone who knows how to read, commanding, "Read this," he says, "I cannot, for it is sealed." If the scroll is given to someone who does not know how to read, commanding, "Read this," he says, "I do not know how to read." (29:11–12)

But this state of affairs can change.

Is it not just a little while before
Lebanon becomes farmland, and farmland is thought of as a forest?
On that day the deaf will hear the words of a scroll,
    while from their deep gloom the blind will see;
The poor will continually rejoice in the Lord, while the needy
    of humanity will celebrate in the Holy One of Israel.

(29:17–19)

"Message," "teaching," and "scroll" refer, on the one hand, to particular pronouncements of the prophet within the book and, at the same time, to the whole book, the vision of Isaiah. The book of Isaiah is a scroll, a teaching, and a prophecy that people have not read or have not been able to read in the past. Now it is presented to a new generation of readers in the hope that they, and perhaps we, will read it and respond to its message. Humans, including individual prophets, come and go, "but the word of our God stands forever" (40:8). The word of God is both particular statements of God reported in the book and the book itself. Nations, prophets, and kings may pass, but the book of Isaiah stands forever. This represents a change displayed by and in the book, a change from a prophet speaking directly to an audience to a work written by a prophet-poet that can be read by any audience, present or future.

The change is represented within the book, many times indirectly. References to "words," "teaching," and "scroll" are allusions to the book itself, allusions to a time when people will read what was spoken and then written long ago. The word and the teaching that go forth from Zion to instruct the nations in the ways of the Lord (2:2–3) are the vision of Isaiah. And as with most of the themes and patterns we have traced in Isaiah, this change is not presented in a neat sequential order in the vision. Isaiah already refers to writing and testimony for the future in chapter 8, and individuals, although anonymous, continue to proclaim God's word in the closing chapters of the book. Isaiah displays his themes and images and their variations throughout his vision; therefore, as noted at relevant points in my work, I draw my examples from diverse points in Isaiah and not just from one part. Shared content, not shared context, ties the examples together.

The Rabshakeh, referring to promises of help from both Egypt and the Lord, asks Hezekiah, "Is a mere word of the lips counsel and strength for war?" (36:5). In the context of chapters 36–37, the mere word from Egypt, a promise of aid, is useless; but the word of the Lord, a promise of deliverance spoken by the prophet Isaiah, is anything but mere. The Assyrian army is soon destroyed. We can, however, apply the Rabshakeh's question to the book of Isaiah and interpret war as a metaphor for life: "Are the mere words of this vision counsel and strength for life?" Readers of Isaiah have to answer the question for themselves.

Corresponding to Isaiah's universal, all-inclusive thrust, the prophet speaks and writes all manner of words. He denounces sin and evil and praises goodness and righteousness; he threatens and declares disaster and promises restoration, peace, and prosperity; he speaks of the past, present, and future. The prophet curses the wicked, praises God, proclaims the rejection of the people, and prays to God to forgive them. He speaks to Israel, to Assyria, to Babylon, and to all nations and peoples, near and far. He speaks for, and at times to, the Lord.

But a prophet is not known by some simple test of what he or she says, whether for woe or for weal. (I say "she" since the prophet refers to a prophetess who bears his child, Maher-shalal-hash-baz [8:3].)[7] Israel and all humanity are faced with the twin choice of accepting or rejecting the prophetic message, the word of God, and of walking or not walking in God's ways. They must choose, and it is a choice with serious consequences, dire or wonderful. It is also a true choice since they are not forced to a preset decision by the contents or form of the message or by God's manifest power. Indeed, Israel questions and rejects the message both when it is a denunciation of evil and announcement of disaster and when it is a proclamation of forgiveness and restoration (45:9–13; see pp. 36–37).

In the discussions of themes and imagery I went into detail on the various ways that people can accept the teaching and walk in the Lord's paths and reject the teaching and the paths. In the opening section of this chapter I talked of the persuasive rhetoric consistently employed by God and prophet to convince their audiences to accept the message and its implications for their lives. The entire book consistently employs the same rhetoric and emotional appeal to convince its readers, of whatever time, to accept its vision and message, its implications for their lives, and to walk in the light of the Lord. Our ways of reading and interpreting Isaiah mirror the ways that people within the book respond.

The Lord, God

God is a unique character in Isaiah. As speaker, God stands in balance with the prophet, but the latter is essentially only a speaker; even the acts of the eighth-century prophet in chapters 7–8 and 20 are symbols that support his spoken message. God is speaker and, at the same time, the initiator of the actions of creation, teaching, punishing, and saving. As an active character God stands in concert and tension first with Israel and then with the host of others, individuals and nations, who appear in the vision. The prophet-poet serves mainly to proclaim the divine acts, past, present, and future. I focus on God as actor but, as with all that we have considered, this is a focus and not an exclusion of God as speaker. All previous citations from Isaiah in some way involve God's acts. Isaiah portrays a divine persona with an incredible range of traits, and this complex persona, both the violent and the compassionate Deity, is present in the first and the last chapters of the vision. Therefore I choose my examples from throughout the book and not in strict accord with its sequential order.

In Hebrew there are two main words used to refer to God. The first is *YHWH*, usually pronounced Yahweh, as in NJB,[8] which is a type of personal name and is used only for Israel's God; following the standard translation, I render it as "the Lord."[9] The other term is *Elohim*, the general word for deity. In English translations, lower-case "god" is used when the term refers to a god other than YHWH, for example, Sennacherib's god Nisrok (37:38), and capital "God" for YHWH, for example, the God of Jacob (2:3). (*Elohim*, which is grammatically plural in Hebrew, can occasionally refer to gods, e.g., "All the images of her [Babylon's] gods" [21:9].) I do not make a distinction in the use of "the Lord" (Yahweh) and "God" (Elohim). They appear in parallel, "Hear the word of *the Lord*. . . . Give ear to the teaching of our *God*" (1:10; see 2:3), and in apposition, "the Lord your God" (7:10) and "the Lord, the God of Israel" (17:6).

I use the divine titles in Isaiah as an entrance into the portrayal of the Lord since they are both names and descriptions: who God is and what God does. "The Holy One of Israel" is frequent: "They have despised the Holy One of Israel" (1:4). "They call you, City of the Lord, Zion of the Holy One of Israel" (60:14). (The title can be "the Holy One of Jacob" [29:23] or simply "the Holy One" [5:16; 40:25].) To be holy is to be separate and other. The Holy One is totally other than anything created, including supposed "gods."

> Thus says the Lord, the King of Israel, and his Redeemer,
>   the Lord of Hosts:
> "I am the first and I am the last; there is no god but me. . . .
> Is there any god but me? There is no other rock; I know none!"
>   (44:6–8)

God is utterly separate from this world, but is present in it in ways that do not compromise God's holiness. The seraphs that Isaiah hears in the temple combine the Lord's holiness and worldly presence. "One called to another, 'Holy, Holy, Holy! O Lord of Hosts! The whole earth is filled with his glory!'" (6:3). TNK renders the last phrase "His presence fills all the earth!" The divine presence includes the relationship with Israel.

> For I am the Lord your God, who upholds your right hand,
> Who says to you, "Fear not! I will help you.
> Fear not, O worm Jacob, O men of Israel!
> I will help you"—says the Lord, your Redeemer, the Holy One
>   of Israel.
>   (41:13–14)

The second recurrent title is "the Lord of Hosts,"[10] which occurs in some of the preceding passages: "If the Lord of Hosts had not left us a few survivors, we would have become like Sodom" (1:9). "The Lord of Hosts is his name" in 54:5 is the last occurrence of the title in the book. The title is military and refers to God as creator and leader of the hosts, that is, the armies, of heaven and of earth, especially the army of Israel: "The Lord of Hosts is mustering a host [an army] for battle" (13:4; see 40:26). The title stresses divine power, not otherness or holiness; the two are combined in 6:3: "Holy, Holy, Holy! O Lord of Hosts!" NIV and GNB render the title as "the Lord Almighty" to convey the sense of power and sovereignty.

This is the plan determined for the whole world;
This is the hand stretched out over all nations.
For the LORD Almighty has purposed, and who can thwart him?
His hand is stretched out, and who can turn it back?

(14:26–27 NIV)

The Lord is creator of the entire earth (37:16; 40:28; 42:5) and sustains the creation.

The Lord is God forever, the creator of the ends of the earth.
He does not weary or grow faint; there is no limit to his understanding.
He gives strength to the weary and great vigor to the powerless.

(40:28–29)

Israel is a particular creation. "And now, thus says the Lord, who created you, O Jacob, and who formed you, O Israel" (43:1). To "form" is the term used for God's making the human in Genesis 2:7, and it refers to working with clay to make pottery: "We are the clay and you are our potter [the one who forms us]" (Isa. 64:8).

As maker (17:7; 51:13), God is ruler. "I am the Lord, your Holy One, the creator of Israel, your king" (43:15). (Most of the examples contain more than one of the titles or characteristics of God.) The Lord is "the king, the Lord of Hosts" (6:5), and judge, king, and savior (33:22), the king of Israel and of Jacob (41:21; 44:6).

As king, God punishes rebellious subjects, whether humanity in general or Israel in particular. We have seen several illustrations of chastisement and outright destruction. This is the God of justice who rewards the good and punishes the wicked.

Tell the righteous that it is good, for they will eat the fruit
of their work.
Woe to the wicked! Evil will be repaid to them
for what their hands have done.

(3:10–11)

Humanity is bowed down, everyone is brought low,
and the eyes of the exalted are humbled.
And the Lord of Hosts is exalted by justice
and the Holy God shows himself holy by righteousness.

(5:15–16; see 2:9–22)

This is the brutal and violent Deity who is described in passages in Isaiah that can be most difficult for a reader to hear. But this is part of the all-inclusive vision of Isaiah, who presents a God with a great variety of characteristics, many of which stand in sharp contrast.

> Yes, the Lord's wrath is against all the nations,
>   and his fury against all their armies.
> He has doomed them, he has given them to the slaughter.
> Their slain are thrown out, and their corpses: their stench goes up.
> The mountains melt with their blood,
>   and all the armies [hosts] of heaven rot;
> The heavens roll up like a scroll, and all their armies [hosts] wither
> Like leaves wither from the vine, like withering leaves
>   from the fig tree.
>
>   (34:2–4)

> Look! The Lord comes in fire, and like a whirlwind his chariots,
> To repay with his wrathful anger and to rebuke with flames of fire.
> Yes, by fire the Lord judges—by his sword—all flesh;
>   and many are those slain by the Lord.
>
>   (66:15–16)

The Lord, at the same time, is Savior and Comforter. Salvation is a central theme in the book of Isaiah; the Hebrew name Isaiah itself means "the Lord saves."

> I give thanks to you, O Lord, for though you were angry with me,
> Your anger turned away, and you comforted me.
> Surely God is my salvation; I trust, and I am not afraid,
> For my strength and my might is Yah the Lord;[11]
>   he has become my salvation.
>
>   (12:1–2)

> Yes, this is our God. We wait for him so that he will save us.
> This is the Lord; we wait for him. Let us be glad and let us rejoice
>   in his salvation.
>
>   (25:9)

> I am the Lord, your God, the Holy One of Israel, your Savior.
>   (43:3)

The Lord comforts his people, and has compassion
  on his suffering ones.

(49:13)

"To save" and "salvation" mean to give victory and success by delivering from disaster, natural or human, or military defeat. The words are also translated as "triumph," "victory," and "deliverance." For example, TNK renders 12:2:

Behold the God who gives me triumph!
I am confident, unafraid;
For Yah the LORD is my strength and might,
And He has been my deliverance.

People are rescued from the paralyzing fear that so often limits human life. "Do not fear" is an encouragement to the king (7:4; 37:6), to the prophet (8:12), and to the people (10:24; 41:10; 44:2). True to Isaiah's all-inclusive reach, God's salvation is for all.

Turn to me and be saved, all ends of the earth!
For I am God and there is no other.
By myself I have sworn; from my mouth has gone forth truth,
  a word, and it will not return:
"To me every knee will bend, every tongue will swear."

(45:22–23)

TNK renders the first phrase, "Turn to Me and gain success."
  God's promises of victory can be trusted and relied on. God is a sure rock (17:10; 26:4; 30:29) whose actions are reliable: "Fathers tell their children of your faithfulness" (38:19).

O Lord, my God, you, I exalt you and I praise your name,
For you have performed wonders, plans of old, entirely reliable.
  (25:1; NRSV translates the last phrase "faithful and sure")

Truly the Lord waits to be gracious to you; truly he rises
  to be compassionate to you.
For the Lord is a just God and happy are all who wait for him.

(30:18)

"To wait," "to hope," and "to trust" in the Lord have similar meanings of relying on God and living life with the confidence that the divine promises will come to be. "You know that I am the Lord; whoever hopes in me will not be put to shame" (49:23).

But, on a grimmer note, divine consistency includes the certainty of punishment following upon arrogance and rebellion. In one example the Creator is neither caring nor merciful.

For there is a day for the Lord of Hosts
Against all that is high and raised; against all that is elevated and low.
(2:12)

For this is a people without understanding; therefore, he who made them will not have compassion on them, and he who formed them will not have mercy on them. (27:11)

You who forsake the Lord, who forget my holy mountain . . .
I destine you to the sword; all of you will kneel down
    to be slaughtered.
(65:11)

In a paradoxical sense, the Lord has to save both Israel and all humanity from the disasters that the Lord has brought upon them. This highlights the sharp tension that exists between justice and mercy in Isaiah.

I will not always accuse, and I will not be angry forever. . . .
Because of their sinful greed I was angry; I struck them, I hid,
    and I was angry,
But they kept returning to their heart's ways.
I have seen their ways and I will heal them; I will guide them
    and provide them full comfort. . . .
Peace, peace to the near and the far—says the Lord—
    and I will heal them.
But the wicked are like the tossing sea that cannot rest;
    its waters toss up mire and mud.
There is no peace—says my God—for the wicked.
(57:16–21; see 48:22)

To return to a positive note, God is both Savior and Redeemer (41:14; 44:6; 49:7). "Our Redeemer—the Lord of Hosts is his name—

is the Holy One of Israel" (47:4). "All flesh will know that I am the Lord, your Savior, your Redeemer, the Mighty One of Jacob" (49:26; also 60:16). (God is the Mighty One of Israel: 1:24.)[12] To redeem or ransom is to buy back property, whether land or house, that was sold to another or to rescue a family member who has fallen into bondage or slavery. The property is usually family property that should not be sold to one outside the family.

> I give Egypt as a ransom for you [Israel], Cush and Seba
>   in exchange for you.
> Because you are precious and honored in my sight, and I love you,
> I give people in exchange for you and nations in return for your life.
>   (43:3–4)

God dwells on high (33:5), on Mount Zion, the holy mountain (8:18; 24:23), and is also present in this world.

> Thus says the one who is high and lifted up, who dwells in eternity,
>   whose name is Holy.
> "In a high and holy place I dwell and also with one broken
>   and of humble spirit.
>
>   (57:15)

God is pictured with a body (38:17). God has a head (59:17) with a face (8:17; 65:3), nostrils (65:5), mouth (1:20; 62:2), lips and tongue (30:27), breath (30:33), and eyes and ears (1:15–16; 37:17). God has arms and hands (1:25; 5:25; 40:10; 66:2), palms (49:16),[13] and feet (60:13; 66:1).

God is depicted as male; that is, the poet uses masculine verbs, pronouns, and adjectives in reference to God. I use the masculine pronouns "he," "him," and "his" in my translations, but I avoid specific gender references to God in my discussions of the texts. God is, at a few points, portrayed as father:

> Children I rear and bring up.
>   (1:2)

> For you are our father. . . . You, O Lord, are our father;
> from ancient times Our Redeemer is your name.
>   (63:16)

But now, O Lord, you are our father!
We are the clay and you are our potter; all of us are the work
   of your hand.

(64:8)

Although not directly called mother, God is associated with being
a mother through the use of similes: "I cry out like a woman in labor"
(42:14). Even to compare God to a woman is unusual in the Hebrew
Bible, and this strong feminine aspect of God's character in Isaiah's
portrayal is striking.[14]

Woe to whoever says to a father, "What are you begetting?"
   or to a woman, "Why are you in labor?"

(45:10)

As a woman comforts her child, thus I, I comfort you—
   you will find comfort in Jerusalem.

(66:13)[15]

God is the major force in the book. Divine and prophetic speech
overlap and even merge, but God is still the ultimate source of the
speech, the one who initiates the divine-prophetic relationship. The
prophet is necessary to present the divine message in human language
to other humans, but the Lord has the first say. The prophet does not
start speaking and then invite God to join in. The book opens: "Hear,
O heavens, and give ear, O earth! For the Lord speaks," and not "For
I [Isaiah] speak."

The Lord created the entire world, both the physical place and its
inhabitants, that is the scene for the book of Isaiah. The Lord is in
charge of the events, the history, that transpire over time in that world.
The creation includes the divine word and teaching that all must
respond to, and their response determines, in various ways, their
futures and their fates. The book of Isaiah revolves around the many
ways that humans, particularly Israel and Israelites, have responded to
or have not responded to the Lord's word and actions, and how the
Lord and the prophet in turn respond to them. God may be the major
force within the vision but is not in total control; Israel, and the rest
of humanity, can and do resist and rebel.

God is so consistently present in the book that all that I have talked
about to this point and that I will talk about after this, including the
passages cited, relate in some way to the Lord and the divine rela-

tionships with humans, particularly with Israel. People respond (righteousness) or not (sin); they can turn to the divine ways (obedience) or they can reject them (rebellion); God can punish them (justice) or forgive them and start the cycle anew (mercy). The Lord and the prophet can exhort them to return to the just ways and can threaten them with further disaster if they do not.

Stories of past (or even present) sin and punishment, recent and long ago, and predictions of future sin and punishment make up a large portion of the divine-prophetic speeches calling for change. The rhetoric of persuasion, whether encouraging or menacing, is one reason for the large amount of repetition in Isaiah. In a simple sense, the same story keeps repeating itself. Humans never do learn to walk only and always in the Lord's ways; they may for a while but then they return to their customary ways of rebellion and sin. The Lord never does learn how to effectively reform humans for once and for always; from the divine point of view, reform works for a while but then fails, and the people return to their ways of rebellion and sin. And there are a large number of divine strategies. The Lord threatens, disciplines, punishes, and even destroys; the Lord beats, cuts down, floods, and tramples in the dust; the Lord burns, both to destroy and to cleanse and purify; the Lord promises, supports, leads, and restores; the Lord bandages and heals, builds up and raises on high; the Lord is light and brilliance, saving and glorious.

Israel

The next two sections treat the major characters involved with God as active agent, Israel and the nations. The presentation of Israel is not in depth since most of the passages and discussions to this point and in the rest of my book bear, directly or indirectly, upon Israel. Israel is a general, inclusive name for the people of God without geographical or national distinctions. In this use Israel is Jacob (2:3, 5–6; 40:27). Israel, the general name, includes Judah, the southern kingdom (1:1; 9:21; 40:9), and Israel, the northern kingdom. The latter two can be at odds with each other as when Israel, with Aram, attacks Judah (7:1), or they can be in parallel as two parts of the larger whole.

> The vineyard of the Lord of Hosts is the house of Israel,
> And the people of Judah his pleasant planting.
>
> (5:7)

The distinction between the northern and southern kingdoms is barely, if at all, visible in chapters 40–66. "Judah" appears in parallel with "Jacob" and "Israel" as the name of an ancestor of the people.

> Hear this, O house of Jacob, who are called by the name Israel
> and who sprang from the loins of Judah.
>
> (48:1)

> I bring forth descendants from Jacob,
> and from Judah heirs for my mountains.
> (65:9)

The northern kingdom is called Ephraim in the first half of the book (7:2; 28:1–3).

> Ephraim's jealousy departs, and Judah's hostilities are stopped;
> Ephraim is not jealous of Judah, and Judah is not hostile
> toward Ephraim.
>
> (11:13)

Israel is male and is both a plural group (e.g., chap. 1), and a singular group (e.g., 33:17–24; 40:27–28). I do not make the distinction a major issue since it is often unobservable in English, which does not distinguish plural and singular in the second person pronoun "you" (see p. 165). Israel is God's people chosen in Egypt at the event of the exodus.

> There will be a highway for the remnant of his people
> that remains from Assyria,
> As there was for Israel when he came up from the land of Egypt.
> (11:16; see 63:10–14)

This choice and election provide the background, the reasons, for God's expectations that the people will respond and act in certain ways and not others. They should walk in the light of the Lord (2:5) and not rebel and forsake the Lord (1:28).

> I place water in the wilderness, rivers in the desert
> To provide water for my people, my chosen,
> the people I formed for myself who will proclaim my praise.
> But you did not call upon me, O Jacob; you are indeed weary of me,
> O Israel! . . .

You have burdened me with your sins; you have wearied me
    with your iniquities. . . .
I profaned the holy princes; I gave Jacob over to total destruction
    and Israel to condemnation.

(43:20–28)

Israel, the personification of the nation, can be chosen and can be
righteous as a whole, or, at the other extreme, can reject the Lord as
a whole: "Israel does not know; my people does not understand" (1:3).
Israel can be divided into the righteous and the wicked, those who
walk in the Lord's paths and those who choose their own ways. The
possibility of the distinction is introduced in the first chapter.

Cease to do evil. Learn to do good. . . .
If you are willing and you listen, the good of the land you will eat;
But if you refuse and rebel, by a sword you will be eaten.

(1:16–20)

Zion, by justice, is redeemed, and her repenters, by righteousness.
But rebels and sinners are destroyed together, and forsakers
    of the Lord are consumed.

(1:27–28)

The distinction is connected with that between corrupt rulers and
exploited, oppressed people.

The Lord rises to argue his case; he stands to judge peoples.
The Lord enters into judgment with the elders of his people
    and their princes:
"It is you who have devoured the vineyard; the spoil of the poor
    is in your houses.
What do you mean by crushing my people, by grinding the face
    of the poor?"

(3:13–15; also 56:9–12)

Israel is spoken about (he or they) and spoken to (you) by the Lord
and the prophet; the change between third and second person can
occur from one verse to the next without comment (see 1:4 to 5–7,
and 27–28 to 29–31). In the first passage that follows, from chapter
29, the change is from "this people" to "you"; in the second passage,
from chapter 59, it is from "you" to "they."

The Lord says, "Because *this people* approaches me with their mouths,
And with their lips honor me while their heart is far from me,
And their fear of me is a human practice learned by rote,[16]
Therefore I am about to do wonderful things with *this people*,
    wonderful wonders:[17]
The wisdom of their wise perishes, and the discernment
    of their discerners is hidden.
Woe to those who would hide their plans too deep for the Lord,
    whose deeds are done in the dark, and who say,
"Who sees us? Who knows us?"
You pervert everything as though the clay could be thought equal
    to the potter.

(29:13–16)

For *your* palms are defiled with blood, and *your* fingers with iniquity;
Your lips have spoken lies, *your* tongue mutters wickedness.
No one brings suit righteously, *no one* seeks justice truthfully;
They trust in empty pleas, *they* speak lies,
They conceive mischief, and *they* beget depravity.

(59:3–4)

The Nations

Egypt as a character, whether the king or the whole nation, appears mainly in chapters 19–20; the other references scattered throughout the book deal more with the actual nation than with a character in a vision. Egypt is closely identified with Cush or Ethiopia, which lies south of Egypt (see 20:3–5); I am not going to distinguish them in my treatment.

In the ancient world Egypt was a symbol of wisdom and knowledge. Even in the eighth century B.C.E. Egypt was ancient, since the Old Kingdom, the time of the great pyramids, lay fifteen hundred and more years in the past. Egypt was the kingdom of the Nile. In the period spanned by the book of Isaiah, about 735–500 B.C.E., Egypt's power and prosperity waxed and waned. Isaiah refers to its wealth. "Egypt's wealth and Cush's trade and the Sabeans, tall people, will come to you and be yours; they will follow you, coming in chains" (45:14).

One of the main strategies of Egypt's foreign policy was involvement with the small states in Syria-Palestine to use them as a buffer against whatever empire, Assyrian or Babylonian, was in power in the east. The states, including Judah and Israel, would tie down the empire's forces through their rebellions. Egypt would instigate rebellion by promising, but seldom delivering, military aid. In Isaiah Egypt is mainly an unreliable ally despite its reputation for power and wisdom.

> Complete fools are the princes of Zoan; the wisest of Pharaoh's
>   counselors give stupid counsel.
> How can you say to Pharaoh, "I am a child of wise men,
>   a child of kings of old"?
> Where now are your wise men?
> Let them tell you, let them discover, what the Lord of Hosts
>   has planned against Egypt.
> The princes of Zoan are fools, and the princes of Memphis
>   are deluded;
> the chiefs of her tribes have led Egypt astray.
> The Lord has poured into her a confused spirit,
> and the leaders have led Egypt astray in all they do,
>   just as a drunkard staggers in his vomit.
> Nothing is to be done in Egypt whether by head or tail,
>   palm branch or reed.
>
> (19:11–15)

> Pharaoh's refuge will be your shame, and seeking shelter
>   in Egypt's shadow, your disgrace. . . .
> Egypt's help is worthless and empty.
>
> (30:3, 7)

> Egypt is human, not divine, and their horses are flesh, not spirit.
> The Lord stretches out his arm; the helper stumbles
>   and the helped falls; together they all perish.
>
> (31:3)

Egypt is "the staff made of a broken reed that, when someone leans on it, pierces their hand" (36:6).

Egypt plays the role of an idol, a human product, or a creature of the world that people turn to for help rather than looking to the Lord. As an idol, Egypt is useless, and what is said of idols in the next two passages applies also to Egypt and its promises of aid.

On that day people will turn to their Maker and their eyes will look to the Holy One of Israel. They will not turn to the altars that their fingers made, and they will not look to that which their fingers have made. (17:7–8)

> They pour out silver from the purse, and gold they weigh
>   in the scales; they hire a smith who makes it into a god—
>   they bow down, they even worship.
> They lift it on their shoulders, they carry it; they put it down
>   and it just stands there; it cannot budge from its place.
> If one cries out to it, it does not answer, it does not save one
>   from distress.
>
> (46:6–7)

Finally, on a positive note, Egypt is part of the trio blessed by the Lord: "Blessed is my people Egypt; the work of my hands Assyria; and my heritage Israel" (19:25). Assyria, second in the trio, is our next topic.

Assyria appears as the Assyrian king in 7:17, 20; 8:4, 7, and as the nation in 7:18; 10:5, 24. Actual kings are named: in 20:1, Sargon; chapters 36–37, Sennacherib; and 37:38, Esarhaddon. Assyria continues in both roles, king and nation, through 38:6,[18] and is portrayed as a male. Assyria is the instrument brought to devastate the people.

> The Lord is bringing upon you . . . days such as have not been since Ephraim split from Judah—the king of Assyria. On that day the Lord will whistle for the fly at the sources of the rivers of Egypt and for the bee in the land of Assyria. . . . On that day the Lord will shave, with a razor hired from beyond the Euphrates— the king of Assyria—the head and the hair of the feet and the beard as well. (7:17–20)

Woe, O Assyria, rod of my anger—the club in their hands is my fury.
Against a godless nation I send him; against the people of my wrath
    I commission him,
To despoil spoil and to plunder plunder, to turn them into trodden
    ground like mud in the streets.

(10:5–6)

As an instrument, Assyria belongs with the others that the Lord employs to punish or to save Israel or all humanity: "He is raising a signal for nations from afar . . . from the end of the earth" (5:26).

The Lord of Hosts is mustering an army for battle;
They come from a far country, from the end of the heavens,
The Lord and his weapons of fury, to destroy the entire earth.

(13:4–5)

Israel is a threshing tool and is analogous to Assyria at that point.

I now make you a threshing board, new with sharp teeth.
You will thresh the mountains and crush them;
   the hills you will make like chaff.
You will winnow them, and the wind will carry them off,
   the whirlwind will scatter them,
But you will rejoice in the Lord; in the Holy One of Israel
   you will revel.

(41:15–16)

Assyria, however, does not accept the status of mere instrument, of being only an insect or a razor. God sends Assyria to trample down only one people.

But he does not intend to do this, nor is his mind thinking of it,
For destruction is on his mind, cutting down nations
   and not just a few.
He says, "Are not my generals all kings?
Is not Carchemish like Calno? Is not Hamath like Arpad?
   Is not Samaria like Jerusalem? . . .
As I have done to Samaria and her idols, shall I not do to Jerusalem
   and her images?" . . .
For he says, "By the strength of my own hand I have done it
   and by my own wisdom, for I am perceptive."

(10:7–13)

But this is the tool thinking that it is as good as, if not better than, the one using it.

Does the ax think itself better than the one who hews with it,
   or the saw magnify itself over the one who handles it?
As though a rod should handle him who raises it,
   or a club raise one who is not wood.

(10:15)

Assyria symbolizes the proud and arrogant who do not just disregard the Lord but who think that God's work through them is their own accomplishment. Pride and haughtiness, raising oneself on high, is a major category of sin (see pp. 48–49). Any human being can be guilty of arrogance.

> Humanity is humbled; people are brought low; do not forgive them!
> Go into the rock; hide in the dust before the terror of the Lord
>   and his dread majesty.
> The haughty eyes of humanity are brought low;
>   proud people are humbled;
> the Lord alone is exalted on that day.
>
> (2:9–11)

> We have heard of Moab's pride—how incredibly proud!—
>   of his arrogance, his pride, and his insolence, of the sin in him.
>
> (16:6)

Tyre is "the exultant city whose origin lies in days of old," but the Lord has planned its destruction "to defile all proud beauty, to shame all the honored of the earth" (23:7–9).

The proud and arrogant are symbolized in chapters 24–27 by the city of chaos (24:10), the fortified city (25:2; 27:10), and the lofty city (26:5). The fate of this city is the fate of all, individual or people, who are haughty and insolent. They are smashed (24:10) and turned into a heap, a ruin (25:2).

> He has humbled those who live on the heights,
>   the lofty city he brings down,
> He brings it down to earth, he lays it in the dust.
> A foot tramples it, the feet of the poor, the soles of the needy.
>
> (26:5–6)

The city is then "solitary, a deserted pasture, forsaken like the wilderness" (27:10).

Israel can be proud and assert themselves against the Lord in the same ways that Assyria does. Again Israel stands parallel with Assyria.

> Woe to those who would hide their plans too deep for the Lord,
> Whose deeds are done in the dark, and who say,
> "Who sees us? Who knows us?"

You pervert everything, as though the clay could be thought
    equal to the potter.
Can the made say to its maker, "You did not make me"?
Or the formed say to its former, "You do not understand"?
                              (29:15–16)

They even question the call of Cyrus to save them.

Woe to whoever quarrels with the one who forms him,
    pottery with the potter.
Does clay say to the one forming it, "What are you making?"
  or "Your product has no handles?"
Woe to whoever says to a father, "What are you begetting?"
  or to a woman, "Why are you in labor?"
Thus says the Lord, the Holy One of Israel, the one who forms him:
"Will you question me about the future, about my children?
Will you give me orders about the product of my hands?
I, I made the earth and I created humanity upon it. . . .
I, I aroused him [Cyrus] in righteousness, and I straighten out
    all his ways."
                              (45:9–13)

To return to Assyria, his pride does not go unnoticed by the Lord:
"I will punish the arrogant mind of the king of Assyria and the overweening haughtiness of his eyes" (10:12).

Assyria will fall by a sword that is not of a human;
    a sword not of a mortal will devour him.
He will flee from the sword; his warriors will be consigned
    to slave labor.
His fortress will pass away in terror; his officers will collapse in panic.
                              (31:8–9)

The angel of the Lord went and struck 185,000 in the Assyrian
camp; when morning arrived, there were only dead corpses.
                              (37:36)

But Assyria is not subjected to total destruction: "I am turning you
[Sennacherib] back on the road by which you came" (37:29). Sennacherib's sons kill him and one of them, Esarhaddon, rules in his place
(37:38). The Lord has blessed Assyria; I close with the quotation I

opened with: "Blessed is my people Egypt; the work of my hands Assyria; and my heritage Israel" (19:25).

Babylon: With the exception of Merodach-baladan, who sends messengers of sympathy to Hezekiah (chap. 39), no other king or official of Babylon is mentioned in Isaiah (see pp. 25 and 33–34). In the vision, Babylon has less connection with the historical people and nation than do Egypt and Assyria. Assyria is introduced in connection with the events of the Syro-Ephraimite War of 734–732 B.C.E. Babylon first appears at the close of the description of the Lord's cosmic army and the resultant cataclysm for the entire world. It is a graphic description of the desolation of a city, a geographical area.

Babylon, most beautiful of kingdoms, the proud splendor
    of the Chaldeans will be
Like Sodom and Gomorrah overthrown by God.
She will never be lived in, and she will not be dwelt in for all times;
No Arab will tent there, and shepherds will not rest their flocks there.
Demons will rest there, and howling creatures will fill their houses;
Ostriches will dwell there, and hairy demons will cavort there.

(13:19–21)

The final scene is reminiscent of the devastation described in chapter 34.

A brief proclamation of God's restoration of Israel follows the horrific scene; Israel is then to recite a taunt over the king of Babylon (14:4–21). The taunt uses terms such as "club" and "rod" and images such as unbridled wrath, terms and images similar to those used against Assyria.

The Lord has smashed the club of the wicked, the rod of rulers
That struck people in wrath, striking without cease,
That ruled nations in anger, persecuting without relenting.

(14:5–6)

Babylon is not an instrument sent on a mission to punish Israel or any other nation. At a later point in the vision, God speaks of handing over the people, not of sending Babylon as a divine instrument.

I was angry with my people, I defiled my heritage.
I gave them into your power; you showed them no mercy.

(47:6)

On the other hand, Babylon is guilty of pride that far exceeds that of Assyria. Babylon does not just smash nations in wrath but claims to be God's equal. In the taunt the king of Babylon reaches for the highest height but instead falls into the lowest depth.

How you are fallen from heaven, O Shining One, son of Dawn![19]
You are cut down to earth, O destroyer of nations!
Indeed, you said in your heart, "I will scale the heavens.
Above the stars of God I will set up my throne.
I will sit on the mount of assembly in the uttermost parts
   of Zaphon.[20]
I will scale the heights of the clouds. I will be like the Most High."
But you are brought down to Sheol, to the uttermost parts
   of the Pit.

(14:12–15)

In chapter 47 the poet addresses a woman called "daughter Babylon" and "daughter Chaldea," who is mercilessly humiliated by God and prophet for her pride and lack of mercy. The Israelites interrupt the denunciation to gloat.

Come, sit in the dust, maiden daughter Babylon!
Sit on the ground dethroned, daughter Chaldea!
For they will never again call you Tender or Delicate.
Take a hand mill and grind grain;
   remove your veil, strip off your robe, bare your legs,
   pass through rivers.
Your nakedness is revealed, even your shame is seen.
I take vengeance, and no one can intercede with me.
Our Redeemer! The Lord of Hosts is his name,
   the Holy One of Israel.
Sit in silence; go into darkness, daughter Chaldea!
For they will never again call you Mistress of Kingdoms.
I was angry with my people, I defiled my heritage.
I gave them into your power; you showed them no mercy.
You made your yoke exceedingly heavy on the aged.
You said, "I will be mistress forever."
You did not take these things to heart; you did not remember
   their inevitable outcome.
But now hear this, O voluptuous woman, you who reign securely,
You who say in your heart, "I am and there is none other but me.

I do not reign as a widow; I do not experience the loss of children."
Both of these will happen to you in a moment, in one day:
The loss of children and widowhood will happen to you
    in full measure,
Despite your many enchantments and the great power
    of your spells.

(vv. 1–9)

Lady Babylon's statements, "I will be mistress forever" and "I am and there is none other but me," are claims to the immortal rule and uniqueness that belong only to the Lord.

Do you not know? Have you not heard?
The Lord is God forever, the creator of the ends of the earth.

(40:28)

So that you can know and trust in me and understand that I am he.
Before me no god was formed, nor will any be after me.
I, I am the Lord, and besides me there is no savior.

(43:10–11)

Unlike Egypt and Assyria, who are depicted as male, Babylon is portrayed as both a man (e.g., the king of Babylon in chaps. 14 and 39) and a woman. This is analogous to male Israel and female Zion. Personified Babylon appears first in 13:19–22 and then in 21:9: "Fallen, fallen is Babylon, and all the idols of her gods lie shattered on the ground." In my next chapter I will return to the denunciation of Lady Babylon in Isaiah 47 (see pp. 204–06).

Character as Type

In prose narrative, people are distinguished by name and by their character attributes. We cannot always make such clear distinctions among characters in Isaiah. Even God is impossible to define except with contrasting and contradictory attributes. On the other hand, a number of named characters are flat and one-dimensional; they are types, symbols, of a particular attribute or fate. I have already noted that Assyria symbolizes anyone employed as a divine instrument and also the proud and haughty. The nations Moab and Philistia are further examples. The advancing army crushes them, and the prophet and others lament their fate.

> Wail, O gate; cry, O city; quake, O Philistia, all of you!
> For smoke comes from the north, and there is no straggler
>   in its ranks.
>
> (14:31)

The proper names in the following are sites in Moab; the speaker, the one who says "I," is ambiguous. God, prophet, and even an Israelite can say this.

> Therefore as I weep for Jazer, I weep for the vines of Sibmah;
> I drench you with my tears, O Heshbon and Elealeh!
> For the cheers over your fruit harvest and your grain harvest
>   have fallen silent.
> Joy and gladness have vanished from the farmland;
>   in the vineyards none sing and none shout;
> No more does the treader tread wine in the vats;
>   I have silenced the harvest cheers.
> Therefore my heart moans for Moab like a lyre,
>   and my very soul for Kir-heres.
>
> (16:9–11)

Shebna and Eliakim are types of the proud and successful whose day in the sun is limited (see p. 30). They fit the pattern in which the fall of one enemy leads to the short-lived success of another. The advance of the divine force, the cosmic army, is unstoppable. The pattern is seen in chapters 36–39. Sennacherib is stopped at the walls of Jerusalem; the city is saved. Both city and king are given a temporary reprieve. Hezekiah has another fifteen years of life and Jerusalem about another century. Assyria is halted, but Babylon replaces it. "Days are coming when all that is in your palace, all that your ancestors have stored up until today, will be carried off to Babylon; nothing will be left" (39:6).

King Ahaz stands for all fearful people, especially Israelites, who turn to their own devices rather than trusting God. Ahaz does not even stand as an individual distinct from the monarchy, the house of David. (This is *synecdoche*, the figure of speech in which a part stands for the whole, but here the part and the whole are not distinct; see p. 13.)

In the days of *Ahaz*, . . . king of Judah, Rezin, king of Aram, and Pekah, . . . king of Israel, besieged Jerusalem, but they were not able to capture it. When *the house of David* was told, "Aram has allied with Ephraim," his heart and the heart of his people shook. (7:1–2)

The Lord spoke again to *Ahaz*, "Ask a sign from the Lord your God. Make it as deep as Sheol or as high as heaven." *Ahaz* answered, "I will not ask and I will not test the Lord." And he said, "Hear, O *house of David*! Is it not enough for you to weary humans that you also have to weary my God?" (7:10–13)

This passage is an example of how God and prophet, here the individual Isaiah, overlap in their statements. God begins the speech, but Isaiah, who says "my God," apparently asks the last question.[21] The rupture of the relationship between Ahaz or the whole monarchy and the Lord is marked by the change from "the Lord *your* God" to "*my* God."

The actions of Ahaz typify those of the people in general who, in their fear, turn to others than the Lord for help. I noted this in applying 22:8–11 to Ahaz in an earlier discussion (see pp. 113–14); the following also employs Egypt, the type of useless aid.

Woe, rebellious children, says the Lord,
For devising a plan that is not from me, for forming an alliance
    that is not my will,
so that you add sin to sin.
Who set out to go down to Egypt without consulting me,
To seek refuge with Pharaoh and to seek shelter in Egypt's shadow.
But Pharaoh's refuge will be your shame, and seeking
    shelter in Egypt's shadow, your disgrace.

(30:1–3)

Woe to those who go down to Egypt for help and rely on horses.
They trust in the numbers of chariots and in the great strength of
    horsemen,
But they do not look to the Holy One of Israel, and they do not
    inquire of the Lord.

(31:1)

Whom do you dread and fear that you lie?
    You do not remember me or pay me mind.

Is it not because I have been silent for so long that you
    have not feared me?

(57:11)

Hezekiah, a major character in chapters 36–39, contrasts with
Ahaz. He is the trusting king who turns to God in times of distress,
both national and personal. He stands in opposition to Ahaz; the two
together form a pair of contrasting types. On the other hand,
Hezekiah symbolizes the eventual destruction of Jerusalem and the
exile of the people and, at the same time, points beyond them to return
and restoration. His additional fifteen years are like the additional
century for Jerusalem and its people. Hezekiah's prayer in 38:10–20
contains themes and images of both exile (death) and return (life); the
final two verses illustrate the near identity of Hezekiah, "I," and the
people, "we."

I have been consigned to the gates of Sheol for the rest of my days.
I thought, I will not see Yah, Yah[22] in the land of the living;
I will not look upon mortals among the world's inhabitants.
My dwelling is pulled up and removed [exiled] from me
    like a shepherd's tent. . . .
The living, the living, they praise you as I do today;
    a father proclaims your faithfulness to his children.
O Lord, save me; we sing to you on my stringed instruments
    all the days of our lives at the house of the Lord.

(38:10–12, 19–20)

The house of the Lord, the temple, symbolizes both the land of Israel
and the land of the living, that is, life lived in God's presence. The
story in chapter 38 ends with Hezekiah's pregnant question, "What is
the sign that I will go up to the house of the Lord?" Being able to go
up to the house is itself a sign of return and restoration.

As noted earlier, the story of Hezekiah's illness is narrated in 2
Kings 20:1–11 in a somewhat different form (see pp. 34–35). The
psalm in Isaiah 38:10–20 is not in the Kings text, and the latter
includes details not in Isaiah. For example, Isaiah is not even out of
the king's court when the Lord speaks to him (2 Kgs. 20:4), and the
king will go to the Lord's house on the third day (20:5, 8). Hezekiah's
question about what sign he will be given precedes the prediction that
the sundial will go in the reverse direction (20:8–11). In Isaiah the sign

is provided and the question is placed at the end of the story (38:21–22) to emphasize the connection between the Lord's house and life and to form a contrast with the king's house in Isaiah 39, a house that is to be emptied by Babylon.

Hezekiah's depiction ends on an ambiguous note. He shows everything to the ambassadors of the Babylonian king Merodach-baladan: "There was not a thing in his house or in his entire realm that Hezekiah did not show them" (39:2). This anticipates the Babylonian destruction of Judah and Jerusalem, but the narrator leaves it an open question whether Hezekiah thinks that he is doing anything wrong. The story ends with his ambiguous response to Isaiah's prophecy.

> Hezekiah said to Isaiah, "The word of the Lord that you have spoken is good." And he said/thought, "For there will be peace and security in my days." (39:8)

This can be taken as a self-serving remark, "Who cares about the future as long as I am safe now?" It can be a passive acceptance of the state of affairs or even a prayer, "Let there be peace in my life."

Cyrus is my final example of a type. Beyond his name, Koresh in Hebrew, and the references to the conquest of Babylon and the release of captured prisoners, there are no other specifics linking this poetic figure to the historical king of Persia. Persia, in fact, is not named in Isaiah. Cyrus shares a poetic, symbolic status with Babylon. He is not a historical character in Isaiah in the sense that Hezekiah and Sennacherib are.

Like Assyria, Cyrus is a divine instrument but one used for Israel's benefit. He is a type for one who is not of Israel and who is yet called to perform the Lord's service, to be a servant of the Lord. The Lord calls him in 41:2–4, 25; 45:12–13; 46:8–11; and 48:14–16; and by name in 44:24–45:6. Several passages that speak of one sent by the Lord (e.g., 42:5–7 and 61:1–11) refer on one level to Cyrus, since he fills this role.

The Lord calls Cyrus from the east and overwhelms all who stand in his way (41:2–3, 25). The Lord says of him, "He is my shepherd; he fulfills all my plans" (44:28). He is called to return the people and to rebuild Jerusalem. "For the sake of my servant Jacob and Israel my chosen, I have called you by your name" (45:4). This leads to universal recognition of the Lord: "so that they [humanity] may know . . . that there is not another besides me" (45:6).

Who Speaks? Who Is Spoken To?

God and prophet often quote Israel. These are usually short citations that illustrate Israel's rebellious attitudes and behavior.

> Woe! You who drag iniquity with cords of falsehood,
>   and as with cart ropes, sin.
> You who say, "Let him make haste, let him speed his deed that
>   we may see it;
> Let the plan of the Holy One of Israel hasten to fulfillment,
>   that we may know it!"
>
> (5:18–19)

> Therefore hear the word of the Lord, you men of mockery,
> Who rule this people in Jerusalem,
> For you have said, "We have made a covenant with Death,
>   and with Sheol we have sealed a pact.
> When the raging flood passes through, it will not reach us,
> For we have made deceit our refuge, and in a lie we have
>   hidden ourselves."
>
> (28:14–15)

> Tell my people their rebellion, and the house of Jacob their sins. . . .
> They delight to approach God,
> "Why do we fast and you pay no attention?
> Why do we afflict ourselves and you know nothing of it?"
>
> (58:1–3)

Others are similarly indicted through their own words. The above discussions of Egypt, Assyria, and Babylon include quotations of all of them.

> Because Aram, with Ephraim and the son of Remaliah, has planned evil against you, "Let us attack Judah to invade and conquer it for ourselves and to make the son of Tabeel king of it."
> (7:5–6)

Positive assertions are also cited, but these are less frequent than the self-condemning statements.

> All nations flow to it; many peoples come and say,
> "Let us go up to the mountain of the Lord,
>   to the house of the God of Jacob,

That he may teach us his ways and that we may walk in his paths;
For teaching comes forth from Zion, and the word of the Lord
      from Jerusalem."

(2:2–3)

They [Egyptians and Cushites] will bow down to you [Zion],
    and they will plead with you,
Only with you is God; there is no other, no other God but him.
You are certainly a God who conceals himself,
    O God of Israel who saves.

(45:14–15)

Most translations close the first assertion with quotation marks and make the final assertion about the hidden and saving God a direct exclamation by the prophet or other speaker. I leave off quotation marks to preserve the ambiguity of speaker: Egyptian, prophet, or other?

Most positive assertions are spoken outright and not as a citation in another statement. In 63:7–64:12 Israel speaks without quotation formulas (see p. 57). Speaking first as "I" in 63:7–15 and then as "we" in 63:16–64:12, Israel recounts the story of past grace, sin, punishment, and renewed mercy. "Thus you guided your people to make for yourself a glorious name" (63:14). Despite this last mercy, Israel feels betrayed and abandoned by the Lord amid desolation.

Why, O Lord, do you make us stray from your ways,
    make our hearts too hard to fear you?
Return for the sake of your servants, the tribes that are your very own.
Although for a short while your holy people were in possession,
    our enemies now trample your sanctuary.

(63:17–18)

In chapter 64 Israel pleads with the Lord for deliverance based on their misery and their status as God's chosen people. This special status and its relation to justice and mercy were discussed in chapter 2 above.

In 59:1–8 the prophet denounces the people for their persistent evil. In verses 9–15a the people admit that their pitiful state is the result of their sins.

Therefore justice is far from us, and righteousness
    does not reach us. . . .

We wait for justice, and there is none; for victory, and it is
    far from us.
For many are our crimes before you, and our sin testifies against us;
Indeed, our crimes are with us, and we know well our iniquities:
Transgressing, and denying the Lord, and turning back
    from following our God,
Speaking oppression and revolt, conceiving and muttering
    lying words from the heart.

(59:9–13)

In response to the denunciation and the confession, the Lord puts on
the armor of vengeance. "According to their deeds, so he repays:
wrath to his adversaries, requital to his enemies, to the coastlands—
he repays requital" (59:18).

Israel is the obvious object of the accusation and the subject of the
confession in chapter 59. But, unlike 63:7–64:12, the people who
appear in 59:1–15a are not named. Only in verse 20 does the poet
name Zion and Jacob, and they are the Lord's goal, not necessarily the
site and people of the preceding denunciation and confession.

He comes like a pent-up river that the wind of the Lord drives on.
He comes to Zion, a Redeemer, for those in Jacob
    who turn from crime.

(59:20)

Chapter 59 can, therefore, be concerned with any people, their sin,
and God's violent reaction. Israel is a primary example of such a people but not the only one. The chapter highlights the play between the
general and the particular in Isaiah. To put it simply, sinners are sinners and God reacts against them whether they are Israelite, Assyrian,
or any humans. This is part of the all-inclusiveness of Isaiah; although
the story and fate of Israel are central to the vision, they are only part
of the much larger story of God's ways with the entire world.

Reading with different possible speakers can be applied to the
speeches in chapters 24–25. After the description of the worldwide
devastation in 24:1–13, the poet informs us that some rejoice in its
midst. They suddenly speak on their own, saying "we," and are as suddenly interrupted and contradicted by another, saying "I," who does
not share the optimistic mood.

They raise their voices; they sing of the majesty of the Lord;
    they shout from the sea:

"Therefore honor the Lord with lights in the coastlands of the sea,
    the name of the Lord, the God of Israel."[23]
From the edge of the earth we hear songs:
    "Glory to the righteous."[24]
And I say, "I waste away, I waste away! Woe to me!
For the treacherous act treacherously, the treacherous act
    very treacherously."

                                                                    (24:14–16)

Rather than trying to assign particular identities to those saying
"we" and "I," one can read this as the expression of opposing reactions
to the devastation by groups or individuals who remain unidentified.
One group sees justice being carried out, but another is dismayed
because the evil and its punishment are far from over. At the start of
chapter 25, a voice praises the Lord for the ruin of the ruthless and
the care of the poor. This is another speaker or perhaps the same voice
from 24:16 now realizing the ultimate victory of the Lord.

O Lord, You are my God! I exalt you; I praise your name.
For you have performed wonders, plans of old, entirely reliable.
Indeed, you turned the city into a heap, the fortified city
    into a ruin. . . .
For you were a fortress for the poor, a fortress for the needy
    in their distress,
a shelter from the storm, shade from the heat.

                                                                    (25:1–4)

Related examples where we can leave the speaker unidentified are
the songs of thanks in chapter 12; 26:1–6; and 38:10–20. They fit in
their immediate contexts and are also general expressions of thanks to
God for deliverance from the powerful or from death. The third song
is ascribed directly to Hezekiah as a prayer following his recovery. We
have already discussed that it, and Hezekiah, mirror the future fate of
Israel and Jerusalem, lost in exile and destruction but hoping to be
again in the land of the living, in the house of the Lord.

Personification

Personification is a figure of speech that is central to characterization in Isaiah (see p. 13). Nations and cities are addressed and
portrayed as personages in the grand vision. There is a change in

emphasis in the mode of personification within the book, especially between chapters 1–39 and 40–66. This is one of the instances in which I follow the sequential order of Isaiah. Personifications that retain strong ties with the actual nation or city portrayed are in the majority in chapters 1–39; in 40–66 there are more in which the characters stand on their own with weaker ties to the actual entities or people portrayed. This is a strong tendency within the book, but it is not a total contrast, since both types of personification appear in both parts of Isaiah.

This is part of the shift from the numerous particulars of much of chapters 1–39—named individuals and places, historical people and events—to the more sweeping presentations of 40–66 with their marked decrease in the number of named individuals and places (see pp. 34–35). In chapter 47 we have a woman named Lady Babylon, but she is not a named character in the sense that Shebna, Hezekiah, and Sennacherib are. Nonetheless, we have as much, if not more, character portrayal of her as of the previous three, particularly Shebna. The decrease in named individuals is balanced by an increase in the number of independent personifications. These brief comments serve as introduction to the depiction of Zion-Jerusalem in the next section and to the presentations of my final chapter.

Jerusalem-Zion

Jerusalem is the capital of Judah captured by David from the Jebusites (2 Sam. 5:6–10). It is the site of the temple and the home of the Davidic dynasty. Zion is the plateau on which Jerusalem is located, hence the name Mount Zion. In Isaiah, as in the rest of the Hebrew Bible, Jerusalem and Zion parallel each other with little distinction between them. I treat the two as one, Zion-Jerusalem, and usually refer to Zion or Jerusalem to avoid the awkward Zion-Jerusalem or Jerusalem-Zion.

Jerusalem is named in the first verse of the book in connection with Judah and its kings (see Isa. 2:1). At times the city stands threatened with destruction or it is in actual ruins.

> Now look! The Sovereign, the Lord of Hosts,
> Is taking away from Jerusalem and from Judah
> Support and staff: all support of bread, and all support of water.
> (3:1)

[The Lord] who says of Jerusalem, "She will be inhabited,"
And of the cities of Judah, "They will be rebuilt; I will raise
up their ruins."

(44:26)

Your holy cities have become a wilderness.
Zion has become a wilderness, Jerusalem, a desolation.

(64:10)

In other instances the city and its inhabitants are equivalent to Israel, the people, and what was said about the latter applies to Jerusalem and those who live there. The statements can be negative or positive.

Jerusalem stumbles and Judah falls,
Because their speech and their deeds are against the Lord
to defy his glorious presence.

(3:8)

He [Eliakim] will be a father to the inhabitants of Jerusalem and
to the house of Judah; I will place the key to the house of David
on his shoulder. (22:21–22)

O people in Zion, inhabitants of Jerusalem,
you certainly will weep no more.

(30:19)

Sinners in Zion are frightened; trembling has seized the godless:
"Who of us can live with a devouring fire?
Who of us can live with an everlasting blaze?"

(33:14)

Zion is a special place for the righteous, the cleansed, the remnant. "Zion, by justice, is redeemed" (1:27).

Whoever is left in Zion and remains in Jerusalem will be called
Holy, all who have been recorded in Jerusalem for life, when the
Lord has washed the filth of the daughters of Zion and has
cleansed the bloodstains of Jerusalem from her with a just spirit
and a fiery spirit. The Lord will create over the whole site and
assemblies of Mount Zion a cloud by day and smoke with flaming fire by night. (4:3–5; see 12:6)

> Envision Zion, our festive city! Your eyes see Jerusalem:
> A quiet homestead, a tent not to be moved
>
> (33:20)

> The surviving remnant of the house of Judah will again strike
> root downward and bear fruit upward, for a remnant will leave
> Jerusalem, and a band of survivors Mount Zion. (37:31–32)

This status is connected with the Lord's protection of Jerusalem: "I will protect this city to save it for my own sake and the sake of my servant David" (37:35).[25]

> Like one who is hungry dreams of eating but wakes up empty,
> And like one who is thirsty dreams of drinking but wakes up tired
>   and parched,
> So it will be for the mass of all the nations who are fighting
>   on Mount Zion.
>
> (29:8)

> As a lion, a fierce lion, growls over its prey, and,
> When a band of shepherds gather against him,
> Is not frightened by their shouts or bothered by their noise,
> So will the Lord of Hosts descend to fight upon Mount Zion
>   and upon its hill.
> Like hovering birds will the Lord of Hosts shield Jerusalem:
>   shielding and delivering, sparing and rescuing.
>
> (31:4–5)

Zion is the divine dwelling, the holy mountain (66:20). In the ancient world, God or the gods were thought of as dwelling on a mountain or in the mountains. The king of Babylon resolves to "sit on the mount of assembly in . . . Zaphon . . . the heights of the clouds" (14:13–14; see p. 166). Isaiah calls attention to Mount Zion and the holy mountain Jerusalem (11:9; 65:11): "Let us go up to the mountain of the Lord" (2:3); "This is from the Lord of Hosts who dwells on Mount Zion" (8:18); and "the Lord of Hosts is king on Mount Zion and in Jerusalem" (24:23).

> Those lost in the land of Assyria and those driven into the land
> of Egypt will come and worship the Lord on the holy mountain
> in Jerusalem. (27:13)

Height, being on high, in this usage is acceptable and the exact opposite of the elevation of pride and arrogance: "In a high and holy place I dwell and also with one broken and of humble spirit" (57:15).

In these passages Jerusalem is presented with little or no personification; this is the city, whether real or ideal. In the latter half of the book, true to the pattern of increasing personification, Jerusalem is at times spoken to as a woman who appears as a rounded character in her own right. There are a few suggestions in some of the poems that this is a city personified (see pp. 158–59).

> Comfort, comfort my people, says your God.
> Speak to the heart of Jerusalem and cry to her
> That her term is filled, that her penalty is paid,
> That she has received from the Lord's hand double for
>   all her sins. . . .
> Get up on a high mountain, O Zion, herald of good news!
> Raise your voice in a loud shout, O Jerusalem, herald of good news!
> Raise it; fear not; say to the cities of Judah, "Here is your God!"
>
> (40:1–2, 8–9)

The section 40:1–49:13 ends with the celebration of the Lord's comforting the people, and 49:14–54:17 opens with Zion's counterclaim that the Lord has abandoned her.

> Sing, O heavens, and rejoice, O earth! O mountains, break into song!
> For the Lord has comforted his people, and has compassion
>   on his suffering ones.
> But Zion says, "The Lord has forsaken me,
>   my Lord has forgotten me."
>
> (49:13–14)

The Lord assures Zion that she has not been abandoned and that she will have so many children even in her time of bereavement that they will say:

> "The place is too crowded for me; make room for me to settle."
> And you will say to yourself, "Who bore these for me?
>   I was bereaved and barren, exiled and driven off.
> Who, then, raised these for me?
> I was left all alone. Where, then, were these?"
>
> (49:20–21)

Zion fears mere humans because "you forget the Lord, your maker, who stretches out the heavens" (51:12–13), but her time of punishment is over.

> Rouse yourself, rouse yourself! Stand up, O Jerusalem!
> You have drunk from the hand of the Lord his cup of wrath,
> You have drunk to the dregs the bowl, the cup of staggering. . . .
> Therefore listen to this, miserable one, drunk but not from wine:
> Thus says your Lord, the Lord, your God who defends his people:
> "Look, I have taken the cup of staggering from your hand;
> You will drink no more from the bowl, my cup of wrath,
> but I will put it into the hands of your tormentors,
> Those who have commanded you, 'Get down so that we may
>   walk over you.'
> And you made your back like the ground, like a street for
>   those walking over you."
>
> (51:17, 21–23)

Chapters 60–62 are a high point in the proclamation of restoration. Chapter 60 is addressed to a woman; all the second person pronouns are feminine singular. The poet describes a woman whose children are returning and who is being enriched.

> Arise! Shine! For your light comes, and the glory of the Lord
>   rises upon you. . . .
> Lift your eyes and look around: they all gather, they come to you,
> Your sons come from far away and your daughters,
>   at their nurses' side.
> You see and you glow; your heart thrills and throbs,
> For the abundance of the sea passes to you, and the wealth
>   of nations comes to you.
>
> (60:1, 4–5)

Isaiah moves from addressing the woman to describing the place where she dwells. The site is the Lord's altar, a glorious house (vv. 7, 13; see 56:7). The mention of walls and gates in verses 10–11 indicates that this is the city personified: "Your gates are always open; day and night they are not shut." Zion is then explicitly named: "They call you 'City of the Lord, Zion of the Holy One of Israel'" (v. 14). Her walls are named Salvation and her gates Fame or Praise (v. 18).

I will discuss chapter 61 in my next chapter since it deals with an anonymous person whom the Lord sends to aid Jerusalem and her people. Chapter 62 opens as the poet or perhaps the anonymous speaker of chapter 61 addresses Zion.

> For Zion's sake I will not keep silent, and for Jerusalem's sake
>   I will not rest,
> Until her victory goes forth as a bright light,
>   and her salvation burns like a torch.
> Nations see your victory and all kings your glory;
> You are called by a new name that the mouth of
>   the Lord designates.
>
> (vv. 1–2)

Chapters 60–62 end on a grand note for both Jerusalem and Israel; it is reminiscent of the opening of chapter 40. But, typical of the powerful contrasts in vision of Isaiah, the imposing climax is followed by the depiction of the bloodstained Lord who has trampled peoples.

> Pass through, pass through the gates, prepare a way for the people.
> Build, build the highway, clear it of rocks, lift a signal
>   over the peoples.
> See, the Lord has proclaimed to the end of the earth:
> Tell daughter Zion, "See, your salvation comes;
> See, his reward is with him and his recompense before him."
> They call them, "The Holy People, The Redeemed of the Lord."
> And you are called, "Sought Out, A City Not Forsaken."
> Who is this coming from Edom, in crimsoned garments,
>   from Bozrah?
> This one, splendidly attired, striding in his great might?
>
> (62:10–63:1; see pp. 83–84)

Jerusalem's final appearance as a character is the picture of a mother comforting her many children. The speaker addresses Jerusalem and her children, the people. ("You" is masculine plural.)

> Be glad for Jerusalem, sing with her, all you who love her!
> Rejoice, rejoice with her, all you who have mourned for her,
> So that you may suck and be satisfied at her comforting breast,
> So that you may drink with delight from her glorious bosom.
> For thus says the Lord:

"I am now extending to her peace like a river and,
like a flooding stream, the wealth of nations,
And you will suck and be carried on her hip and dandled
    on her knees.
As a woman comforts her child, thus I, I comfort you;
you will find comfort in Jerusalem."

(66:10–13)

Endnotes to Chapter 4

1. The royal armory; see 1 Kgs. 7:2–5.
2. The ambiguity of the Rabshakeh's addressee appears in the textual evidence. The MT has singular "you" (Hezekiah) while 4QIsaᵃ, the Greek, and the parallel text in 2 Kgs. 18:22 have plural "you" (the Jerusalemites and Hezekiah). In 2 Kgs. 18:22, however, the Greek has singular "you" in contrast to MT's plural.
3. For the first two phrases, see 28:13–14; 38:4; 39:6; 66:5; and for the second pair, 1:11, 18; 3:15; 40:25; 45:13; 66:22–23. The phrase "says the Lord" represents two different phrases in Hebrew that are not clearly distinguished in English translations, including mine.
4. Also 7:7; 18:4; 28:16; 30:12; 45:14; 66:1.
5. The allusion to Gen. 3:14 does not occur in the parallel text in Isa. 11:6–9. The final two chapters of Isaiah are marked by sharp contrasts between the wonderful fate for those who tremble at the Lord's word (66:2, 5), his servants, and the horrors in store for "you who forsake the Lord, who forget my holy mountain" (65:11). The contrast is in this brief description of the peaceable kingdom; the serpent is a symbol for those who forsake the Lord.
6. English has one second person pronoun, "you," and does not distinguish masculine from feminine as in the third person, "he" and "she," or singular from plural, as in "he" and "they." Hebrew has four forms of the second person pronoun and distinguishes masculine and feminine, singular, and plural. Isaiah employs three of these regularly. Israel, the people, are both masculine singular and plural; Zion-Jerusalem is feminine singular as in 1:21–26. "You" in 1:5–20 is masculine plural and masculine singular in 33:17–24. The plural is seen in a reflexive form: "Wash yourselves; make yourselves clean" (1:16). Otherwise these distinctions are not available in English translation except by using archaic forms or by indicating gender and number in parentheses. Watts employs a sizable number of such parentheses in the translation in his commentary. This is an unavoidable limitation of an English translation but not an insurmountable problem in reading and understanding Isaiah. I mention it for information and deal with it in limited fashion at other points.
7. This is another child with a symbolic name: Speeding-Spoil-Hastening-Prey. It is ironic that some in Israel want the Lord to speed and hasten "his work that we may see it" (5:19).
8. In the Masoretic scribal tradition, the divine name YHWH (the Tetragrammaton: four-lettered) was not to be pronounced. When these four consonants appear in the manuscripts, they are supplied with the vowels for *'adonai*, "my lord," which is the word to be pronounced. Early English translators misunderstood this and rendered

the name as Jehovah ("J" and "v" replace "Y" and "W" of YHWH). "Yahweh" is assumed to be close to the proper pronunciation.

9. The word "Lord" is usually printed in capitals, LORD, or small capitals, LORD, in most translations to distinguish it from "lord," *'adon*, which I translate as "the Sovereign."

10. NJB renders this as a transliteration of the Hebrew: Yahweh Sabaoth. Sabaoth is the Hebrew word for "hosts, armies."

11. This is literally "Yah Yahweh." Yah is a shortened form of Yahweh that is occasionally used in the HB; see p. 211.

12. See pp. 105–06 for other uses of the Hebrew term for Mighty One, including the phrase "bulls in heart."

13. Hebrew uses three different terms to indicate (1) the entire arm; (2) the forearm, translated "arm" or "hand" depending on the context; and (3) the hand, which can be translated "palm" in a context such as 49:16. The rendering of the second and third terms varies between translations so that "arm" in one may be "hand" in another.

14. See "Isaiah" by Susan Ackerman, pp. 161–68 in *The Women's Bible Commentary*, ed. Carol A. Newsom and Shannon H. Ringe (London: SPCK; Louisville: Westminster John Knox Press, 1992). Also Phyllis Trible, *God and the Rhetoric of Sexuality*, 50–71, and John F. A. Sawyer, *The Fifth Gospel*, 198–219.

15. The human family, its members and its life, whether peaceful or hostile, weaves its way through Isaiah's vision, but I do not make it a focus of my readings. See Katheryn Pfisterer Darr, *Isaiah's Vision and the Family of God* (Louisville: Westminster John Knox Press, 1994).

16. The first three lines employ singular and plural forms for the people. Most translations choose the plural throughout. TNK employs the singular, e.g., "Because that people has approached [Me] with its mouth and honored Me with its lips."

17. Ironically the Lord's wonders are the people's punishment; REB renders, "I shall shock this people yet again, adding shock to shock." This is the same term that occurs in "Wonderful Counselor" (9:6).

18. The only mention of Assyria after 38:6 is in 52:4, where the Assyrians, in parallel with the Egyptians, are oppressors of Israel.

19. This probably refers to a divine character in an ancient myth that we no longer have. I follow TNK. Others translate the first name as "Day Star" (NRSV, NJB) or "morning star" (NIV, REB, NAB). The Latin Vulgate translates it "Lucifer," Latin for "bearer of light."

20. In many poetic texts in the Prophets, Psalms, and Job, God is depicted as dwelling with an assembly or council of other gods or divine beings on Zaphon, a mountain in the north. This is similar to the Greek image of the gods dwelling on Mount Olympus, and it is a common motif in Canaanite and Mesopotamian myths.

21. NRSV, NIV, and TNK use "Isaiah" in the introductory "and he said." Both NRSV and TNK note that "Isaiah" is not in the Hebrew.

22. The repetition is in the Hebrew, and my translation is similar to TNK: "I shall never see Yah, Yah in the land of the living." See p. 211.

23. In translating "the sea" and "with lights" I follow TNK. Other translations render "west" (referring to the Mediterranean Sea) and "east" (taking lights as a metaphor for sunrise).

24. I follow TNK, NAB, and others in translating this final phrase as a quotation. NRSV does not have a quotation: "songs of praise, of glory to the Righteous One." I follow TNK and KJV with "the righteous," who are both human and the Lord. NRSV, NIV, NAB, and NJB refer to the Lord by capitalizing the title, e.g., the Righteous One. Both REB and GNB refer to the righteous nation.

25. See B. C. Ollenburger, *Zion, the City of the Great King: A Theological Symbol of the Jerusalem Cult* (Journal for the Study of the Old Testament Supplement 41; Sheffield: Sheffield Academic Press, 1987), for details on the role of Zion in the HB, its connection with the Davidic dynasty, and discussion of some relevant extrabiblical parallels.

Chapter 5

The Lord's Holy Mountain

A Child, a Shoot,
a Servant, and a Woman

The passages and issues of this chapter are significant both in my reading of the vision of Isaiah and in the history of the interpretation of Isaiah. Messianic passages, whether or not they refer to a specific Messiah, have been interpreted in a variety of ways in Jewish and Christian interpretation. I discuss mainly some Christian interpretations, but read the particular passages in themselves in the ways employed in this work and in relation to the whole book of Isaiah. The chapter, to a great extent, is a summary of and a conclusion to my book. It contains the most detailed and developed readings and follows the order of Isaiah, although I do draw many parallels and illustrations from many other places in the book. Through the readings, I provide an overview of Isaiah's vision of the Lord's holy mountain, Jerusalem (66:20), Mount Zion the divine dwelling place (24:23), God's house of prayer, altar, beautiful house, and holy courts (56:7; 60:7; 62:9). Isaiah's imaginative depiction of the ideal holy site and of those who live there combines the themes, characters, and imagery that we have looked at to this point. True to Isaiah's all-inclusive reach, however, those who cannot or will not live on the mountain are part of the picture, including the places they actually dwell.

I am reading Isaiah as a single work, a vision expressed in poetic language, with a focus on both what is said and how it is said. I emphasize imagery, the picture displayed by Isaiah. But I am not attempting to interpret images and the passages that embody them as referring solely to particular individuals or groups either in their ancient historical context or in any subsequent historical context.

The Anointed

The word "messiah" is based on a Greek approximation for the Hebrew term for "anointed" (*mashiach*), which is used of priests and kings.[1] References to the anointing of a priest are restricted to texts in Exodus, Leviticus, and Numbers that detail the consecration of the tabernacle and the priests who serve there. The consecration includes anointing the tabernacle and its altar with oil (Exod. 40:9–11; Lev. 8:10–11) and then Aaron and his sons as priests (Exod. 40:13–15; Lev. 7:36; Num. 3:3). "The anointed priest" specifies the priest as ordained (Lev. 4:3–16; 6:22), but a priest is not referred to as simply "the anointed."

The anointing of a king has special significance; a king can be called "the anointed." We first hear of anointing a king in Jotham's parable against Abimelech (Judg. 9:8–15): "The trees went out to anoint a king over themselves" (9:8). Hannah refers to the Lord's anointed in parallel with the king: "The Lord judges the entire earth; he gives strength to his king; he exalts the power of his anointed" (1 Sam. 2:10). Samuel anoints Saul (1 Sam. 10:1) and David (16:3–13), Nathan anoints Solomon (1 Kgs. 1:34–45), and an unnamed prophet anoints Jehu (2 Kgs. 9:1–12).

The king is the Lord's anointed. It is a sin to touch him, let alone kill him. David is stricken when he simply cuts a piece off of Saul's robe (1 Sam. 24:1–7; see 26:9–23), and he executes the Amalekite soldier who claims to have killed Saul (2 Sam. 1:1–16). Abishai wants to put Shimei to death for cursing King David (2 Sam. 19:21).

Beyond this the king, the anointed, both as an individual and as a representative of the Davidic dynasty,[2] has a special status in many places in the Hebrew Bible as God's chosen ruler for the people: "I took you from the pasture, from guiding the sheep, to be prince of my people, of Israel" (2 Sam. 7:8). The Davidic dynasty is assured stability and permanence.

> Your dynasty and your kingdom will be made sure forever; your throne will be established forever. (2 Sam. 7:16; see 2 Sam. 23:5)

> Forever I will guard my love for him [the Davidic king],
>   and my covenant with him will be sure;
> I will make his dynasty last forever, and his throne,
>   as long as the heavens exist.
>   (Ps. 89:28–29)

The Davidic king is guaranteed victory and sovereignty over his enemies and other peoples. In Hannah's song, the Lord, who judges the entire earth, supports the power of the king, the anointed (1 Sam. 2:10); the king's power may extend to the entire earth.

> You delivered me from war with people;
>   you made me head of nations;
>   people whom I had not known served me.
> (Ps. 18:43; see Ps. 2; 89:22–23; and Isa. 55:5)

Let him [the Davidic king] rule from sea to sea, from the River
   [the Euphrates] to the ends of the earth.
Let desert tribes bow before him; let his enemies lick the dust.
Let the kings of Tarshish[3] and the coastlands bring tribute;
   let the kings of Sheba and Seba[4] offer gifts.
Let all kings worship him; let all nations serve him.
                                   (Ps. 72:8–11; see Isa. 60:11–12)

The king establishes the peace and prosperity and the justice and righteousness promised by God for Israel and for all humanity. The following from Psalm 72 is similar to the description of "the shoot" in Isaiah 11:1–5, including defense of the poor and destruction of the wicked.

O God, grant the king your justice, your righteousness
   to the king's son.
That he may judge your people rightly and your poor justly.
Let the mountains yield peace for the people, the hills righteousness.
Let him defend the poor among the people; let him save the needy;
   let him crush the oppressor.

                                                        (Ps. 72:1–4)

The royal power is based in the Lord's power that is manifested in the creation of the world. Psalm 89 has parallels with Isaiah, especially passages such as the Song of the Arm (Isa. 51:9–11) that names Rahab (see pp. 100–01).

O Lord, God of Hosts, who is like you, O Mighty Yah?
   Your faithfulness surrounds you.
You rule the raging of the sea; when its waves surge, you still them.
You, you crushed Rahab like one slain; with your powerful arm
   you scattered your enemies.

The heavens are yours and the earth too; the world and all
    that is in it—you established them. . . .
Righteousness and justice are the foundation of your throne;
    steadfast love and faithfulness march before you.
                                     (Ps. 89:8–14)

Monarchy appears in a different light when placed in its ancient Near Eastern context revealed in texts from Canaan, Mesopotamia, and Egypt. In these cultures kings, in varying ways, claimed that a god or the gods had founded kingship as part of the created order of the world. They had granted kings the power to conquer their enemies, if not the whole world, to establish peace, and to rule their subjects justly and fairly.[5]

The above texts from the Hebrew Bible represent the claims of the kings for the divine basis of their authority and the claims for what they were going to do with that power and authority. Like kings elsewhere and throughout history, however, kings in Judah were usually much more concerned with keeping and increasing their power and authority than with building a just society with peace and prosperity for the people. The sad and violent story of the kings of both Judah and Israel in the books of Samuel and Kings ends in the destruction of both rulers and ruled.

In my reading, Isaiah is aware of this history of kings and wants little to do with actual kings, but he is impressed with their grand claims to divine establishment and to the wonderful society that they will rule. It is these royal claims and the terms and vivid images that express them that I refer to as messianic. I speak of messianic imagery and theology and not of a messiah; even Isaiah 9:2–7 and 11:1–9 focus on the resultant society and not on a specific identity for the child or the shoot that will produce this society. Isaiah says nothing specific about a king, whether real or ideal, bringing about this new world of peace and justice. In short, Isaiah takes these royal claims, especially their powerful imagery of creation, peace, and justice, and employs them as part of his vision of the Lord's holy mountain. He takes the terms and images of the royal claims, and he separates them from an actual king, a specific anointed one. "Messianic," then, goes beyond royal and becomes ideal, future, yet-to-come. Many writers use the term "messianic" to refer to any of Isaiah's pictures of an ideal and peaceful time; they do not limit it to the pictures based in royal terms and imagery.

The Holy Mountain

I begin with a description of the divine mountain presented in exodus imagery, not royal terms. We have already encountered the description in its rich imagery (see p. 88).

> The Lord will create over the whole site and assemblies of Mount Zion a cloud by day and smoke with flaming fire by night. Indeed, over all the glory there will be a canopy and a pavilion that will serve by day as shade from the heat, and as a refuge and a shelter from the storm and the rain. (4:5–6)

The "canopy and pavilion" (NRSV, TNK) or the "shelter and protection" (NAB) emphasize openness. This is a canopy or a tent, not a walled city or fortress. The pavilion does mark out a site that is special, but it does not rigorously or physically isolate it from the natural or human surroundings. This image of an open and expansive site is central to Isaiah's vision of the Lord's holy mountain, the Righteous City, the Triumphant City. It is truly a special place for a special people, but a place that is, at the same time, open and accessible to others.

> "My house will certainly be called a house of prayer
>   for all the peoples"—
> A statement of the Sovereign, the Lord,
>   who gathers the outcasts of Israel—
> "I will yet gather more to those already gathered."
>   (56:7–8)

This is another example of the contrast and tension encountered in other ways in Isaiah: God of justice and God of mercy; God of Israel and God of all humanity; Israel the righteous and Israel the rebellious.

Isaiah does not depict the ideal site, whether the Lord's holy mountain or redeemed Jerusalem, as a fortified city in which walls and closed gates are there to keep others out. A strong city symbolizes security and reliability, not fortification to exclude all others.

> On that day this song will be sung in the land of Judah:
> We have a mighty city; he makes victory its inner and outer wall.[6]
> Open the gates so that a righteous nation may enter,
>   one that keeps faith. . . .[7]

Trust in the Lord forever, for in Yah the Lord[8] you have
an eternal rock.

(26:1–4; see 33:16)

Your gates will always be open; they will close neither day nor night,
So that the wealth of nations may be brought to you,
and their kings come in procession.

(60:11)

Violence will no longer be heard in your land, havoc
or destruction within your borders;
You will call your walls Salvation and your gates Praise.

(60:18)

The opening vision of chapter 2 has been cited to illustrate its themes and imagery (see pp. 72 and 85–86). The mountain is special because it is the highest, but it is accessible, since nations and peoples flow to it; the image of water flowing uphill highlights the ease of approach. Zion is not a closed fortress but the site from which the divine teaching and word go forth.

This will be in the latter times:
The mountain of the house of the Lord is established
As the tallest of the mountains, as the highest of the hills,
And all the nations flow to it, many peoples come and say,
"Come, let us go up to the mountain of the Lord,
to the house of the God of Jacob,
That he may teach us his ways and that we may walk in his paths,
For teaching comes forth from Zion, and the word of the Lord
from Jerusalem."
He judges among the nations and decides for many peoples;
They beat their swords into plowshares and their spears
into pruning hooks;
Nation does not lift a sword against nation, and they
no longer learn war.

(2:2–4)

The passage closes with the messianic imagery and themes of universal justice and peace, but there is no human king, real or ideal. God alone, or God through the impact of the teaching,[9] judges all, not just Israel, and all enjoy the peace that follows from the establishment of justice. The images, some of the most familiar from the Hebrew Bible, speak for themselves.

Accessibility is also a central feature of Isaiah's references to the temple and to the more generic "house of the Lord." Although the temple is a symbol of the Lord's presence for life, as in 2:2–3 and 38:20–22, as a building with walls it can also symbolize restriction and exclusion.[10] The Lord questions efforts to rebuild the temple if it means the latter.

> The heavens are my throne, and the earth my footstool.
> What, then, is this house you are building for me?
> This place, then, is it to be my resting place?
> My hand made all these things, and they all exist[11]—says the Lord.
> This is the one I look upon: the poor and broken in spirit,
>   the one who trembles at my word.
>
> (66:1–2)

The Lord stresses openness and acceptance in 56:1–8. House, mountain, and even walls represent the special character and inclusiveness of the site that is just as much a state of being as a physical place.

> For thus says the Lord:
> To the eunuchs who keep my Sabbaths and who choose that
>   in which I delight, holding fast to my covenant,
> I give within my house and within my walls a monument
>   and a name better than sons and daughters;
> An everlasting name I give them that cannot be cut off.
> Foreigners who are joined to the Lord to minister to him,
>   to love the name of the Lord and to be his servants—
> All who keep the Sabbath, not profaning it and who hold fast
>   to my covenant—
> I will bring them to my holy mountain and make them happy
>   in my house of prayer.
> Their burnt offerings and their sacrifices are acceptable on
>   my altar;
> For my house will be called "a house of prayer for all the peoples"—
> A saying of the Sovereign, the Lord, who gathers
>   the outcasts of Israel—
> "I will yet gather more to those already gathered."
>
> (56:4–8)

At the close of the book the Lord speaks of a parallel between "my holy mountain Jerusalem" and "the house of the Lord." Their reference and meaning are expanded. The "holy mountain" is the actual city and the temple and, at the same time, the symbol of being in the Lord's presence and the state of life there. This is life lived according to the teaching and the light of the Lord.

> They [the nations] bring all your kin from all nations, on horses, in chariots and wagons, and on mules and camels, as an offering to the Lord on my holy mountain Jerusalem, says the Lord, just as the Israelites bring the offering, in clean vessels, to the house of the Lord. (66:20)

Immanuel

On the one hand, rule by children can be a curse. The Lord removes the normal leaders, and "I make boys their princes and babes rule over them" (3:4; see v. 12). The young are inexperienced and ignorant: "the boy will be insolent to the elder" (v. 5). On the other hand, Isaiah does not restrict himself to only one meaning for a given image or motif. At the time of the invasion of Aram and Israel, Ahaz refuses assurances of deliverance and instead relies on his own resources. He does not want a sign because that might prove the Lord's assurance and force him to give up his preparations. But a sign is still provided, a sign that includes the motif of a child.

> My Lord himself will assuredly give you a sign: Look, the young woman is pregnant and about to give birth to a son and she will name him Immanuel. He will be eating curds and honey by the time he knows how to reject the evil and choose the good. For before the boy knows how to reject the evil and choose the good the land whose two kings you fear will be abandoned. The Lord will bring upon you and upon your people and upon the house of your father times such as have not happened since Ephraim broke away from Judah—the king of Assyria. (7:14–17)

Because Matthew (1:22–23) cites verse 14 from this passage in relation to the birth of Jesus, the passage has been the object of controversy over the centuries as part of debates between Jews and Christians and among different groups of Christians. I digress into issues of the translation and interpretation of the passage. My goal is not to solve the interpretive problems but to read the passage and to shed light on some of the textual reasons for the debate, including why the controversy continues without resolution. The debate concerns the identity and marital status of the young woman (or the virgin), the time of the pregnancy and birth (i.e., the tenses used in the translation), and the identity of Immanuel.

"The young woman" is the preferred translation of the Hebrew term, which refers to a sexually mature woman who is marriageable (GNB, NRSV, REB, NJB, and TNK; see Exod. 2:8; Song 1:3; 6:8; Prov. 30:19). "The virgin" occurs in the Septuagint, which is the version used by Matthew; other ancient Greek translations render the term with "the young woman." KJV, NAB, and NIV use "the virgin," but NIV notes that the term "may refer to a young woman betrothed to Isaiah. . . . In Ge 24:43 the same Hebrew word (*'almah*) refers to a woman about to be married."*

The traditional Christian interpretation, beginning with Matthew, is that the virgin is Mary and the son, Immanuel, is Jesus. This interpretation prefers translations that use a future tense throughout the verse (e.g., "The virgin will be with child," NAB, NIV), rather than the present tense of many translations. In its Isaianic context the immediate reference of verse 14 is to the boy's youth, not to his identity or the significance of his name, since Isaiah stresses that Israel and Aram will be in ruins before the boy reaches the age of moral choice.[12] Some contemporary interpretations see the mother as a young woman who is pregnant at the time of the Syro-Ephraimite crisis (ca. 734–733 B.C.E.). In this reading the sign concerns not a miraculous birth of a unique child in the distant future but a birth in the immediate future and then deliverance from the attack shortly after the birth. The sign stresses the shortness of time before this rescue.

Commentators debate whether the woman is a wife of King Ahaz (the son could be Hezekiah) or of Isaiah, an unidentified woman, or, in a collective sense, any woman pregnant at the time. In these interpretations, the sign is the pregnant woman and the identity of the son, beyond the name Immanuel, is not significant. One intriguing suggestion, which accords well with my way of reading Isaiah, is that this is Zion giving birth to the remnant.[13] If we focus on the time span

---

*This is a note to 7:14 contained in the *NIV Study Bible* (Grand Rapids: Zondervan, 1985), 1027.

from the declaration of the sign to the birth to Jerusalem's deliverance, then the identity of the woman or of the child is not crucial, and we can keep the ambiguity and richness of these different interpretations.

The child's name is symbolic in itself without any further identification of the bearer. Immanuel means "God with us" and can be a wish, "May God be with us," or an assertion, "For God is with us" (see 8:9–10). In 7:14–16 God is with us for salvation, because the enemies are soon to be destroyed. Typical of Isaiah's multiple use of a theme, God is also with us for destruction in verses 17–20. Both an infestation of insects and a razor are images of the onrushing army. They are Isaiah's poetic version of the events of 735–701 B.C.E. The Assyrians sweep down from the north and wipe out Damascus (733–732), Israel (722), and the cities of Judah (701), but stop at the walls of Jerusalem and do not destroy it (chaps. 36–37). The flood reaches only to the neck (8:8).

This story of the sign for Ahaz has royal overtones, but it does not unequivocally refer to the birth of a prince who will be instrumental in the deliverance. It does not even refer to royalty solely in a positive sense; chapter 7 as a whole does not paint Ahaz or the house of David in a favorable light. The strictly messianic reading of the chapter, especially as a literal reference to and prediction of Jesus, begins with Matthew and is expanded by subsequent Christian commentators on the Gospel and on Isaiah.

A Child Is Given to Us:
The Wonderful Counselor

In the joyful proclamation of 9:2–6, the people come out of darkness into light, into the joy of harvest and of military victory. Victory fittingly precedes the people's declaration of the birth of a new ruler: "you have smashed the rod that was on their shoulder." The motif of the child continues from chapters 3 and 7, now with emphasis on innocence and beginnings. The people's declaration contains several messianic themes: dominion, might, peace, the throne of David, justice, and righteousness. Most regard the four-part name as a coronation or throne name used for Davidic kings.

For a child has been born to us, a son given to us,
And dominion[14] rests on his shoulders, and his name will be:
Wonderful Counselor, Mighty God, Eternal Father, Peaceful Prince.[15]

For the increase of dominion and for peace without limit
Upon the throne of David and upon his kingdom,
To establish it and uphold it in justice and righteousness from now
  and forevermore.
The zeal of the Lord of Hosts will accomplish this.

                                                              (9:6–7)

I translate literally to accentuate the ambiguity of the Hebrew text. The poet does not establish clear and explicit relationships, especially of cause and effect, between the increase of dominion and peace, the throne of David, and its establishment in justice. This is ultimately the work of the Lord, as is the rescue of Jerusalem and its remnant, for which the same phrase is employed (37:32). Translations of the passage differ widely, but they generally work to remove the ambiguity.

> His [the child's] authority shall grow continually,
>   and there shall be endless peace
> for the throne of David and his kingdom.
>   He will establish and uphold it
> with justice and with righteousness
>   from this time onward and forevermore.
> The zeal of the LORD of hosts will do this.
>
>   (NRSV)

> Of the increase of his government and peace
>   there will be no end.
> He will reign on David's throne
>   and over his kingdom,
> establishing and upholding it
>   with justice and righteousness
>   from that time on and forever.
> The zeal of the LORD Almighty
>   will accomplish this.
>
>   (NIV)

This vision of unending peace and justice is far grander than the immediate deliverance coming after the birth and naming of Immanuel. It is a powerful messianic vision that focuses more on the ongoing result, everlasting justice and peace, than on the child, the son, who bears another symbolic name and who, in unstated fashion, ushers in the new age.

The presentations of the children, Immanuel and this son with the glorious name, are both followed immediately by announcements of judgment. In 7:17 the Lord brings the king of Assyria; in 9:8; 10:5–6; and 10:16 the Lord sends first a word against the people, of Israel, then Assyria against the people, and finally a wasting disease, a burning, against both the people and Assyria. God the light turns into a fire.

> The Light of Israel becomes a fire and his Holy One a flame.
> It burns and devours his thorns and briers in one day.
> (10:17; see p. 50)

Characteristically the devastation is not total; the poet reintroduces the motif of the child: "The remnant of the trees of his forest will be so few that a child could write them down" (10:19). The child symbolizes inexperience and lack of ability but also alludes to the positive significance of Immanuel and of the royal child in this grim scene. The prophet displays a hopeful side in verses 20–27.

> In that day the remnant of Israel and the surviving band of the house of Jacob will no longer lean for support on the one who struck them but will faithfully lean for support on the Lord, the Holy One of Israel. (10:20)

A Shoot from the Stump of Jesse

At the close of chapter 10 the divine forester is hacking down the thick forest, but a remnant remains in the shoot or sprout growing from a stump and roots. The poem continues in 11:1–9 and details the attributes of the shoot, its actions, and the wondrous results of those actions. In my translation, I keep the shoot as the main character in verses 1–5; I use "it" in verses 1–2 and shift to "he" in 3–5 because "it" is too severe. I use the present tense to heighten the effect of the vision Isaiah presents us. We see the vision now, although it is of a world to come, a world yet to be. Finally, I begin the text with 10:33, instead of 11:1, to offer another example of how chapters and verses influence our reading.

Even though the poem is messianic in its royal themes and imagery, I do not speak of the shoot as a king, real or ideal. This is an aspect of a literal reading of Isaiah. The poet describes a shoot, a sprout, and the peaceable world (I deliberately avoid the loaded phrase "peaceable kingdom") that follows from the shoot's just treatment of the righteous and the wicked. For readers, ancient and modern, the shoot and the entire poem have had and still have many possible interpretations and applications, including seeing the shoot as an ideal king, Jesus, the word of the Lord, or the book of Isaiah. I leave it to my readers to choose and develop their own interpretation.

The shoot comes from the stump of Jesse, David's father. This can refer to the Davidic monarchy or to a replacement for the Davidic monarchy, a replacement pictured by a need to return to its roots for renewal. I favor the latter reading because the rest of chapter 11 says nothing about kings or monarchy. Chapter 11 portrays a world that kings have promised but a world now without kings. The shoot is endowed with four types of spirit, a list of many of Isaiah's most important positive qualities. Four indicates completion, as in the four corners of the earth or the four winds (v. 12; see Jer. 49:36 and Ezek. 37:9). Hebrew *ruach* means "spirit," but also "wind" and "breath" (Isa. 11:4); the four winds are, in a sense, the four spirits.

> Now look! The Sovereign, the Lord of Hosts,
>   is violently lopping off the boughs;
> The tallest trees are cut down; the lofty crash down.
> He hacks down the thickets of the forest with an ax,
>   and the Lebanon, in its majesty, topples.
> A shoot goes forth from the stump of Jesse,
>   and a sprout blossoms from its roots.
> The spirit of the Lord rests upon it, a spirit of wisdom
>   and understanding,
> A spirit of counsel and strength, a spirit of knowledge
>   and fear of the Lord.
>
> (10:33–11:2)

Verses 3–5 depict the shoot's actions in the world. Judging and deciding are what the Lord or the teaching of the Lord do in the vision of the mountain and the approaching nations in 2:2–4. I follow TNK's translation by reading the first sentence of verse 3 as an introduction to verses 3–5, not as the final clause in verses 1–2. Other translations reflect the latter understanding. In my rendering, the sentence explains how the shoot can judge by other than what he sees and hears; his reverence for the Lord gives him the uncanny ability to decide rightly and truthfully. The shoot performs the royal functions of justice, but he does not rule. Defense of the poor and destruction of the wicked are constant themes in Isaiah. In this aspect, the vision is not that far removed from our world. In terms of imagery, there are body parts, the rod (Assyria in 10:5; Babylon in 14:5), and clothing (see 59:6, 17).

His inspiration lies in fearing the Lord:[16]

> He does not judge by what his eyes see nor does he decide
>   by what his ears hear,
> But he judges the poor in righteousness, and he decides
>   with fairness for the weak of the land.
> He strikes the land with the rod of his mouth, and he kills
>   the wicked with the breath/spirit of his lips.
> Righteousness is a belt around his waist, and truthfulness a belt
>   on his hips.
>
> (11:3–5)

In verses 6–9 the poet returns to the paradisiacal world described at the close of Genesis 1, when animals and humans ate different grasses and not each other. The wild and the domestic join in the pastoral image of feeding and lying down. Isaiah's encyclopedic quality manifests itself in the number of terms for the animals (thirteen in two verses) and in the three different words for the child. The motif of the child connotes the innocence and vulnerability of the infant combined with the child's leadership. The child is part of the world that follows upon the shoot's unfailing justice and is not equated with the shoot. I am not equating Immanuel, the child born to us, the shoot, and this child. They are all part of Isaiah's grand vision, and there are varied and complex relationships between them and the society or worlds described in association with them.

The poet closes the poem with a vision of the Lord's holy mountain free of evil (see 1:4) and filled with knowledge (see 1:3 and 6:3). "My holy mountain" and "the earth" are a parallel pair accenting the expanse, the openness, and the accessibility of the site; it is like the sea. (I leave it to the reader to ponder how much of the poem is in fact spoken by the Lord, who says "*my* holy mountain.") Waters totally cover the sea, unlike the destructive flood that reaches only to the neck.

> The wolf dwells with the lamb, and the leopard lies down with
>   the kid, the calf, the young lion, and the fatling all together.[17]
> A small child leads them.

The cow and the bear graze, while their young lie down together;
    the lion[18] eats straw like the ox.
The nursing infant plays over the asp's hole, and the weaned child
    places its hand on the adder's lair.
They do neither evil nor corruption on my holy mountain,
For the earth is filled with the knowledge of the Lord as
    the waters cover the sea.

                                    (11:6–9)

Messianic Interludes

The image of the tent, which is analogous to that of the canopy or pavilion of chapter 4, occurs in a short passage in the midst of the poem proclaiming and lamenting the destruction of Moab. In 16:1–4a a Moabite remnant appeals to the ruler in Zion for refuge and shelter (see 4:5–6); their approach is described in verses 1–2 and their request voiced in verses 3–4a. The people as a whole reject the appeal. "We have heard of Moab's pride—how incredibly proud! . . . Therefore let Moab wail! Let all in Moab wail!" (vv. 6–7).

However, verses 4b–5 lie between the request and the refusal. Commentators debate who is speaking here and whether the speech is a positive or negative response to the refugees. Because of the ambiguity I present verses 3–5 without quotation marks. However we may understand verses 4b–5 in their context, they do present a scene of peace and of justice similar to those in chapters 9 and 11. The throne is in the tent of David, not a city or palace, and it is a judge, not a king, who presides there. This is another messianic passage that downplays, if not rejects, actual kings. In 11:1–9 the shoot judges and decides. The Hebrew terms for "judging" and "deciding" in the passage belong to the verbal roots for "justice" and "righteousness" (see pp. 51–54).

    "Give counsel; make a decision;
    Make your shade like night, even though it is high noon.
    Provide shelter for the outcasts;
    Do not expose the fugitive;
    Let the outcasts of Moab take asylum with you;
    Be a shelter to them from the destroyer."
    For the oppressor is gone,
    Destruction has ceased,
    The marauder has vanished from the country—

> A throne is established in love
> And on it will sit, in truth and in the tent of David,
> A judge, one who pursues justice and is prompt to act rightly.
>   (16:3–5)

In another dreamlike scene the prophet sees a king and princes; the terms, images, and themes of the dream are familiar.

> See! A king reigns with righteousness, and princes rule with justice.
> Each of them is like a refuge from the wind, a shelter from the storm,
> Like streams of water on dry ground, like the shade of a massive
>   rock in a thirsty land.
> And the eyes of those who see will not be sealed; the ears of
>   those who hear will pay attention;
> The minds of the thoughtless will gain understanding
>   and knowledge; the tongues of stammerers will speak fluently.
>   (32:1–4; see 29:17–24)

After denouncing fools and complacent women, the poet closes chapter 32 with a seductive picture of a transformed world of justice, peace, and security. It is a scene of farms, forests, and pastures, not fortified and walled cities. "My people live in a peaceful pasture, in secure dwellings and quiet resting places" (v. 18). And the transformed world is the result of "a spirit from on high [or from heaven] poured out on us" (v. 15), not of the work of a king or prince.

In chapter 33 the poet presents a mixture of proclamations of destruction and salvation spoken by the poet, the Lord, and the people. The Lord fulfills Isaiah's hopes.

> The Lord is exalted; indeed, he tents on high.
> He fills Zion with justice and righteousness; . . .[19]
> Abundant salvation, wisdom, and knowledge;
> The fear of the Lord, that is his treasure.
>   (33:5–6; see 11:3a)

"Tents" is usually translated "dwells" or such. I use "tents" to draw attention to the parallel with the imagery of tents and pavilions in 4:2–6 and 16:4b–5. The Lord "tents on Mount Zion" (8:18; see 57:15), and the upright "tents on high places, and rock fortresses are his exalted site" (33:16). My wooden translation brings to light the literal parallels of "high" and "exalted." Finally, the Lord declares that his servants will tent on his mountain (65:9). The image of God's mountain and the description of life on it are central to both Isaiah and this chapter in my book.

The prophet briefly mentions looking at "a king in his beauty" (33:17) but gives far more attention to the wondrous sight of Zion. He speaks as one of the people and leaves no doubt as to who the actual king and ruler is.

> Look at Zion, our festive city! Your eyes see Jerusalem:
> A quiet pasture, a tent[20] not to be moved, whose pegs will never
>   be pulled up, and none of its ropes will ever break.
> Indeed, the majestic Lord will be there for us: a place
>   of broad rivers and streams,
> Where no ship with oars can go, and no majestic ship pass through.
> For the Lord is our judge, the Lord is our lawgiver,
>   the Lord is our king, the Lord saves us.
>
> (33:20–22)

Prophet and Servant

Since much of the following discussion revolves around chapters 40–66, I need to speak further about these chapters in themselves and in their relation to 1–39. Chapters 40–66 are more sweeping in their proclamations, they no longer refer to specific named individuals, and their style is more conversational and argumentative. The chapters repeat themes and images of 1–39 with change and development. I do not overemphasize the differences between these two parts of the book of Isaiah; in fact, chapters 40–66 share most of the characteristics just listed with 24–27 and 34–35.

The eighth-century prophet Isaiah, son of Amoz, appears by name in chapters 1–39 (1:1; 2:1; 13:1; chaps. 7; 20; 37–39) and not at all in chapters 40–66. As I noted above, Isaiah, the poet and author of the book, is concerned more with prophecy and the role of prophet than he is with any particular prophet, including Isaiah son of Amoz (see pp. 126–27). The prophet is a messenger of the word of God who both reports and interprets the message in terms relevant to the particular audience. If one looks at the entire book, the prophet, who is a poet, writes a book, the vision of Isaiah, to present the message in a form that can be read by many audiences both then and in following ages.

The concern with the prophet's role, and not with a specific prophet, is evident in the anonymity of the opening proclamation of chapter 40. We do not know who is quoting God or to whom they are speaking, but a group and not an individual (the imperatives are plural) is commissioned as prophet to carry the divine message to Jerusalem. " 'Comfort, comfort my people,' says your God. 'Speak to the heart of Jerusalem. . . .'" The anonymity continues in the next verses; the imperatives "prepare" and "make straight" are both plural.

> A voice cries:
> "In the wilderness prepare the way of the Lord, make straight
>   in the desert a highway for our God. . . ."
> A voice cries, "Cry!" And he said,[21] "What shall I cry?"
> "All flesh is grass, and all their constancy like the flower
>   of the field. . . .
> The grass withers, the flower fades; but the word
>   of our God stands forever."
> Get up on a high mountain, O Zion, herald of good news;
> Raise your voice in a loud shout, O Jerusalem,
>   herald of good news;
> Raise it; fear not; say to the cities of Judah, "Here is your God!"
> (40:3–9)

Zion is appointed prophet to Judah's cities. The word of God passes through a prophetic chain until it reaches personified Zion. The "word of God that stands forever" refers first to the immediate message of comfort and salvation, then to other statements of God in the book, and finally to the book of Isaiah itself. Humans, including individual prophets, wither and fade, but the word of God, and the book of Isaiah, last forever.

The Servant Songs

The Lord's servant is another role, related to prophet, that the poet presents and expands in chapters 40–66. Chapters 40–41 depict the power of the Lord and of the divine word. The power is both creative and destructive, comforting and punishing. By contrast, idols and the gods they represent are powerless whether for weal or for woe. The Lord has both called Cyrus and has foretold it; the gods and their idols have done nothing like this (41:25–27). The last verses of chapter 41 and the first of 42 sharply contrast the gods with the Lord's servant. By printing the following passage without verse numbers or chapter break, I illustrate how such additions to a text partially obscure contrasts and connections between chapters. In addition, I read chapter 42 in the same way I read chapter 59, that is, as a chapter with general reference and not just to Israel (see pp. 156–57).

> I look and there is no one; among all these [gods and their idols],
>   there is no adviser who, when I ask, can answer anything.
> See, all of them are nothing; their works are zero;
>   their statues are an empty void.
> Here is my servant whom I uphold, my chosen in whom I delight.
> I have put my spirit upon him; he will bring justice to the nations.[22]
> He will not cry out or raise his voice or make it heard in the street;
> A bruised reed he will not break and a dim wick he
>   will not snuff out;[23]
> unfailingly he will bring justice.
> He will not dim nor will he bruise until he establishes
>   justice in the earth,
> and the coastlands look for his teaching.
>
> (41:28–42:4)

At the end of the nineteenth century the German commentator Bernhard Duhm isolated four parts of Isaiah 40–55 and maintained that they were independent poems by a different poet than the one who wrote the rest of Isaiah 40–55 (see p. 2). They present an individual servant of the Lord who is not obviously Israel personified as in 41:8–10: "You, O Israel, my servant!" He called the four poems The Servant Songs. His four songs are 42:1–4; 49:1–6; 50:4–9; and 52:13–53:12. Since Duhm, much ink has been spilled debating the extent of the poems; many feel that the first two can be 42:1–7 and 49:1–7 or even 49:1–12. Others have questioned whether the poems were originally independent of their context. Today few, if any, see the poems as the work of another poet or even as radically distinct poems within Isaiah; the poems are intense personifications that are an integral part of Isaiah. This is how I read them; I do not debate their extent, since I am not trying to isolate them as in any sense independent poems.

There is still extended debate about the identity of the servant. Proposals include a collective interpretation (e.g., all Israel or some part of Israel), an individual interpretation (e.g., a prophet such as

Jeremiah or a postexilic ruler), or a combination of the two. An example of the last regards the two poems in chapters 42 and 49 as Israel personified and the two in chapters 50 and 53 as the prophet.[24]

In the first part of Isaiah three people, representing prophecy and royalty, are called "servant of the Lord": Isaiah (20:3), Eliakim (22:20), and David (37:35). Isaiah is both servant and prophet; therefore, it should be no surprise that these are not distinct figures in chapters 40–66. To be the Lord's servant means both to carry out a divine commission or perform divine work, and to serve and worship the Lord. Anyone, even a foreigner, can be a servant of the Lord; anyone can perform divine tasks and worship God. As in the treatment of the prophet, I focus on what a servant does, on what the role of a servant is in Isaiah, and not on trying to identify a specific figure, real or ideal, group or individual, that the poet is trying to describe. A servant can be an individual, a group, or an entire nation. The Lord's holy mountain, the house of prayer, is open, accessible, and can include all.

> Foreigners who are joined to the Lord to minister to him,
>   to love his name, and *to be his servants*—
> All who keep the Sabbath by not profaning it and hold fast
>   to my covenant—
> I will bring them to my holy mountain and make them
>   happy in my house of prayer.
>
> (56:6–7)

Cyrus is an example of a foreigner joined to the Lord. He is the Lord's shepherd and anointed (44:28–45:1); both are royal, messianic titles. This is the only time that Isaiah uses the noun "the anointed," the messiah, and it refers to a foreign ruler, not a Davidic or Israelite king.

> Cyrus [is] my shepherd, and he will carry out all that I want.
> Thus says the Lord to his anointed [his messiah], to Cyrus,
>   whose right hand I grasp.
>
> (44:28–45:1)

Isaiah employs messianic themes and imagery in presenting his vision, but the vision does not revolve around a king, real or ideal, who is to appear in the future, near or distant. Cyrus is a servant not because he worships the Lord, but because he carries out the divine purpose by returning the people and restoring the city (44:28; 46:10). Cyrus is a type of the non-Israelite called to do the Lord's work. On one level, the prophet describes him and his achievements in the first servant poem in 42:1–4.

God chooses and supports the servant and places the divine spirit on him. This is reminiscent of that other strange and anonymous entity, the shoot.

> A shoot goes forth from the stump of Jesse. . . .
> The spirit of the Lord rests upon it. . . .
> He judges the poor in righteousness and he decides
>   with fairness for the weak of the land.
>
> (11:1–4)

The servant is not as violent as the shoot. He neither breaks nor is broken, but he works unceasingly and quietly to bring about justice, the way of the Lord. The servant's work involves all the earth (see 41:1).

After the initial servant poem, the poet continues in chapter 42 in this inclusive, anonymous vein. In verses 6–7 and at other points in the chapter, God speaks to, not about, the one called who is sent and who therefore is both servant and prophet, that is, one who acts and one who speaks. Prophet and servant are not two distinct roles, since delivering the word is performing the Lord's work.

> Thus says the God, the Lord, who creates the heavens,
>   who stretches them out, who spreads the earth
>   and what springs from it,
> Who gives breath to the people on it and spirit to those
>   who walk in it.
> "I, the Lord, I have called you in righteousness; I have taken
>   you by the hand;
> I have guarded you; I have given you as a covenant of people,
>   as a light of nations,†
> To open eyes that are blind, to bring the prisoner from
>   the dungeon, from the prison those who sit in darkness."
>
> (42:5–7)

---

†The meaning of neither of these phrases is clear. Translations and interpretations vary.

Because of these liberating actions, all will "sing to the Lord a new song," including the sea, the desert, and their inhabitants (vv. 10–12). The wide range of those who praise emphasizes that chapter 42 is not confined to speaking only to or about Israel.

The quiet, persistent efforts of the servant are not the only way to deal with the world, for the Lord turns to the way of war and acts like a warrior, a soldier (v. 13). God is "like a woman in labor" whose gasping "lays waste mountains and hills" (vv. 14–15). The violence is ultimately for the benefit of the blind, those in darkness.

> I lead the blind on a road they do not know;
>   on paths they do not know I guide them.
> The darkness before them I turn to light, the rough places
>   into level ground.
> These things I do; I do not abandon them.[25]
> Driven back and utterly ashamed are those who trust in a carved idol,
>   those who say to a molten idol, "You are our gods."
>   (42:16–17)

God condemns idol makers who know nothing and who bow down to a piece of wood, to a lie (44:18–20); this, at times in Isaiah, applies to Israel. By contrast, the Lord supports and rescues the blind because they are in need and in darkness, not because they are righteous and worthy of rescue.

> The poor and the needy are seeking water and there is none;
>   their tongue is parched with thirst.
> I the Lord answer them; I the God of Israel do not forsake them.
>   (41:17)

This too, many times in Isaiah, applies to Israel.

The close of chapter 42, verses 18–25, is a fine example of the complexity of Isaiah in terms of who is speaking, of who is spoken to and about, and of the relation of the general and the particular. In verses 18–20 the Lord addresses the deaf and blind, who are like, yet different from, the servant. God protects the blind and the servant, whoever they may be, but that does not make them perfect or deserving.

> You who are deaf, listen; and you who are blind, look up and see!
> Who is so blind as my servant, or so deaf as my messenger
>   whom I send?

Who is so blind as the special one,[26] so blind as the servant
    of the Lord?
Although you see many things, you take no heed;
    although his ears are open, he does not hear.

The shift from second to third person in the last line is in the Hebrew
(see KJV). It is addressed to the deaf and blind, who are like the Lord's
servant: you do not see and he does not hear. This is ironic. Those
who are called to listen and see are told that they do no such thing;
the prophet's initial commission includes the same paradox (see
6:9–10). The complexity continues in 42:21–25.

    The Lord is pleased, for the sake of his saving justice,
        to magnify and glorify the teaching.[27]
    But this is a people preyed upon and plundered,
        all of them trapped in pits, hidden in prisons;
    They have become prey with none to rescue; plunder
        with none to say, "Give back!"
    Who among you will listen to this, pay attention,
        and hear from now on?
    Who gave up Jacob for plunder and Israel to those
        preying upon him?
    Was it not the Lord whom we have sinned against?
    They were not willing to walk in his roads; they would
        not hear his teaching.
    And he poured upon him wrath, anger, and the fury of war;
    It blazed all about him, but he did not know; it burned him,
        but he did not take it to heart.

                                       (42:21–25)

    The plundered people are the imprisoned that God sent the ser-
vant to release (42:6–7). Israel is a prime example of such a people, but
they are not the only ones; they are a particular manifestation of the
general category. The poet or God questions the deaf about their lack
of attention. The process of questioning and the explicit question,
Who? stress the theme of knowledge. God cares for all needy, "so that
all may see and know, may consider and understand that the hand of
the Lord has done this" (41:20). Knowledge may be God's intention,
but it is not always the result. "Israel does not know, my people do not
understand" (1:3).
    The poet finally turns to Jacob-Israel, a specific people preyed upon

(see 10:5–6) and an example of how any people can be imprisoned. Israel is a plural group ("they" in 42:24) and a single nation ("he" in v. 25). "We," who sin against the Lord, are the deaf and blind addressed in verses 18–20. "They" are both like the servant ("you do not see and he does not hear") and like Jacob ("we sin and they do not follow the Lord"). Although punishment falls upon Israel and upon all who ignore the teaching, the result is still ignorance. People, Israelite and non-Israelite alike, are often unable to learn, whether for good or for evil. "The wicked is shown compassion—he does not learn righteousness" (26:10).

This lengthy analysis of one chapter in Isaiah exemplifies the complexity and ambiguity of speeches in Isaiah, especially, in this instance, who is spoken to and about. In addition, the discussion exemplifies different ways that translations deal with the complexities. My translation is literal and fits my present purposes, but this is not a claim that my translation is better than the others. The analysis illustrates why there are different translations and interpretations of this chapter, of other parts of Isaiah, and of the book as a whole. The tension and play between the particular and the general, the named and the anonymous, are the source of much of the richness and complexity of Isaiah.

The Servant Speaks for Himself

At the opening of chapter 49, the servant speaks personally and quotes the Lord extensively.

> Listen to me, O coastlands! Pay attention, O far peoples!
> The Lord called me in the womb; while in my mother's belly
>   he pronounced my name.
> He made my mouth like a sharp sword; in his hand's shadow
>   he hid me.
> He made me into a polished arrow; in his quiver he concealed me.
> He said to me, "You are my servant, Israel, in whom I am glorified."
> And I, I said, "I have wearied myself for nothing, for utter futility
>   I have spent myself."
> But it is not so. My cause is with the Lord, and my reward
>   with my God.
> Now the Lord, who formed me in the womb to be his servant,
>   has promised
> To restore Jacob to himself so that Israel will be gathered to him.

I am honored in the eyes of the Lord, and my God is my strength.
   He said,
"It is not enough that you are my servant,
that you raise up the tribes of Jacob, that you restore
   the survivors of Israel,
For I also make you a light of nations to extend my salvation
   to the end of the earth."

(49:1–6)

This picture is more like that of the shoot of chapter 11—both have deadly mouths—than that of the pacifist servant of chapter 42. Nor does this servant have the same patience as the latter; he feels that his efforts are wasted. In both poems the servant is a light of nations. Chapters 42 and 49 describe different ways to be the Lord's servant, different roles that a servant can fill. I see no reason to try to decide whether these are separate servants or one servant.

   The servant identifies himself as Israel, whom God formed in the womb (44:2, 24). The servant is to restore Israel, but how does Israel gather Israel? This increases the mystery of the servant. Is he perhaps not Israel but another character who is named Israel? Is this an instance of the distinction between an ideal and a real Israel, so that the servant is an ideal or symbolic Israel who restores the actual Israel to the Lord? Or do we posit a change of speaker, so that yet another servant, not personified Israel, starts speaking with "Now the Lord who formed me in the womb . . ."? Discussion reveals the richness and complexity of Isaiah without leading to only one way to read a given passage. I ask questions and provide no sure answers.

   Verses 7–12 continue the complexity and ambiguity. Verses 7 and 8 are separate quotations, both introduced by "Thus says the Lord"; this speech formula, so frequent throughout Isaiah, mixes the roles of prophet and servant. God speaks first to "one despised, abhorred by the nation, the slave[28] of rulers." Combined with the servant's frustration, this terminology forms part of the image of the Suffering Servant whose afflictions continue in 50:4–9 and 52:13–53:12. His ultimate vindication is indicated in the present context:

"Kings will see and rise up; princes, and they
   will prostrate themselves;
Because of the Lord who is faithful, the Holy One of Israel—
   he has chosen you."

Thus says the Lord, "In a favorable time I answered you,
    and on a day of salvation I helped you;
I formed you and appointed you a covenant of people
    to raise up the land, to allot the desolate heritages."
Saying[29] to prisoners, "Come out!" to those in darkness,
    "Show yourselves!"

                                      (49:7–9a)

Exodus imagery marks verses 9b–12: they—Israel and other captives—return from all parts of the earth. God is both spoken of and a speaker.

They pasture by roads, and by bare trails they have pasture.
They neither hunger nor thirst, and neither wind nor sun
    batters them,
For he who loves them leads them, and to springs of water
    he guides them.
I turn all my mountains into a road, and my highways
    are built up.
See these, they come from afar; see these, from the north
    and the west; and these, from the land of Sinim.[30]

The rest of chapter 49 focuses on Zion, a woman in a debased condition that is similar to that of the servant, a man. "Zion says, 'The Lord has forsaken me, my Lord has forgotten me'" (v. 14). Her ultimate vindication is anticipated. (The same pattern of destruction and restoration is present in the first reference to Jerusalem in 1:21–26.) The Lord does not forget her, and her children return in droves.

Your adversaries I contend with, and your children I save. . . .
All flesh will know that I am the Lord, your Savior,
    your Redeemer, the Mighty One of Jacob.
(49:25–26; the second person pronouns are feminine singular)

Isaiah portrays people and city, man and woman, as first broken and humiliated and then restored and vindicated. The pattern fits with themes of both justice and mercy and adds to the richness of Isaiah. God punishes and restores because the responses are merited by sin and by repentance; God destroys in anger and restores because of love and privilege—these are God's people. The servant, the man, speaks in 50:4–9, and perhaps in verses 10–11. He is called, disgraced, and then vindicated.

> The Sovereign, the Lord, has given me a skilled tongue
>   to know how to sustain the weary with a word.[31]
> Every morning he wakens my ear so that I might listen
>   as the skilled do. . . .
> I gave my back to those beating me, and my cheeks to those
>   pulling out my beard;
> I did not turn my face from disgrace or spit.
> But the Sovereign, the Lord, he helps me. Therefore I am
>   not disgraced.
> Therefore I have set my face like flint, and I know that
>   I will not be ashamed. . . .
> Yes, the Sovereign, the Lord helps me! Who can convict
>   me of anything?
> All who do will rot like clothing; the moth will eat them.
>
> (50:4–9)

Although he is not to be convicted, the servant has no trouble condemning others.

A Man and a Woman

Jerusalem, the woman, is addressed and her restoration promised at points in 51:17–52:10. The woman is a counterpoint to the servant, the man. The contrast of the man and the woman reaches a high point in chapters 53 and 54. The great Servant Song, 52:13–53:12, has received large amounts of attention over the years, not so the Song of the Woman in chapter 54. This certainly reflects, in part, the fact that most commentators have been men with a decided male focus. I want to join efforts to counter this heavy male focus. And, consistent with my interpretive purposes, my goal is to reveal the intricacies and the wealth to be found in reading the vision of Isaiah and not to establish only one way to read Isaiah, only one way to identify the servant and the woman.

Both poems reveal the surprising treatment that one specially chosen by God may have to undergo. The treatment can be at the hands of God or of humans. In regard to such treatment of the chosen, no distinction is made between a man and a woman. I stress the anonymity of those portrayed in these poems; they present patterns for God's ways with the world and not just with Israel and Israelites. Both poems reveal the tensions and even the contradictions that exist between expectations of justice and mercy. They are inspiring and shocking, comforting and troubling, and this is a major source of their fascination for readers. Isaiah, as usual, does not present us with a vision of a perfect world of peace and justice.

David Clines has read our first poem in terms of the four pronouns in it without trying to identify them with characters beyond this poem.[32] "I" (who says "my" servant) is the Lord, who speaks in the beginning (52:13) and at the close (53:11–12). "He" is "my servant" when the Lord speaks (52:13; 53:11), and just "he" to the other speakers. Unlike chapters 49 and 50, here the servant does not speak on his own. He is presented to readers only through the eyes of others. The third group are "they," who, like the Lord, appear at the beginning (52:14–15) and at the end (53:9–12). "We," a fourth group or perhaps "they" speaking, speak in 53:1–6.

The Lord declares the servant's victory. Height recalls Jerusalem (2:2) and the Lord (6:1). Whether the Lord continues to speak beyond this opening is not clear; the prophet-poet could easily pronounce the rest of the passage.

> See how he prospers, my servant; he is high, lifted up,
> very exalted.
> Just as many were shocked by him[33]—
> So marred was his appearance that he was not a person,
> and his form that he was not human—
> So he startles[34] many nations, and kings clamp
> shut their mouths because of him;
> For what they have not been told they see,
> and what they have not heard they understand.
>
> (52:13–15)

There is a distinction between the one, the servant, and the many, the nations and kings. At the end of the poem, the servant carries the sins of the many (53:11–12). Part of the fascination of the poem is the stark contrast of the solitary servant, and his God, with all those around him who thought they knew God's ways but who are now amazed at the servant's status.

The verses hint at a distinction between appearance and reality and assume that a change has occurred over time, a change from misery to glory. Change is a central hope and proclamation of the vision of

Isaiah; it is the promise that a time of suffering and disaster will pass and will be replaced by times of joy and prosperity. The promise stands in tension with the fact that humans, whether Israel or the nations, do not always change and that their continuing resistance to the divine and prophetic word blocks this positive change from misery to glory. The final statement is reminiscent of, although the opposite of, the paradox of the Lord's message to the prophet that stresses lack of change: "Listen carefully but do not understand; look closely but do not know" (6:9).

Chapter 53 opens as "we" speak. The distinction of the many, "we," and the one, "he," continues. "They," of the close of chapter 52, and "we" may be the same. "We" may have heard and now know, since "the Lord bared his holy arm in the sight of all the nations" (52:10). There are no solid reasons, however, to think that the nations and kings have to be those now speaking; "they" and "we" can be two different groups standing over against the servant. That leaves open the identity of "we," which is a familiar situation encountered while reading Isaiah.

The statement in 53:1–6 is a quotation (marked as such in TNK). I assume that the prophet and/or the Lord speak in verses 7–10 and that the Lord definitely speaks in verses 11–12, although another source of the difficulty of the poem is the question of just who is speaking in verses 7–10. This group, "we," confirm that they were misled by the servant's pathetic appearance; the reality of his status is totally different. They testify that, despite powerful human resistance, change can happen, people can see and understand, "they can turn and be healed" (6:10). What is not stated is how and why this group experienced the change, how they came to realize that the appearance is not the reality. This lack underscores that the possibility of change is the issue, not how or why it comes about.

> Who would believe what we have heard?
> To whom has the arm of the Lord been revealed?[35]
> He grew up before him like a sapling, like a root from dry ground;
> He had no form, no beauty, that we should look at him,
>   nor appearance that we should find him pleasing.
> He was despised and shunned by others; a man of suffering,
>   familiar with disease;
> As one who hid his face from us,[36] despised, we thought
>   him worthless,

Yet it was our diseases that he bore, our suffering that he carried.
Still we, we thought him stricken, battered, and afflicted by God,
But he, he was wounded for our transgressions,
    crushed because of our guilt.
The punishment that restored us was upon him,
    and by his bruises we were healed.
All of us, like sheep, have wandered off; we have gone
    our own ways.
But the Lord laid upon him the guilt of all of us.

(53:1–6)

Even though this is God's servant, it is God who has punished and crushed him. His miserable state is a result not of his own sin, as in much of Isaiah, but of that of many others. This is an unexpected twist on themes of justice and mercy; sin is punished, but the punishment falls on another. "We" are correct in thinking that God has afflicted him, but it is for "our" guilt, not his. It is not just that one suffers because of the sins of another, but that the suffering of one somehow results in the restoration and cure of all these others. Jerusalem bears the effects of her children's evil. "It was because of your sins that you were sold, and because of your transgressions that your mother was sent away" (50:1).

Because of the references to this Isaianic text in the Gospels, a long-standing Christian interpretation of Isaiah puts this poem in a christological context, reads the servant as Christ, and sees this as a process of vicarious suffering and atonement. "That is, that through his [the servant's] own unmerited suffering he enabled others to escape the divine punishment that they deserved."[37] In Isaiah people are punished and suffer for their own iniquity. A large portion of Isaiah's vision declares that the iniquity has been forgiven and that the time of desolation is over or soon to be over. In Isaiah and in the rest of the Hebrew Bible, there is no hint that God will accept the suffering of the innocent and righteous in place of the punishment of the guilty and wicked. People may well suffer unjustly or excessively—Jerusalem "has received from the Lord's hand double for all her sins" (40:2)—but not in place of the deserved punishment of others.

Wisdom of Solomon 4:20–5:23 contains an ancient Jewish interpretation of this Servant Song. (Scholars usually date Wisdom in the first century B.C.E. or first century C.E.) The servant is the righteous taken as a group. The unrighteous realize the error of their previous view of the righteous and also the error of their sinful ways. The righteous are with the Lord, and the unrighteous perish in their lawlessness. There is no hint of the vicarious suffering of the righteous in this interpretation.

To return to the Isaianic poem, the servant has borne and suffered for the sins of the many, whether "we" or "they." These others express their sheer amazement at this turn of events and at their past gross misunderstanding of what was happening to the servant; this is the thrust of the poem, and not whether they have also suffered and borne the effects of their iniquity. Indeed, that "we" speak of being restored and healed (53:5) assumes previous affliction. The human surprise at the error of having taken appearance for reality is expressed by God in other words:

> Indeed, my thoughts are not your thoughts nor are your ways
>   my ways—says the Lord.
> For as the heavens are higher than the earth, so are my ways
>   higher than your ways and my thoughts than your thoughts.
>   (55:8–9)

The poem is, then, an enigmatic and intense illustration of this divine utterance.

The remainder of the poem details the servant's agony and eventual vindication by God. I discuss omitted portions in notes because the Hebrew text is too uncertain to translate. One of the uncertain lines, 53:10a, is central to an interpretation of the servant's fate as vicarious suffering, and therefore I discuss it in the main text, not a note. NRSV renders:

> Yet it was the will of the LORD to crush him with pain.
> When you make his life an offering for sin,
>   he shall see his offspring. . . .

TNK:

> But the LORD chose to crush him by disease,
> That, if he made himself an offering for guilt,
> He might see offspring. . . .

(Both note: "Meaning of Heb. uncertain.") It is not certain that the servant is portrayed as actually dead in the passage. Being cut off from the living and having his grave prepared certainly imply death, but they can be expressions of extreme agony. The servant is on the verge of death, and others treat him as already dead by readying his tomb.

> He was maltreated and afflicted, but he did not open his mouth.
> Like a lamb led to slaughter, like a ewe before its shearers,
> He was silent and did not open his mouth.
> He was arrested, sentenced, taken away;[38] who could imagine
>   his fate?[39]
> For he was cut off from the land of the living, stricken because
>   of the transgression of my people.
> They placed his grave among the wicked, and his tomb
>   with the rich
> Although he had done nothing violent, and no deceit
>   was in his mouth. . . .
> He sees his descendants; he prolongs his life; the Lord's pleasure
>   prospers through him.
> Despite his anguish, he sees it [the Lord's pleasure];
> an innocent man, my servant, declares the many innocent,
>   and their guilt he bears.
> Therefore I allot him a portion among the many, and with the
>   strong he divides booty,
> Because he poured out his life to death[40] and was counted
>   among transgressors.
> And he, he bears the sin of many and intercedes for transgressors.
>   (53:7–12)

The book of Isaiah would be a different book and we would read this poem in a different way if the book ended here. Isaiah's vision reaches compelling high points and then continues on, repeating what has gone before, including the high points. The high points are not final conclusions. The two-part poem of chapters 34–35 is a good example of a high point of destruction and restoration that is not a conclusion. This formal feature of the vision reflects the inclusive nature of Isaiah, the drive to say as many things as possible, even if cryptic or contradictory, about a topic or a character. In chapter 53, in this poem of intense agony and ultimate exaltation, we are given one view, which is formed from the combination of several perspectives, of the servant. It is a significant view, but it is not the only one, and it is not a summary view that ties everything up in one neat bundle.

A lengthy poem of encouragement to a barren and depressed woman follows this enigmatic poem. Although her husband abandoned her in a fit of rage, he said nothing about any wrong that she did to merit this treatment. The husband returns and offers her compassion and love and, reading between the lines, asks her to forgive and forget, to accept his offer despite the past. This can be troubling for a modern reader familiar with the pattern of wife beating by an angry, abusive husband. The image joins the other violent images of God in Isaiah that similarly shock and disturb. Isaiah roots his vision in the human reality of this world and includes the extremes of human good and evil and all that is in between; Isaiah portrays God in the terms and images of this world and all its good and evil.

As in my discussion of the servant, I leave open the question of the woman's identity. This is not obviously Zion-Jerusalem personified as a woman; this was the case in 49:14–26.[41] In the latter passage, Zion's children return to her; this woman's are yet to be born. Despite the grim past, her fortunes are taking a decided turn for the better. She, with the servant, illustrates the possibility of change that underlies calls for repentance and divine promises of restoration. Just as Israel and Israelites are one manifestation of being a servant, Zion is one manifestation of this woman. But it is the pattern of divine and human ways that is central to both of these poems, not who the woman or the servant might be. In the Hebrew Bible the woman who has borne no children can be Sarah or Hannah just as well as Jerusalem.

> Sing, O barren woman who has borne no children;
>   break into song, shout, you who have not labored!
> For the children of the desolate woman will be more than those
>   of the married woman—says the Lord.
> Enlarge the site of your tent; let the walls of your tents stretch out.
> Do not hold back: lengthen your ropes and drive your pegs in firmly,
> For you are bursting out on the right and the left.
> Your descendants will dispossess nations and will again live in
>   the now desolate cities.
>
>   (54:1–3)

The once barren woman becomes the mother of a large nomadic tribe who are now living in tents but who will soon drive out the nations inhabiting desolate cities. The event is reminiscent of Israel's wilderness and conquest traditions in Numbers and Joshua. Before the woman can rejoice in this imminent future, she must be freed from her violent and shame-ridden past. In verses 4–10 the poet addresses these concerns, and, as so often in Isaiah, we have a mix of divine and prophetic speech.

> Do not be afraid, for you are not shamed; do not feel disgraced,
>   for you are not humiliated.
> You will indeed forget your youthful shame and no longer
>   remember the dishonor of being a widow.
> Because your husband is your maker: the Lord of Hosts
>   is his name!
> Your Redeemer is the Holy One of Israel: he is called God
>   of the Entire Earth!
> Yes, the Lord calls to you as though you were a wife abandoned
>   and deeply distressed,
> a rejected wife married when one was young—says your God.
> For a brief moment I abandoned you, but with great love
>   I bring you back.
> In an outburst of rage I hid my face from you for a moment,
>   but with everlasting mercy I love you—
> says your Redeemer, the Lord.
> For this is the time of Noah for me—
> Just as I swore that the waters of Noah would never again
>   cover the earth,
> I swear the same concerning my rage toward you
>   and my rebuke of you:
> "The mountains may shake and the hills crumble, but my mercy
>   for you will never be shaken, nor will my covenant of peace
>   ever crumble"—says your lover,[42] the Lord.
>
> (54:4–10)

To promote human change, the Lord promises divine unchangeability. To put it simply, "I will not do that again!" Yet, as we have seen in Isaiah, these merciful attributes are only one aspect of the portrayal of God, and they stand in tension with just and punishing attributes and with overflowing wrath (v. 8 NRSV; see 30:27–28).

In verses 11–17a the Lord addresses the woman with city images that strengthen the connection with Zion but that do not turn this into a simple personification of the city. The intent of the final verses, 15–17a, is difficult to determine. Although God asserts that the woman will be far from any oppression or terror, some may still attack her. Although God does not send them and although they fail, they will attack. The Lord creates smiths, who in turn fashion instruments of destruction; the latter allude to Assyria and Babylon, the rod and club, who wreaked havoc on Israel and the rest of humanity. But now no attack will be effective against this woman.

> O you miserable woman, storm-tossed and uncomforted,
> Look at me! I am setting your stones with the finest mortar[43]
>   and laying your foundations with sapphires;
> I make your towers with gleaming rubies, your gates
>   with precious stones, and your walls with gemstones.
> All your children are taught by the Lord, and great is their
>   happiness.
> You are established through righteousness.
> You are far from oppression—fear nothing!—and from terror—
>   it will not come near you!
> If anyone should attack you, they are not sent by me;
> whoever does attack you will fall before you.
> See I, I have created the smith who blows on the burning coals;
> He produces a tool fit for its work, and I, I have created
>   an instrument of destruction:
> Any tool fashioned against you will not succeed; any tongue
>   that rises to accuse you, you will refute.
>
> (54:11–17a)

These grand promises of compassion and of peace apply to all servants of the Lord.

> This [the grand promises] is what comes to the servants of the Lord,
>   and it is what they have a right to expect from me[44]—says the Lord.
>
> (v. 17b)

The plural "servants" occurs in the rest of the book; the singular "servant" does not occur after 53:11. The servants, just as any one servant, are those who serve the Lord in proper worship and who do the divine work and will. In Isaiah 55–66 they stand in contrast to the Lord's enemies, those who go their own way and reject the Lord. The poems in chapters 53–54, however, with their enigmatic portrayals of the servant and of the woman, remind us that God's ways are not so simple and that the world is not so clear-cut.

As an example, the initial verses of chapter 55 follow immediately upon the passage just cited, and they continue the note of mercy but soon return to the theme of justice. The themes of listening and eating what is good recall the choice of following the Lord or not, issued by the prophet in 1:19–20.

> Ho! All who thirst come to the waters; all without money come!
> Buy and eat; come, buy wine and milk without money, without cost.
> Why spend your money for what is not food, and your labor
>   for what does not satisfy?
> Listen closely to me, and then eat what is good and delight
>   in rich food.
> Bend your ear and come to me; listen so that you may have life
> And so that I may make an everlasting covenant with you,
>   the enduring loyalty promised to David. . . .
> Seek the Lord while he is to be found; call to him while he is near.
> Let the wicked forsake their way and the worthless their thoughts;
> let them return to the Lord that he may have mercy on them,
>   and to our God, for he pardons abundantly.
> Indeed, my thoughts are not your thoughts, nor are your
>   ways my ways—says the Lord.
>
> (55:1–8)

Before turning to Isaiah 61, I briefly depart from the sequential order of Isaiah and return to chapter 47. At several different points, I have detailed Isaiah's rich portrayals of both Zion and Babylon as characters. Here, in concert with my reading of the woman in chapter 54 and of the man in chapter 53, I focus on some similar elements in these portrayals. The Lord declares to the woman, "For a brief moment I abandoned you. . . . In an outburst of rage I hid my face from you for a moment" (54:7–8). This is similar to the declaration to Lady Babylon in which the Lord sharply distinguishes Babylon from Israel.

> I was angry with my people, I defiled my heritage.
> I gave them into your power; you showed them *no mercy*.
> You made your yoke exceedingly heavy on the aged.
>
> (47:6)

The Lord stirs up the Medes against Babylon, and "they have *no mercy* on infants and no pity on children" (13:18). As for the chosen people:

> The Lord *does not* spare their youths or *have mercy*
>   on their orphans and widows,
> For all of them are ungodly and evil, everyone speaks
>   only impiety.
>
>   (9:17)

The chosen are "a people without understanding; therefore, he who made them *will not have mercy* on them, and he who formed them will not have compassion on them" (27:10).

Beyond the association of Babylon and the chosen people, symbolized at times by Zion, I only note and do not pursue the very troubling parallel between Babylon and the Lord, both of whom can refuse to show mercy. We have encountered portrayals of God as both a brutal and violent and a comforting and merciful Deity, and we have seen Israel and Jerusalem as faithful and rebellious and as glorious and desolate. Similar to the presentation in chapter 54, in the last half of chapter 47 the poet condemns a confident and arrogant woman. The condemnation counters the reassurance of the barren woman in chapter 54. Although chapter 47 begins as a denunciation of Lady Babylon, verses 8–15 are against any proud woman or city personified: Zion, Tyre, or Babylon. In fact, other than the name Babylon, nothing in chapter 47 connects the woman directly with a city.[45] In chapter 48 the prophet picks up on a reading as Zion and denounces "the house of Jacob," "those who name themselves after the Holy City" (48:1–2).

> But now hear this, O voluptuous woman, you who reign securely,
> You who say in your heart, "I am and there is none other but me.
> I do not reign as a widow; I do not experience the loss of children."
> Both of these will happen to you in a moment, in one day:
> The loss of children and widowhood will happen to you
>   in full measure,
> Despite your many enchantments and the great power
>   of your spells.
> You trust in your evil; you say, "No one sees me."
> Your wisdom and your skill, they lead you astray,
> And you say in your heart, "I am and there is none other but me."
> But evil happens to you that you cannot conjure away;
> Disaster falls upon you that you are unable to avert;
> Ruin happens to you suddenly, and you had no hint of it.
> Stand firm in your spells and in your many enchantments,

Which you have practiced to exhaustion from your youth;
Perhaps you will be able to succeed; perhaps you will strike terror—
You are worn out with your many consultations.
Let them stand and save you, those who study the heavens
    and gaze at the stars,
Those who predict at each new moon what will happen to you.
But look, they are like stubble, fire burns them;
They cannot save themselves from the power of the flame.
This is not a coal to warm oneself by, nor a fire to sit before!
Such to you are they with whom you have exhaustively traded
    from your youth—
Each wanders on his own way—there is none to save you!

(47:8–15)

The Anointed, Once Again

Chapters 60–62 are a centerpiece in the final section of Isaiah (see pp. 39–40). They glow with images of light, abundance, gardens, and brilliant jewels and garments; and they are replete with themes of joy, return, triumph, salvation, and restoration. In the middle of the piece, an anonymous speaker announces that the Lord has designated him or her for an awesome mission. The chapter is an excellent summary of most of Isaiah's positive themes, with a hint of the negative. Rebuilding ancient ruins presumes the time that grand cities of the past were turned into these ruins.

The speaker's anonymity accords with Isaiah's concern for what any prophet or servant of the Lord may be and may do. Many people and even things in Isaiah fill, or at least partially fill, the role of this speaker: a prophet, the prophet Isaiah, a servant of the Lord, Israel, Cyrus, Zion, and even the book of Isaiah. I detail what the chapter says and depicts and do not argue for one specific identity for the speaker. Although in my reading I assume Israel as the primary recipient of the divine mission and beneficence, I do not thereby exclude other peoples as worthy recipients of the same.

In the opening of chapter 61 (vv. 1–4), the speaker defines the commissioning, the mission itself, and the result. The terms, the imagery, and the themes are familiar and call to mind many of the passages that we have discussed. The commissioning involves the divine spirit, anointing and sending; the mission is a series of seven infinitives ("to announce," etc.); the result is a pronouncement of the renaming and the rebuilding.

The spirit of the Sovereign, the Lord, is upon me because
    the Lord has anointed me;
He has sent me to announce good news to the poor,
    to bind up the brokenhearted,
To proclaim release to captives and liberty to prisoners,
To proclaim a year of favor for the Lord and a day of vengeance
    for our God,
To comfort all mourners, to provide for the mourners of Zion,
To give them a glorious crown in place of ashes,[46] festive oil
    in place of mourning, a choice cloak in place of a despairing spirit.
They will be called The Righteous Oaks, The Lord's Planting,
    to glorify him.
They will rebuild the ancient ruins; the old desolate sites
    they will erect;
They will restore the ruined cities that have been desolate
    for so long.

In verses 5–7 the anonymous speaker may continue or there may
be a change of speaker to the prophet or the Lord. In any case, the
speaker addresses the people ("you" is masculine plural), although he
does shift and speak in the third person in verse 7.

Aliens will stand ready to feed your flocks; foreigners will be
    your farmers and vinedressers.
But you, you will be called Priests of the Lord, Ministers of
    our God you will be named;
The wealth of nations you will eat, and in their riches you will revel.
    . . . .[47]
Therefore in their land they will inherit a double share;
    eternal joy will be theirs.

The aliens and foreigners who once devoured Israel's land and who
could minister to and serve the Lord (1:7; 56:6–7) are farmworkers in
this passage. The people are the Lord's priests and ministers. They
inherit a double share and eternal joy (see 35:10). The double share
may be of the land, of honor, or of joy.

The Lord, who may have uttered verses 5–7, explicitly intervenes
in verses 8–9 to declare his stand and how he will treat the people.

For I the Lord love justice, and I hate robbery covered
    with a burnt offering.[48]

I will give them their due faithfully, and an everlasting covenant
  I will make with them.[49]
Their descendants will be known in the nations,
  and their offspring in the midst of the peoples;
All who see them will recognize them, that they are a race
  [descendants] the Lord has blessed.

Descendants, translated "race" in the last line, and offspring were the recipients of God's spirit and blessing in 44:3 (see pp. 81 and 108). At that point I noted the double meaning of the Hebrew terms, both human and plant seed and produce. Plant imagery is central to verses 3 and 11.

The speaker of the opening announcement, or perhaps the prophet, declares his joy in the Lord's grand accomplishments and his personal resolve that comes from that joy. The latter is the first verse of chapter 62; I regard the chapter as spoken mostly, if not entirely, by the speaker of the closing verse of chapter 61. I restrict my present analysis, however, to only 61:10–62:1.

I greatly rejoice in the Lord; my very being delights in my God;
For he has clothed me in triumphal garments,
  and a victory robe he has wrapped about me,[50]
As a bridegroom dons a glorious crown, and as a bride adorns
  herself with her jewelry.
For as the earth sends forth its sprouts, and as a garden
  makes the sown sprout,
So the Sovereign, the Lord, makes victory and renown sprout
  before all the nations.
For Zion's sake I will not keep silent, and for Jerusalem's sake
  I will not rest,
Until her victory shines forth like a bright light,
  and her triumph burns like a torch.

The clothing imagery alludes, among other texts, to the garb of the shoot (11:5) and of the Lord (59:17; see 59:6). Because the Lord donned armor, the speaker dons robes worn to celebrate triumph. "Triumphal" and "triumph" in the passage translate the Hebrew terms translated "victory," "salvation," and "deliverance" by other translators or in other settings in Isaiah (see pp. 51–54). "Victory" in the passage translates the term also translated "righteousness," "vindication," and "what is to be expected."[51] The passage is another fine example of how Isaiah combines, through the use of the same terms, themes of justice, deliverance, salvation, and victory. The terms carry social, military, and religious connotations. A society, a people, who live justly and righteously will experience deliverance and triumph in all aspects of their lives.

In 62:1 the speaker declares a resolve not to remain silent, a resolve that reiterates the mission to announce and proclaim issued in 61:1–3. Here the speech on Zion's behalf is repeated to the Lord, to Zion, and to all others who can work on Jerusalem's behalf. Light and fire imagery are dominant in chapter 60.

The Worm That Never Dies

I close my book with the close of Isaiah's book. The final verses illustrate many of the issues and problems that we have encountered in reading Isaiah. First are textual and translation concerns. Translations differ on whether they print the verses in prose or poetry. For example, NIV prints all of 66:18–24 in prose, while TNK puts verses 18–21 in prose and 22–24 in poetry. Parts of the Hebrew text itself are unclear. Translations differ on how they deal with the problems; I comment on the most troublesome ones. Second, the passage is a characteristic mix of imagery and themes appearing with positive and negative valuations. The prophet opened the chapter denouncing the plans to rebuild the temple and the sacrifices offered there (vv. 1–3). In verses 20–21 offerings and priests are positive signs. Third, the nations, Israel, and all flesh are presented with no clear distinctions among them. Even in his final scenes, Isaiah maintains his tension and balance between the general and the particular. He maintains his inclusive, universal vision. All who serve the Lord and walk in his light can come to the Lord's holy mountain Jerusalem. All gather to see and to announce the Lord's glory. Isaiah continues his encyclopedic quality in the detailed lists of nations and animals.

> I [know] their deeds and their thoughts;[52] it is coming[53] to gather all nations and tongues; they come and see my glory. I place a sign among them and I send survivors from them[54] to the nations— Tarshish, Pul,[55] and Lud (those who draw the bow),[56] Tubal and Javan—the far coastlands that have not heard of my fame or seen my glory. And they will proclaim my glory to the nations.
>
> They bring all your kin from all the nations as an offering to the Lord—on horses, in chariots, in wagons, on asses, and on

camels—on my holy mountain Jerusalem, says the Lord, just as the Israelites bring the offering, in clean vessels, to the house of the Lord. And I even take from them some to be priests and Levites. (66:18–21)

Isaiah fittingly closes his vision with the juxtaposition of a dream and a nightmare, of salvation and destruction, but the close is unsettling because of this very juxtaposition. I end with it, realizing that my book thereby ends on a similar note. Isaiah does not resolve all the tensions and problems of humans and of God in his vision, and I have not tried to find or to force some resolution in my reading.

The people have the durability of the Lord's word (40:8). All gather for unending worship on the holy mountain, but they are only a short way from the smoldering corpses of the rebels. "Rebels and sinners are destroyed together" (1:28).

As the new heavens and the new earth, which I am making,
    stand before me—saying of the Lord—so does your seed
    and your name stand.
And further from new moon to new moon
    and from Sabbath to Sabbath,
All flesh comes to bow down before me—says the Lord.
They go out and see the bodies of the people who rebel against me.
Their worm will never die; their fire will never be quenched;
    they will be a horror for all flesh.

(vv. 22–24)

Endnotes to Chapter 5

1. In 1 Kgs. 19:15–16 God commands Elijah to anoint Hazael and Jehu as kings of Damascus and Israel and Elisha as a prophet to succeed himself. This is the only mention of anointing a prophet. Only Jehu is actually anointed and then by an unnamed prophet, not Elijah. Elisha foresees Hazael's rule as king, but he does not anoint him (2 Kgs. 8:7–15). Although Elijah grants Elisha "a double portion" of his holy spirit, he does not anoint him (2 Kgs. 1:9–12).
2. The HB refers to the claims of the Davidic dynasty, the rulers of Judah. We do not know if the kings of Israel made similar claims. Beyond Isaiah, I draw on the following texts: 2 Samuel 7; 22 (= Ps. 18); 23:1–7; Pss. 2; 45; 72; 89; 110; 132.
3. This is an unknown place, usually located in the western Mediterranean; see Isa. 23:6; 66:19; Jonah 1:1–3.
4. I follow *Harper's Bible Dictionary* in regarding these as two spellings for the same place, i.e., Saba in southwest Arabia, the area that is now Yemen; see Isa. 43:3 and 60:6. Others locate Sheba in Africa, south of Egypt.

5. See Levenson, *Creation and the Persistence of Evil*; and Ollenburger, *Zion, the City of the Great King* (see p. 167). Hammurabi was king of Babylon from about 1728 to 1686 B.C.E. and is noted in world history for his law code. In the prologue to the code, Hammurabi claims:

> Anum and Enlil [Babylonian sky-god and storm-god, respectively] named me
>   to promote the welfare of the people,
> me, Hammurabi, the devout, god-fearing prince,
> to cause justice to prevail in the land,
> to destroy the wicked and the evil . . .
> Hammurabi, the shepherd . . .
> the king who has made the four quarters of the world subservient. . . .
> When Marduk [god of Babylon] commissioned me to guide the people aright,
>   to direct the land,
> I established law and justice in the language of the land.
> (*Ancient Near Eastern Texts Relating to the Old Testament*, ed. James B. Pritchard;
>   3d ed. [Princeton: Princeton University Press, 1969], 164–65).

6. This is close to TNK. Others reveal different possible meanings: "We have a fortress city, the walls and ramparts provide safety" (NJB); "A strong city have we; he sets up walls and ramparts to protect us" (NAB).

7. Verse 3 is uncertain.

8. This is literally "Yah Yahweh." 12:2 has the same phrase; see pp. 134 and 166.

9. "He judges" can be rendered "It judges," "it" referring to God's teaching and word.

10. "Temple" occurs three times in Isaiah: 6:1; 44:28; 66:6. The word for temple, *hekal*, also means "palace" in Hebrew and occurs in 13:22 and 39:7. The temple, in a sense, is God's palace.

11. This is the Hebrew text. TNK renders, "And thus it all came into being" (see NAB and NIV). NRSV reflects the Greek reading, "and so all these things are mine" (see NJB and REB) and notes that the Hebrew is different.

12. It is not clear what specific age is meant by this phrase. 8:4 indicates a fairly young age, "Before the boy knows how to say 'my father and my mother.'"

13. Gene Rice, "A Neglected Interpretation of the Immanuel Prophecy," *Zeitschrift für die alttestamentliche Wissenschaft* 90 (1978): 220–27.

14. Others translate the term "authority" (NRSV, TNK) or "government" (KJV, NIV). Dominion contrasts with the previous broken rod; both were on the shoulders.

15. I translate each part with a noun and adjective to reflect the repetition of the grammatical phrase in Hebrew; "Prince of Peace" is the traditional translation of the fourth part.

16. The translation is based on NJB. "Inspiration": the term, translated "delight" in NAB, NIV, NRSV, and REB, is similar to the word for spirit and wind. TNK renders, "He shall sense the truth by his reverence for the Lord," and notes that the phrase is uncertain in Hebrew. For "fear of the Lord," see p. 54.

17. The LXX and 1QIsaᵃ have a verb, "to feed," in place of "the fatling." REB renders: "the calf and the young lion *will feed* together." TNK renders: "The calf, the beast of prey, and the fatling together," but notes the other possibility: "the calf and the beast of prey *shall feed*."

18. Isaiah uses a synonym for this second occurrence of "lion." KJV, NAB, and REB translate the synonyms "young lion" and "lion" to show the change in words; GNB uses "lion cubs" and "lions," while TNK employs "beast of prey" and "lion."
19. The final phrase, "he will be the stability of your times" in NRSV, is not clear in Hebrew, and translations differ.
20. Although this is a different Hebrew term than that translated "tents" in the preceding discussion, it belongs to the imagery of tents and openness (see 54:2).
21. "And he said" is the Hebrew. This translation is reflected only in KJV and TNK. The latter reads "Another asks," adding a footnote that 1QIsaᵃ and the LXX read "And I asked." This is in the other translations, and none of them notes that this is a change in the Hebrew text. I keep "and he said" because it fits with the anonymity of the passage. But "and I asked" does not remove the anonymity, since who says "I" is not named, and such an anonymous speaker reappears in 48:16 and 61:1.
22. TNK stresses another aspect of justice: "He shall teach *the true way* to the nations."
23. This is similar to NRSV, NAB, and NIV. The ambiguity is present in the Hebrew. The reed and wick can be objects as in TNK—"He shall not break even a bruised reed, or snuff out a dim wick"—or subjects, i.e., refer to the servant's weakness, as in TNK's footnote—"A bruised reed, he shall not be broken; a dim wick, he shall not be snuffed out."
24. See P. Wilcox and D. Paton-Williams, "The Servant Songs in Deutero-Isaiah," *Journal for the Study of the Old Testament* 42 (1988): 79–102.
25. The phrase has a double meaning. God does not abandon, i.e., leave undone, the saving acts. Also God will not abandon the blind. Since Hebrew *dabar*, "thing," also means "word" or "promise," TNK translates: "These are the promises—I will keep them without fail."
26. The translations differ on this unusual term: "he that is perfect" (KJV); "my dedicated one" (NRSV); "the chosen one" (TNK); "the one who has my trust" (REB); "the one committed to me" (NIV); and "the friend I have taken to myself" (NJB). Both GNB and NAB omit this entire second question.
27. This line, v. 21, is difficult to understand. My translation leaves the relation to context open, similar to KJV, NIV, NJB, and NRSV.
28. The Hebrew term means "servant" or "slave" depending on the context; this context refers to demeaned status that would not be reflected in "servant of kings." In an ironic twist the servant of the Lord is the slave of kings.
29. The subject of "saying" may be either the Lord or the servant. By putting it after the closing quotation mark, I am choosing the Lord as the subject. GNB and REB make this more explicit: "I said to the prisoners, 'Go free'" (REB). NIV and NJB have the servant as the subject: "to return ravaged properties, to say to prisoners, 'Come out'" (NJB). The others leave the ambiguity unresolved.
30. This is a distant land whose location is debated.
31. This is a difficult sentence and translations differ, especially in the rendering of "skilled tongue" (TNK): "a well-trained tongue" (NAB; see NIV); "the tongue of a teacher" or "of those who are taught" (NRSV with note); "the tongue of one who has been instructed" (REB; see KJV); "a disciple's tongue" (NJB); and "the Lord has taught me what to say" (GNB).

32. See David J. A. Clines, *I, He, We, & They: A Literary Approach to Isaiah 53* (Journal for the Study of the Old Testament Supplement 1; Sheffield: Sheffield Academic Press, 1976).

33. Hebrew has "you," which most change to "him" to accord with the context. REB renders: "Time was when many were appalled at you, my people; so now many nations recoil at the sight of him," comparing Israel, "my people," and "him," "my servant." I translate "him" for the sake of simplicity.

34. The Hebrew term is not certain, and this, or a similar word, is the usual translation based on the context.

35. NJB shows a clear relation between the two questions.

> Who has given credence to what we have heard?
> And who has seen in it a revelation of Yahweh's arm?

36. This is TNK and it notes: "i.e., as a leper." NRSV renders, "as one from whom others hide their faces." NJB renders, "one from whom, as it were, we averted our gaze."

37. Whybray, *Second Isaiah*, 77.

38. This is similar to REB; others differ: NRSV: "By a perversion of justice he was taken away"; NJB: "Forcibly, after sentence, he was taken."

39. The Hebrew is uncertain; this is the translation in GNB, NRSV, REB, and NAB.

40. This is similar to KJV, NIV, and NRSV. REB, "because he exposed himself to death" (see NJB, TNK), stresses the threat of death. NAB, "because he surrendered himself to death," stresses the willingness to accept death.

41. For this approach see John F. A. Sawyer, "Daughter of Zion and Servant of the Lord in Isaiah: A Comparison," *Journal for the Study of the Old Testament* 44 (1989): 89–107. Sawyer's comments concern the first part of the poem, 54:1–10; and I extend his observations to the rest of the poem.

42. This is a participle in Hebrew, as are "maker," "husband," and "redeemer" in vv. 5 and 8; I translate it as a noun in parallel with them, despite the shocking tone of "lover" applied to God.

43. This is REB; others use gems, e.g., "antinomy" (NRSV), "agates" (NJB), and "carbuncles" (TNK).

44. For this final phrase, which is also translated "righteousness," see pp. 38 and 52.

45. "It is important to notice that there is not one detail in this chapter that refers explicitly to a city: nothing about walls or gates or sieges. It tells the story of the overpowering and humiliation of a woman. . . . The personification is complete, the story autonomous and consistent" (John F. A. Sawyer, "Daughter of Zion and Servant of the Lord in Isaiah: A Comparison," *Journal for the Study of the Old Testament* 44 [1989]: 91).

46. Ashes poured on one's head as a sign of mourning are replaced by a crown or wreath of flowers. There is a pun in Hebrew: the crown (*pe'er*) replaces ashes (*'eper*).

47. The first half of v. 7 is not clear in Hebrew. Given the result clause in v. 7b, "Therefore, . . ." 7a is saying something about the people's shame and disgrace that is countered in 7b.

48. This is the MT and refers to a robber who tries to atone for his crime by offering sacrifice. Other manuscripts and versions, including the LXX, read "robbery with violence"; the change involves only a slight difference in the text.

49. See 59:21 for reference to the everlasting covenant; note the parallel with the everlasting joy of v. 7.
50. See p. 40 for a different translation.
51. The last phrase is in 54:17; see p. 203.
52. As Watts notes (*Isaiah 34–66*, 361), "the phrase is difficult to place in context." The LXX adds "know," which is adopted by JPS, KJV, NRSV, and REB; I place it in brackets to show that it is not in the Hebrew. JPS and REB place the phrase "for I know their deeds and their thoughts" at the end of v. 17 with a break between it and v. 18b, while NRSV keeps it with v. 18, for "I know their works and their thoughts, and I am coming to gather. . . ."
53. The Hebrew has a feminine participle with no obvious subject. In the context "I," at the start of the verse, is the Lord. The LXX has a masculine participle to fit with "I"; this is adopted by most translators. JPS, however, keeps the MT and supplies a feminine subject, "time," and marks the conjecture with brackets: "[The time] has come to gather. . . ." KJV is similar: "it shall come, that I will gather. . . ." I leave the ambiguity unresolved.
54. The reference of "them" in "among them" and "from them" (here and in v. 21) is open; God chooses from Israel and the nations.
55. The LXX and many translations have Put, as in Jer. 46:9.
56. Because of different interpretations of the Hebrew, translations vary: Meshech (NJB), Mosoch (NAB), and Rosh (REB). NIV creatively renders the phrase "famous as archers."

Further Reading

1. For background and further detail on the historical view of Isaiah and the theory of the three Isaiahs, consult the series of Old Testament Guides from Sheffield Academic Press.

> J. Barton. *Isaiah 1–39* (Sheffield: Sheffield Academic Press, 1995).
>
> R. N. Whybray. *The Second Isaiah* (Sheffield: Sheffield Academic Press, 1983).
>
> Grace I. Emmerson. *Isaiah 56–66* (Sheffield: Sheffield Academic Press, 1992).

2. For more on the why and how of reading Isaiah as a single work, consult:

> Edgar W. Conrad. *Reading Isaiah* (Overtures to Biblical Theology; Minneapolis: Fortress Press, 1991).
>
> Peter D. Miscall. *Isaiah* (Sheffield: Sheffield Academic Press, 1993).
>
> Christopher R. Seitz. *Isaiah 1–39* (Interpretation: A Bible Commentary for Teaching and Preaching; Louisville: John Knox Press, 1993).

3. This is one of the few contemporary commentaries on Isaiah by one person; other series divide the book between at least two different commentators. Watts divides his commentary into chapters 1–33 and 34–66, not the usual 1–39 and 40–66. This is a thorough and scholarly commentary that has considerable detail on historical and interpretive background and on textual and translation issues. He reads the vision as a drama with identifiable and named speakers. I share this dramatic view but do not try to consistently isolate and name the speakers, and Watts does not share my concern with the poetic aspects of Isaiah.

> John D. W. Watts. *Isaiah 1–33* (Word Biblical Commentary 24; Waco, Tex.: Word, 1985).
>
> ———. *Isaiah 34–66* (Word Biblical Commentary 25; Waco, Tex.: Word, 1987).

4. This is an excellent presentation of the changing interpretations, for both positive and negative effects, of Isaiah in Christianity. Sawyer covers written works, art, sculpture, and music.

> John F. A. Sawyer. *The Fifth Gospel: Isaiah in the History of Christianity* (Cambridge: Cambridge University Press, 1996).

5. These provide more detail on the Septuagint and the Dead Sea Scrolls. The work by Tov is the most detailed and up-to-date but is difficult reading because of the detail.

> Ralph W. Klein. *Textual Criticism of the Old Testament: From the Septuagint to Qumran* (Guides to Biblical Scholarship; Philadelphia: Fortress Press, 1974).
>
> P. Kyle McCarter Jr. *Textual Criticism: Recovering the Text of the Hebrew Bible* (Guides to Biblical Scholarship; Philadelphia: Fortress Press, 1986).

Emanuel Tov. *Textual Criticism of the Hebrew Bible* (Minneapolis: Fortress Press, 1992).

6. These dictionaries are up-to-date and present short treatments of many of the specific names, terms, and themes that are discussed in my book. Harper's is a one-volume dictionary and the Anchor is a six-volume work.

   Harper's Bible Dictionary, edited by P. J. Achtemeier (San Francisco: Harper-Collins, 1985).

   The Anchor Bible Dictionary, edited by D. N. Freedman (New York: Doubleday, 1992).

7. This is the best starting place for more on Bible translations; it includes ample suggested readings to pursue the issue further.

   Steven M. Sheeley and Robert N. Nash Jr. *The Bible in English Translation: An Essential Guide* (Nashville: Abingdon, 1997).

8. This is a thorough and readable guide to the present state of the study of Hebrew poetry; it includes references to and discussion of other works.

   David L. Petersen and Kent Harold Richards. *Interpreting Hebrew Poetry* (Guides to Biblical Scholarship; Minneapolis: Fortress Press, 1992).

9. Although other studies and commentaries refer to the imagery that occurs in a specific context in Isaiah, they do not try to trace the imagery throughout the book in the same fashion that I do. Nielsen's work deals with tree metaphors in Isaiah 1–39, but she is more concerned with them as interpretations of political events and situations than as an integral part of the vision of Isaiah. Trible deals with much of the feminine imagery, particularly in her second and third chapters, pp. 31–71.

   Kirsten Nielsen. *There Is Hope for a Tree: The Tree as Metaphor in Isaiah* (Journal for the Study of the Old Testament Supplement 65. Sheffield: Sheffield Academic Press, 1989).

   Phyllis Trible. *God and the Rhetoric of Sexuality* (Overtures to Biblical Theology; Philadelphia: Fortress Press, 1978).

10. Levenson's book discusses the creation stories that involve conflict with Sea, Rahab, etc., and includes references to other works. Coogan presents translations of the relevant Canaanite myths, while Heidel compares and contrasts the Genesis story with the main Babylonian account, the *Enuma Elish*.

    Michael D. Coogan. *Stories from Ancient Canaan* (Philadelphia: Westminster Press, 1978).

    Alexander Heidel. *The Babylonian Genesis: The Story of Creation*, 2d ed. (Chicago: University of Chicago Press, 1951).

    Jon D. Levenson. *Creation and the Persistence of Evil: The Jewish Drama of Divine Omnipotence* (San Francisco: Harper & Row, 1988).

Index of Authors

Index of Biblical Passages